"The megachurch is an attempt to fr[...]
size" is just one of the astute judgm[...] that informs this
book. Church growth strategies are the death gurgle of a
church that has lost its way. Suttle helps us see how God in
our time is making us leaner and meaner. I hope this book
will be widely read.

—Stanley Hauerwas,
Gilbert T. Rowe Emeritus Professor
of Divinity and Law, Duke University

Tim Suttle has written a powerful, passionate, honest word
to the church. He critiques a church too much seduced
by American can-do culture. His gospel alternative is
straightforward:

> faithfulness, not success
> story, not strategy
> virtue, not technique
> cooperation, not competition

The book is directed toward evangelicals who lust after
megachurches. But I hope his book will spill over into the
world of "progressive" Christians where I live. It is a good
word, one that the entire church needs to hear. It draws us
back to the truth enacted by Jesus.

—Walter Brueggemann,
Columbia Theological Seminary

It takes courage to write a book like this. It also takes courage to read a book like this. Tim Suttle calls for a major shift
in how we think about church growth. This conversation
is challenging and empowering; unsettling and comforting;
convicting and, ultimately, inspiring. That tension embod-
ies the gospel itself, as does this refreshing perspective on
congregational leadership. If you're ready to explore ministry

that is rooted in faithfulness and fruitfulness rather than culturally derived models of "success," this is the book you've been waiting for. *Shrink* is full of life-giving good news for those who want to abandon the hamster wheel of western church culture and lead in the way of Jesus.

—Rev. Erin Wathen,
"Irreverin," Senior Pastor,
Saint Andrew Christian Church, Kansas City

In the tradition of the biblical prophets, Tim Suttle boldly but gently calls us out of our American obsession with bigness and greatness toward a vision of church life rooted in faithfulness. *Shrink* is one of the wisest and most significant evangelical books that I've read in the last decade; it is essential reading for every pastor and church leader!

—C. Christopher Smith,
co-author *Slow Church*
and founding editor
of *The Englewood Review of Books*

From the heart of a pastor, the mind of a theologian, and the soul of a prophet comes a word to Christians in North America: *shrink*. Be freed from ambition. Find God's reign again in the daily faithfulness of living together in his kingdom. Few people could deliver this message with the same depth and piercing insight Tim Suttle has shown. In *Shrink*, he helps us face what we've been hiding from. He plows the scorched soil of the American church so we can take roots again and live.

—David Fitch,
BR Lindner Chair of Evangelical Theology,
Northern Seminary,
author *Prodigal Christianity*

SHRINk

Faithful Ministry in a Church-Growth Culture

TIM SUTTLE

 ZONDERVAN®

To the pastors of small churches wherever you are ...

ZONDERVAN

Shrink
Copyright © 2014 by Timothy Suttle

This title is also available as a Zondervan ebook. Visit www.zondervan.com/ebooks.

Requests for information should be addressed to:

Zondervan, 3900 Sparks Dr. SE, Grand Rapids, Michigan 49546

ISBN-13: 978-0-310-51512-8

Cover design: FaceOut Studio
Interior design: David Conn

Printed in the United States of America

14 15 16 17 18 19 20 /DCI/ 21 20 19 18 17 16 15 14 13 12 11 10 9 8 7 6 5 4 3 2 1

CONTENTS

FOREWORD

Shrink is an honest book. It is the confession of a pastor who longed for and worked hard toward becoming a "great" leader, taking "successful" pastors as his model. Eventually, he came to recognize that "greatness" is not a Christian aim. To adapt words of Jesus, "there is one who is Great," and he isn't anyone's local pastor. Leadership in the mode of Jesus is not what most think; rather, it is cruciform (to borrow the words of Michael Gorman, one of America's finest New Testament scholars). Or, in Tim Suttle's memorable words: "Great is the enemy of good." Think about that. Tim is turning everything upside down.

Shrink is an important book and here's why: Tim Suttle wants us to focus on the church—the local church, the kingdom of God at work in the here and now in your local situation. He's not trying to change the world or invade Washington, DC, with new strategies and finer voting plans. Instead, he wants to see a kingdom-kind-of-life established at the local church level. This may spread all over the land, but spreading over the land is not his passion. His passion is faithfulness in the local church. I love that emphasis because, like Tim, I'm tired of global visions that suck the energy out of the local church, of plans to change the world that ignore the local church, and of hopes to be significant at the expense of being faithful in the context of the local church.

Shrink is an intelligent and intelligible book. Tim Suttle is one of the young pastors I am reading and hearing about who are not reading leadership literature—they are reading the Bible and theologians who are working the Bible hard to make it speak to our world today. So we hear from Walter Brueggemann, Stanley Hauerwas, Jürgen Moltmann, Barbara Brown Taylor, Dallas Willard, Dietrich

Bonhoeffer, N. T. Wright, and—you may have guessed it—Eugene Peterson, who are all thinkers I love and have come to appreciate.

Shrink, I'm thinking, will be the go-to book for young pastors who want to jump off the treadmill of bigger, better, faster, and stronger and who instead want cruciform love, justice, peace, and authenticity emerging from the local church. Here smaller just might be the way to go.

Scot McKnight
Professor of New Testament
Northern Seminary

ACKNOWLEDGMENTS

The idea for this book grew out of an article I wrote for the religion section of *The Huffington Post* called "How to Shrink Your Church." The reason I get to write articles such as this is because Paul Raushenbush is generous and kind and has extended his generosity and kindness to me. Thank you, Paul. I will be forever grateful for you and your great family.

That this newspaper article became a book involves more generosity and kindness. I am so thankful to Ryan Pazdur at Zondervan for seeing value in a book like this. For advising me, listening to my ideas, critiquing them, and helping me to refine the vision for this project I am surely in your debt. I appreciate your expertise and support, Ryan. Thanks to everyone at Zondervan who worked on *Shrink*, especially to Verlyn Verbrugge, who offered sound advice and key changes at a critical point in the process. I am so grateful to you all.

Tim Keel and Mike King: I am blessed to have friends like you who know what a vulnerable thing it is to lead and to put pen to paper. Your friendship came in the nick of time, and has become such a source of hope and strength for me … I'd be in the deep weeds without you.

With a grateful heart I send my love and thanks to:

The AMO, Craig Babb, Marta Gillilan, Chris Jehle, Garret Lahey, and Dan Wilburn: thank you for your friendship. Redemption Church staff and elders: I'm so thankful to be serving alongside you in this precious church. Thank you for allowing me the time to write. To Redemption Church: what a beautiful and rare bunch of ragamuffins you are; thanks for never holding anything back as you chase the kingdom of God and pursue faithfulness. Our common life gives me hope. It is a gift to be your pastor.

To my family, Mom and Dad, Jeff and Amy, Kenny and Amy, Oliver and Christy, Pete and Rosie, Matt and Courtney, and all my nieces and nephews: I think about you guys constantly and feel so blessed to be part of such a loving and faithful family.

To Isaac Anderson, Scott Savage, Rustin Smith, Katie Savage, Jon Bowles, Ryan Green, Jovan Brown, Chaim Carstens, Jeff Suttle, and Bill Hill: thank you for being such good friends, and for the many conversations about life, ministry, theology, and writing.

I save my final thanks for Kristin, Nicholas, and Lewis Suttle. You guys have my heart. They need to make up a better word, because *love* just doesn't seem like enough. Nicholas and Lewis, it is a such a dream to be your dad. You are constantly making life beautiful. I pray that you know how much your parents love you; that you will be blessed for the time you let me take away from you in order to write; that you will always be good friends; that you will learn how to listen to your own life; that you will never know a single moment that you don't feel a part of the people of God; and that you will always have the courage to run "further up and further in!"

Kristin, you still take my breath away. You keep this family together with your ceaseless grace and love. I might be the voice, but you are the beating heart of this family. The life we've built together—you, me, the boys, this church, these friendships—it feels so rich and substantial, like ballast for the ship, the weight of which allows us to hang the sails out there and chase the horizon. I cannot see the future, but I dream about it. And when I do, I dream that our days will stretch out like the ocean just as far as the eye can see. They roll and tumble and flow—filled with love and music, laughter and art, pain and grit, sons and daughters, life and death—then they soften into each other, and then into eternity. And when forever comes to swallow up time, when the earth and sky coming crashing into the sea, and you and I and everyone we love washes up on the other side, I know this for sure: you will have been my favorite part of this life; the truest gift I have been given ... for which I am overwhelmed with gratitude.

INTRODUCTION

I could die in peace, I think, if the world was beautiful.
To know it's being ruined is hard.
—Wendell Berry, *Jayber Crow*

I love the church.
I believe in the church.

I believe in the church maybe more than I believe in any other thing in this world. The church is the surest sign I know of that God loves everything he's created; that God is not done with the world. The church is the singular reality bearing faithful witness to the truth that God has not left us here to struggle all by ourselves. God has come for us, to heal our broken hearts and this precious creation no matter how long it takes.

But the church is facing a huge problem, and it is not a problem of resistance or secularity, nor is it a problem of the culture's hostility to the gospel. It is a problem of our own making. We have become enamored with size. We have become infatuated with all things bigger, better, stronger, higher, and faster.

Famed American author, poet, and farmer Wendell Berry often writes about the rhythms and cycles of a well-run farm. The problems Berry sees facing the farm and the farming life mirror the problems facing the church in our time. When I read Wendell Berry's work, I cannot help but think he is teaching me how to be a pastor.

When Berry writes the word *land*, I think *parish*. When he uses the word *farm*, I think *church*.[1]

In his wonderful novel *Jayber Crow*, Berry tells the story of a father and his son-in-law who had different approaches to farming as well as to life. The father—Athey Keith—worked the land with a sense of pastoral reverence. Athey was an older man by the time the story was told. He'd been learning under the tutelage of the land for all his life. Athey recognized that there was an order to the land; there were patterns and cycles that had to be observed. Those patterns and cycles were determined by nature and should be respected. Athey believed that humans could not impose their own patterns and cycles on the land without damaging it.

On the other hand, the son-in-law, Troy Chatham, was determined to be the picture of a modern industrial farmer. Troy seemed to believe that the farm existed to serve his wishes, not the other way around. Patterns could be imposed on the land, and natural cycles could be altered or ignored. Every inch of land had to be plowed. Limits had to be pushed and expanded. Every dime of capital had to be leveraged or spent. Troy's goal was always bigger, better, higher, faster, and stronger.

Athey and Troy couldn't be more different. Their approaches to farming, and to life, stand in stark contrast. As Wendell Berry explains, "Athey said, 'Wherever I look, I want to see more than I need.' Troy said, in effect, 'Whatever I see I want.' What he [Troy] asked of the land was all it had … he was speaking as a young man of the modern age coming now into his hour, held back only by the outmoded ways of his elders."[2]

Sadly, in Berry's story, time was on the side of youth, and Troy's approach to farming began to overtake his father-in-law's. Athey would make his anxious son-in-law walk the land. He'd show him

---

1 I got this understanding of Wendell Berry's work from a similar comment made by Eugene Peterson in his book *Under the Unpredictable Plant* (Grand Rapids: Eerdmans, 1992), 131. Peterson says that when Berry writes the word *farm* he substitutes the word *parish*.

2 Wendell Berry, *Jayber Crow* (Washington DC: Counterpoint, 2000), 181–82.

the outlines of the plow furrows and teach him to appreciate the way the land sloped and how the water should run. He showed him the next year's cropland, now fallow, and the land slated for the year after that, explaining to him the patterns of the farm he had discovered over decades. Athey tried to teach Troy the value of a good garden, of pasture for the milk cows, and grain for the hogs, and he showed him how to cut firewood from the fence rows without depleting them. Troy's only response was, "We need to grow more corn."[3] Berry explains Athey's reaction:

> This brought Athey to a stop. The law of the farm was in the balance between crops (including hay and pasture) and livestock. The farm would have no more livestock than it could carry without strain. No more land would be plowed for grain crops than could be fertilized with manure from the animals. No more grain would be grown than the animals could eat. Except in case of unexpected surpluses or deficiencies, the farm did not sell or buy livestock feed. "I mean my grain and hay to leave my place *on foot*," Athey liked to say. This was a conserving principle; it strictly limited both the amount of land that would be plowed and the amount of supplies that would have to be bought.[4]

There was between Athey and his son-in-law a fundamental difference in how they viewed the vocation of farming. Berry says, "Athey was not exactly, or not only, what is called a 'landowner.' He was the farm's farmer, but also its creature and belonging. He lived its life, and it lived his; he knew that, of the two lives, his was meant to be the smaller and the shorter."[5]

Troy did not share this view. Berry writes:

> Troy went into debt and bought his new equipment because he didn't want to be held back by demanding circumstances. He was young and strong and ambitious. He wanted to be a star. The tractor greatly increased the power and speed of work. With it he could work more land. He could work longer. Because it had electric lights

---

3 Ibid., 184.
4 Ibid., 185.
5 Ibid., 182.

and did not get tired, he could work at night.... And so the farm came under the influence of a new pattern, and this was the pattern of a fundamental disagreement such as it had never seen before. It was a disagreement about time and money and the use of the world. The tractor seemed to have emanated directly from Troy's own mind, his need to go headlong, day or night, and perform heroic feats.[6]

What Athey—the older and wiser of the two—seemed to understand, which his son-in-law did not, was that it is a sin to disrespect the rhythms of nature and God's created order. Troy's deep disrespect of his elders was eclipsed only by his disrespect of the land, which had now become a means to his own ends. Once you make that trade, you place yourself on a collision course with reality as God has created it. And reality will always win, eventually. The earth will lie fallow one way or another until the rhythms of nature and life and humanity are once again respected. What Athey understood was that farming was never meant to be about production, but about *stewardship*.

What Berry writes about the farm is true of the church. What he writes about the land is true of the parish, because tending a farm and tending a church are similar enterprises. After all, they are both the necessary work of the people who have been asked to care for this world.

The church, like a healthy farm, has limits. The pastor/church leader has certain responsibilities to the health of the church and the community in which it lives. For it is not our creation, it is God's. The church was here before we got here and will outlast every single one of us. Our job is *stewardship*: to leave the church better than we found it, and to cause the church to serve the world around us, not the productivity demands of the leadership.

A family farm is a holy thing—a small operation that still knows the value of the land, speaks the language of the land, and understands what the land needs. The church is meant to be a holy thing—which sees the value of the parish, speaks the language of

6   Ibid., 184–86.

the neighborhood, and understands what the community needs in order to flourish.

My tribe is the evangelicals. We've been the "industry leaders" in developing best practices for the realization of the relevant, the powerful, and the spectacular church. Like industrial farmers, we have been so successful that we have actually moved the dial for the mainstream church as well. We have filled the cities and suburbs with monuments to growth without limits. But we have pushed in the wrong direction, and we have pushed too far. We have confused the very nature of what it means to be a part of the people of God.

If we are going to be wise stewards of the church, we need to learn the lessons Athey Keith tried to teach his stubborn son-in-law, Troy Chatham. We will need to recognize what nearly all of our most celebrated contemporary church leaders have failed to teach us: that the church does not belong to us; it is we who belong to the church. We are not making the church; the church is making us. We cannot determine its success, its mission, or its outcomes.

The church will outlive all of us, that much is certain. If we are going to leave the church better than we found it, we are going to have to rediscover the necessity of *margin* and the reality of *limits*. We are going to have to sit in silence for long enough to comprehend finally the word *enough*. We will have to strain to see the tiny seeds of faith at work in the world and hold them in our sweaty palms, hoping against hope that they will germinate and grow and feed us. And we are going to have to stop our incessant need to make things grow the way we want them to grow, whatever the price. In many ways that will most certainly be uncomfortable and challenging for us, because we are going to have to learn how to *shrink*.

I am not alone in this belief. Many church leaders are now faced with a fundamental disagreement about time and money and the use of the world. All around me everyday in my church and my city, I work with people who have chosen the way of *descent*. They labor in beautiful obscurity and have the audacity to imagine a church that depends upon God for its future. These friends forego lucrative careers and the perks of the upwardly mobile in order to serve small congregations faithfully. They are straining to imagine a different future for the church.

I'm writing this book in honor of those friends, to try and give my thoughts on where we went wrong; to think creatively about how to get back on track; to encourage others—maybe even you—to embrace the vision of the kingdom that this church and this world requires of us.

Tim Suttle, Kansas City—Advent, 2013.

Part 1

DON'T

TRY

TO BE

GREAT

Chapter 1
SUCCESS

Perfect is the enemy of good.
—Voltaire

On a chilly November night in 2011, an elite crowd of art aficionados and collectors gathered at Sotheby's Auction House on Manhattan's Upper East Side to try and grab a piece of art history. Sotheby's caters to the most discriminating of art collectors, and although the wine and cheese are free, the art can really cost you.

The auction was just a few minutes old when lot number 11 was called to the block. Named *1949-A-No. 1*, this oil painting was the most anticipated item of the evening. Sotheby's had aggressively outbid their crosstown rival Christie's Auction House for the right to sell this and three other coveted paintings by the same artist. The massive canvas, nearly eight feet tall and six feet wide, was covered in thick, dramatic black oils, and deep, richly textured, velvety reds. A stunning photograph of the piece adorned the dust jacket of the auction's official catalog, and the bidding started at twenty-five million dollars.

The bidders: Christopher Eykyn (a well-known New York art dealer) had a mobile phone stuck to his ear with one hand, his other hand covering his mouth to avoid revealing the identity of the client on the other end of the line. Lisa Dennison (the head of international business development for Sotheby's) was on the phone with an anonymous bidder of her own. It soon became clear that Eykyn and Dennison were both representing buyers who came to play. As the bid passed forty-five million dollars, all other bidders fell by the wayside, and the price continued to climb.

When the gavel finally dropped, the crowd at Sotheby's erupted with applause for Dennison's mystery client, who had placed the winning bid: $61.7 million.

We are, of course, immune to any real shock when it comes to the world of high-priced artwork. What makes this story remarkable is not that a painting sold for over $60 million but that the artist is largely unknown. His name is Clyfford Still, and he is perhaps the most important American artist you've never heard of.

According to *The Art Wolf*, an online art magazine, the top ten most expensive paintings ever sold are by, in order, Cezanne, Picasso, Pollock, de Kooning, Klimt, Munch, Jasper Johns, Picasso, Picasso, and Andy Warhol. The royal family of Qatar reportedly tops the list of auction purchasers for buying Cezanne's *The Card Players* for a record $250 million. Rock and roll magnate David Geffen sold his prized and dramatic drip painting *Number 5, 1948*—by the original hipster Jackson Pollock—for over $140 million. Some think Geffen sold it merely so he could hold the world record for the most expensive contemporary painting ever sold at auction, a record he held for some time.

When the till tops $100 million, one expects to hear names with a bit of sizzle. Cezanne, Van Gogh, and Picasso certainly qualify, but Clyfford Still? Yet, by the time the auction closed that November night at Sotheby's, art collectors had coughed up a total of $114 million for four Clyfford Still originals. How is it that we've never heard of this guy?

Clyfford Still was a pioneer in a movement called abstract expressionism, which was the first chiefly American artistic movement to capture the imagination of the entire art world. Abstract expressionism, also called the New York School, represented a rebellious break with conventional painting techniques and subject matter. The break grew out of a postwar cynicism that eventually developed into the full-blown artistic, intellectual, and philosophical movement we know as postmodernism. The break also managed to put New York City at the leading edge of art for the first time in history. Clyfford Still was the movement's first great master.

Still grew up in the Pacific Northwest and settled in San Francisco, where he was teaching art and painting mostly agricultural themes. In the late 1930s, he began to experiment by simplifying the forms in his paintings. (Forms are the actual subjects, like barns, farmers, etc.) Still's forms became distorted—less realistic. Before long he abstracted the forms altogether, producing massive, dramatic canvases filled with pure emotive expressions of color and texture.

It was a revolution.

Still found instant success, with showings at the two leading galleries of the day: Peggy Guggenheim's the Art of This Century Gallery, and the Betty Parsons Gallery. The art world had finally turned its jaded eyes to New York City, and they were looking directly at Clyfford Still. Critics loved him. His work was emulated, and his paintings sold for more than that of any of his contemporaries.

He had everything an artist could want, when, at the very height of his success, Clyfford Still simply walked away. "To avoid confusion," he wrote to his agent in the fall of 1951, "I will tell you now that I am withdrawing my work from public exhibition."[1]

Why?

The story goes that Clyfford Still's life was beset with insurmountable tension. On one hand, his entire artistic project called into question the culture of materialism, greed, and fame that personified the New York art scene. On the other hand, that self-indulgent, self-congratulatory bunch was celebrating him as their conquering hero. Still felt that the themes and purposes of his work were being undermined by his participation in the world of commercial art. To take their money, to receive their accolades, and to participate in the system would undercut the statement he was making with his art. Still felt he had no choice but to walk away in order to maintain his integrity. So he dropped out.

Still moved with his wife and family to rural Maryland, bought a farm, and spent the next thirty years painting and working in relative

---

1 Jim Spellman, "The Most Influential Artist You've Probably Never Heard Of," CNN.com, June 9, 2012. Accessed August 11, 2012. www.cnn.com/2012/06/09/living/artist-clyfford-still-profile.

obscurity. For the rest of his life, he sold few paintings and held only a few gallery showings.

Here's where the story gets interesting. When he died, Still left a remarkable handwritten will, in which he ensured his legacy: *he would give all of it away.*

Clyfford Still's estate, including 94 percent of everything he had ever produced as an artist, 825 paintings, and over 1,600 drawings, would be given to an American city that would agree to a few conditions. They would have to build a museum in which to house Clyfford Still's entire collection, show it, and never sell or even loan any of it to other museums or collectors. His last will and testament ensured that his collection would never become part of the commercial art world he meant to critique. The museum, which opened in Denver in 2011, was not even allowed to have a cafeteria or gift shop. They were allowed, through what some saw as a legal loophole, to sell four paintings at Sotheby's auction house, which brought them $114 million—enough money to build the museum and endow it for years to come.

Clyfford Still had it all, and yet he walked away rather than compromise his mission. How does a person do that? I'm fascinated by that choice. This book is *all about* that choice; because it is the choice every single Christian needs to learn how to make—especially Christian leaders. How do I stop trying to chase success and chase faithfulness instead?

A NEW LEADERSHIP NARRATIVE

Pastors and church leaders spend hundreds of millions of dollars each year attending conferences, buying books, hiring consultants and advertisers and marketers, all trying to accomplish one thing: *success* ... read: bigger, better, more celebrated, and more talked about.

I'm convinced this is the wrong tack.

In the late 1980s, Bill Hybels began revolutionizing church leadership practices, taking principles developed in the world of business and applying them to the church. I remember sitting in a church leadership conference at Willow Creek in Chicago somewhere around 1995. I had been listening to Hybels speak for years via cassette-taped services. As a young church planter, I was buying everything he was selling. I sat enraptured as he cast his vision for what he called prevailing churches, by which he meant growing, successful churches who are reaching the unchurched. This guy had a church of *twenty thousand people*, a world-class facility, production staff, professional musicians, actors, writers, and directors. Everybody was so put together, so sharp—I was hooked. I began to aspire to ministry greatness. I was willing to do nearly anything to be a part of the kind of ministry he was building.

Here is where I should insert my cautionary tale about how I worked really hard, climbed the ladder of success, and gave it all away just like Clyfford Still. If only it were so.

The truth is I have never been great. I'm no Clyfford Still, and I'm no Bill Hybels. Yet I know what it means to strive to be like them. I know what it means to dream of success, to chase it with all my might, and to make great personal sacrifice—asking the same of everyone around me—and then watch people crash and burn when it doesn't come to fruition. I have succumbed to the temptation to try to become great, and I have sold out in so many ways. I have pushed myself and others to follow a vision of greatness that, I believe, in the end, runs contrary to the gospel story itself.

Here's the thing. I have come to believe that there is much more to Christian leadership than chasing success. I've come to believe that the most important thing about Christian leaders is not that they are leaders, but that they are *Christian* leaders.[2] Leading in the way of Jesus is a particular mode of leadership that must adhere to the pattern of life Jesus recommended.

The Christian leader is called not primarily to be effective, but to be faithful and to practice leadership in the way of Jesus no matter what the perceived results may be. The Christian leader cannot simply take leadership principles from the arena of business and plop them down in a church or ministry, because the business narrative and the Christian narrative are built on two different foundations. The word *Christian* modifies the word *leader* in ways that should

---

2 I am grateful to William Willimon, who often makes this distinction.

make it incompatible with most of the leadership principles found in the world of business, especially when it comes to the primacy of effectiveness and success.

Most of the church leadership conversation today has its footing squarely in the culture narrative, not the Christian narrative. Leadership today is about getting things done and growing a ministry we can be proud of. As a result, Christian leadership has come to focus solely on *best practices*. Leaders want to know what we can do to produce the kind of *results* we desire. We want *effectiveness*. We crave practical advice that will help us to be bigger, better, and so on.

I have come to believe that this entire line of thinking has little to do with the gospel, even less with the life of Jesus Christ, whom we have been called to imitate.

Here's the heart of my ethos and the foundation of everything I will say in this book: there's leadership, and then there's *Christian* leadership. Christian leadership is categorically different from any other mode of leadership.

If you have been involved in any kind of leadership conversation recently, you could probably teach a seminar on what the word *leadership* means. We all know the bullet points: define the mission, assemble a team, cast the vision, set goals, inspire everyone to work together, achieve the goals, celebrate success, adapt to changes, and grow the enterprise. Under this set of assumptions, the way to judge the effectiveness of the leader is by viewing the results. Success is about effectiveness.

Christian leadership operates with a completely different basic assumption. Our most basic conviction is that the kingdom of God has come and is coming in and through Jesus Christ. We cannot accomplish the kingdom of God; it is the work of God. Our job is to be faithful to the ways of Jesus, not the ways of our culture. The Christian leader does not pursue success or results the way the CEO of a Fortune 500 company does. The Christian leader pursues faithfulness. Results, success, and effectiveness are nice when they happen, but they are not the primary pursuit.

Christian leaders are meant to model their lives and leadership practices on the life of Jesus. This means that we can never have the assurance of predictable results. We lead in the way of Christ and leave the results up to God. Faithfulness, not success, is our goal. The goal of Christian leadership is always and only ever *faithfulness to the way of Jesus.*

I once heard a well-known church consultant say, "You can start a church without God if you have four things: entertaining preaching, great worship, a dynamic youth ministry, and a quality children's ministry." Everybody laughed at the joke, but the point was made: churches that build on the foundation of business leadership principles will prosper.

> Faithfulness, not success, is our goal. The goal of Christian leadership is always and only ever *faithfulness to the way of Jesus.*

Many pastors and leaders bought into the idea that we had to do something important and successful. The church leadership culture taught us to aspire to be fresh, intelligent provocateurs — culturally relevant and upwardly mobile. I embraced these aspirations, dreaming of ways my ministry could be worthy of finding its way onto the big stage. With a deep sense of sadness and regret, I confess that I pushed myself, and even worse, I pushed other people to realize my vision of success. When it didn't happen to the extent that I'd planned, I felt like a failure, and I fear I made them feel like failures as well.

I'm trying to reject that narrative. I believe that churches that build on the foundation of business leadership principles are building on assumptions that are simply foreign to the gospel.

I know I'm not alone.

I'm part of a generation of leaders — and among them, again, I am truly nothing special — who have begun to catch wind of a different way to lead. We are tired of the old script, and we want to write a new one.

I have spent the last decade trying to disentangle myself from the church leadership culture, and while my transformation is still in progress, I'm beginning to learn how to talk about my experiences. I'm learning to dig deeply into some of the rich theology concerning what the church really is, what it's for, and what it means to be a

Christian leader. I'm still trying to rewire my thinking about how to lead people toward Christ's vision of the kingdom of God.

So I'm writing this book not because I've got it all figured out but because I'm struggling with my own ambitions and my own sense of inadequacy. I'm trying to think more carefully about what I aspire to as a leader, especially when it comes to words like *greatness* or *success*. I hope you'll think these things through with me.

The church of the future will not depend on leaders who have been shaped by the church leadership culture of the past two decades. The church of the future will be shaped by leaders who are brave enough to make a Clyfford Still–type move—the courage to pursue leadership in the way of Jesus regardless of the perceived results or success.

I have become convinced that the Christian leader's first job is to become a good and virtuous human being and a good and virtuous leader, and then to leave questions of growth and perceived success in the hands of God. Sometimes all God requires of the leader is to do the small things faithfully for the rest of his or her life. How many of us have the tools to even imagine that, much less carry that off?

THE JESUS WAY IS DOWN

The church was never meant to mimic the world in terms of its approach to how we organize our communities and make decisions. This means that Christian leadership is built upon a completely different story than the story upon which leadership in other sectors of our society is built. Because we are completely committed to the lordship of Christ, we are committed to an alternate reality, one in which the last will be first and the first will be last; one in which faithfulness to Jesus and the pursuit of God's will for our lives both as persons and as communities require a relinquishing of ambition and an embrace of descent.

When Christians attempt to consider questions of leadership, we can seldom trust our own instincts, because in most cases they have been thoroughly formed by our culture, often in ways we are totally unaware of and are unable to discern. The Christian's relationship to power, structure, and decision making must be completely different because of our commitment to the lordship of Jesus. This means the most important impact the gospel will have on our leadership is *teleological*: What is the end toward which the church is committed? What is our goal?

I'm writing from a different assumption than most of the leadership books I have read. The typical assumption of most books on church and ministry—even those written more recently in the missional church field—is the idea that the church's job is to grow. A healthy church is a church that grows bigger. My argument is that this assumption is built not on the gospel but on the American narrative.

When we read the New Testament through the lenses of colonialism and consumer capitalism, we cannot help but accentuate those bits of Scripture that portray expansion and growth. This means that it is easy for us to concentrate on the Great Commission and consider this to be the pinnacle of all of Jesus' vision for the church. Interestingly, the most stringent and forceful teaching—the Sermon on the Mount, for instance—can be all but lost in a leadership culture that is committed to growth without limits.

This is a false assumption. The church's job is not to grow. The church's job is not to thrive. The church's job is not even to survive. *The church's job is to be faithful.* Our growth, even our survival, is predicated on the will and power of God. The church's job is to be the church.

> The church's job is not to grow. The church's job is not to thrive. The church's job is not even to survive. *The church's job is to be faithful.*

In their wonderful book *Resident Aliens*, Stanley Hauerwas and Will Willimon consider ways in which the church has made growth their basic assumption. If not numerical growth through conversion, the church seems to want to impact the culture through Christian social involvement. They write that the church has typically fallen into two unhelpful ditches on the side of the road on which Jesus asked us to travel. The first ditch is the *activist* church. Convinced that their job is to help build a better, more just society, the activist church's focus is on the impact the church may have on the culture. Hauerwas and Willimon remind us that "the church doesn't have a social strategy, the church is a social strategy."[3] The focus of the church is on being the peculiar people of God, embodying a different social reality.

The second ditch is the *conversionist* church. Convinced that no amount of tinkering with societal structures can counter the effect of human sin, the conversionist church tries to save as many souls as possible before the whole thing burns to the ground.[4]

Hauerwas and Willimon recommend a third alternative they call the *confessing church*, modeled on the church that stood in such profound contrast to Hitler's Third Reich in Germany during World War II. One must not think that the confessing church is a Hegelian synthesis of the activist and conversionist churches. The confessing church is not merely focused on the transformation of the individual, or on the modification of society, "but rather in the congregation's determination to worship Christ in all things."[5]

The confessing church is the church that has chosen to worship God in everything they do and to worship no other gods, not even the gods of the culture. The confessing church does not reject the idea of results, nor does it reject the necessity of conversion. However, the confessing church believes that results remain the purview of the Father, and conversion is the work of an entire lifetime.

Hauerwas and Willimon insist, "The church exists today as resident aliens, an adventurous colony in a society of unbelief."[6] As resident aliens, the church is our colony. We exist together as one colony (church) in the midst of another colony (culture), whose virtues, desires, and practices will necessarily make us peculiar. The church's job, then, is neither to save the culture nor to save souls. The

---

3 Stanley Hauerwas and William H. Willimon, *Resident Aliens: Life in the Christian Colony* (Nashville: Abingdon, 1989), 43.

4 Ibid., 45.

5 Ibid.

6 Ibid., 49.

church's job is simply to be the church—to be a colony of heaven in a culture of hell.

The contemporary church leadership conversation cannot fund this sort of church leadership. Both activist (typically mainline denominations) and conversionist churches (typically evangelical, charismatic, and fundamentalist churches) have been captivated by the values of a culture that demands progress toward the goals of bigger, better, stronger, higher, faster—cultural markers that are foreign to the gospel story. Hauerwas and Willimon write, "The world has declared war upon the gospel in the most subtle of ways, ways so subtle that sometimes we do not know we are losing the battle until it is over."[7] Both the activist and conversionist churches have allowed the culture to determine their values.

If we honestly and critically assess the basic underlying assumptions on which we operate as Christian leaders, at the heart of the current leadership conversation we will find not the Christian narrative, but the American narrative of growth and expansion. When it comes to the common conception of what the church is and what it is for, we have allowed the culture in which we live to become more determinative than the gospel Jesus preached. Even the gospel has been adapted to fit the culture. Crisis evangelism and the reduction of the gospel to a means of getting into heaven when we die are both examples of the way the gospel has become purposefully adapted to our culture.

We need a better story.

We need a leadership narrative built not on the American vision of success but on Jesus' vision of the kingdom. The Jesus way is always down, always the way of descent. We need a leadership that is built on the gospel and the way of life Jesus lived and taught. We need leaders who have enough confidence in God that they will pursue faithfulness without having to engineer growth.

> The Jesus way is not about success, but faithfulness.

For most of us who love the church and are involved in its life,

---

7 Ibid., 152.

learning to make this transition requires major surgery. If what I'm arguing so far is new to you, I urge you to read on. Just give me a chance to convince you that the Jesus way is not about success, but faithfulness.

If you have already begun the journey toward the kind of leadership I'm talking about, I hope this book will serve as a good resource for you as you attempt to switch paradigms. Remember that it usually takes a decade to leave one narrative and join another, so gear up for the long haul. If you are already with me, my hope is to encourage you and resource you with a fresh imagination for what it means to be the people of God.

> The church's job is not to thrive or even to survive. The church's job is to be the church — to bear witness to the lordship of Jesus Christ in the way we organize our common lives.

I will say this over and over in the book. The church's job is not to grow. The church's job is not to thrive or even to survive. The church's job is to be the church — to bear witness to the lordship of Jesus Christ in the way we organize our common lives — which will always involve a lot of dying on behalf of each other, the world, and the gospel.

What it takes to lead in the way of Jesus in our present context is nothing less than a radical transformation of our vision of the world and the church's place within that world. For us to become truly Christian leaders, formed in the image of Christ, committed to the lordship of Jesus, and ready to pursue the kingdom of God and not our own success, we have to leave the narrative of consumerism, individualism, and nationalism and cling to Jesus and the gospel. This truly is major surgery. I'm aware that I'm trying to convince you that up is down. I'm trying to sell powerlessness to those who have already learned to navigate power with great success.

Chapter 2

GREAT IS THE ENEMY OF GOOD

*What good will it be for someone to gain the whole
world, yet forfeit their soul? Or what can
anyone give in exchange for their soul?*
—Jesus in Matthew 16:26

*If your life is motivated by your ambition to leave a
legacy, what you'll probably leave as legacy is ambition.*
—Rich Mullins

When Tyler Hamilton was a boy, his father told him that if they had a family crest, it would contain only one word: *honesty*. It was their central family value. Generations of tough, Northeastern, blue-collar, hardworking skiers and outdoorsmen had forged a Hamilton family legacy that held these few things close to their hearts: no cheating, no shortcuts, and no job too small to give it your best. That's what it meant to be a Hamilton. His father and mother placed few demands on Tyler and his siblings, except that they always tell the truth.

Once a year the Hamilton family would take a break from their commitment to honesty and fair play in order to host their annual Mountain Goat Invitational Crazy Croquet Tournament. The contest had only rule: cheating was strongly encouraged. Anything short of chucking an opponent's ball into the sea was legal, and even that was not entirely out of the question. In the end the winner was always crowned, then immediately disqualified for cheating. The tournament was all in good fun, but the message behind it was clear. One day a year cheating was allowed. For the rest of their lives, honesty was at the heart of what it meant to be a Hamilton.

Tyler grew up in a family of adventurers and snow skiers. His parents actually met while back-country skiing a place called Tuckerman Ravine—a notoriously dangerous Northeastern ski slope you had to hike up to ski down. As a young man, Tyler was a pretty good downhill skier. He actually became an Olympic hopeful and was a part of the University of Colorado downhill skiing team until he broke his back in a training accident. Hamilton did much of his rehab on a bike, and soon cycling—not skiing—became his obsession.

"I'm good at pain," Hamilton wrote in the opening line of his memoir *The Secret Race*. "The tougher things get, the better I do ... because I've got a method. Here's the secret: You can't block out the pain. You have to embrace it."[1] Within the year Hamilton rode his ability to embrace pain to a national collegiate championship. A year later he turned pro.

This was about the same time that Lance Armstrong was making his famous comeback from cancer. Most of us know his story. What most of us don't know is that Armstrong's ride to seven straight Tour de France victories was closely tied to the career of Tyler Hamilton.

Hamilton and Armstrong were as close as two cyclists could be. They were on the same professional cycling team. They trained together every day. They roomed together on the road. Their families were friends and even lived in the same building in Italy. Armstrong would confide in Hamilton about his dream of becoming a tour champion, and Hamilton would help push Armstrong and the whole U.S. Postal Cycling Team to unimagined heights.

A couple of years into it, Hamilton started to feel as if he was falling behind his teammates. He seemed to be tiring more easily than the others; doing the same workouts, pushing himself just as hard, performing just as well, but his body wouldn't recover like the rest of the team. He was able to race at the same level but could not bounce

---

1   Tyler Hamilton and Daniel Coyle, *The Secret Race: Inside the Hidden World of the Tour de France* (New York: Bantam, 2012), 15.

back as quickly. Hamilton had what is often called *sports anemia*—low red blood cell count due to overexercise—which is an inevitable part of competing in three-week-long bike races. The question was why didn't his teammates have the same problem?

Hamilton began to notice these curious white paper bags that were handed out to Lance Armstrong and some of the other elite team members at the end of a long day of training. The riders who received the little white bags could always bounce back. It didn't take Hamilton long to figure out they were doping.

Hamilton was already a good rider. He was an elite cyclist making a good living on the bike. He was also one of the most beloved riders in the peloton—salt of the earth, humble, considerate, and courageous. His teammates used to perform a skit in which they would poke fun at Hamilton's legendary kindness. One rider would pretend to be Tyler Hamilton crumpled on a road after a bad crash. Another teammate played the doctor who would race up to Hamilton and shout, "Are you okay, Tyler? Your leg, it has been cut off!" To which the one playing Hamilton would reply, "Oh, don't worry, I'm fine ... how are *you* feeling today."[2]

On top of that, he was tough as nails. During the 2002 Tour of Italy, Hamilton fractured a collarbone early in the race. Most riders would have quit, but he soldiered on. When it was all said and done, Hamilton had finished second, and he had ground eleven of his teeth down to the roots coping with the pain. They had to be surgically repaired.

But virtue and toughness simply weren't enough. Riding clean he was already challenging the elite riders—all of whom were doping—but there was no way he could keep it up long term. If he wanted to compete, it meant doping, which meant cover-ups, which meant lying, which meant he would have to break the cardinal Hamilton rule.

Nobody asked Hamilton to cheat. Initially he stayed true to the family motto: honesty. He rode *paniagua*, or "bread & water"—the cycling world's way of saying the rider is not doping, but soon he could see the handwriting on the wall.

---

2 Ibid., 7.

"Here's an interesting number," Hamilton wrote. "One thousand days. It's roughly the number of days between the day I became professional and the day I doped for the first time. Talking to other riders of this era and reading their stories, it seems to be a pattern: those of us who doped mostly started during our third year. First year, neo-pro, excited to be there, young pup, hopeful. Second year, realization. Third year, clarity—the fork in the road. Yes or no. In or out. Everybody has their thousand days."[3]

The moment Tyler Hamilton took his first performance-enhancing drug, *great* became the enemy of *good* in his life. The pursuit of greatness began to undermine the virtues the Hamilton family held dear for generations.

It's easy to hate Lance Armstrong—he's the quintessential self-absorbed, brash, arrogant professional athlete—but not Hamilton. Everybody loved Tyler because he was deep down good—virtuous, honest, down to earth, hardworking, and kind. Hamilton was also a good racer—extremely talented and strong, with a legendary ability to embrace pain.

Nevertheless, Hamilton lied to everyone he cared about. He allowed the lies and deceit to eat away at his soul. Eventually his pursuit of greatness cost him his marriage, his career, and his Olympic gold medal. And in the end he and his entire team forfeited every single Tour de France win.

> The enduring power of greatness is its ability to entice human beings to trade the good for the great.

If Clyfford Still is an example of a person who understood how the pursuit of greatness could undermine everything he was pursuing with his art, Tyler Hamilton is his mirror opposite. What makes the juxtaposition most striking is that Hamilton was such a kind and good person, while Clyfford Still was notoriously self-centered and self-aggrandizing. Hamilton never seemed to realize what doping was doing to him, to his own soul, until it was already done.

---

3 Ibid., 46.

Hamilton, I believe, is a testament to the enticing allure of greatness. There is a sense in which *great is the enemy of good*. The pursuit of greatness can actually drive out goodness from the human heart.

What good does it do to gain the whole world if in the process that person forfeits their soul? What can anyone give in exchange for their soul?

Great is not necessarily good. In fact, if we learn anything from stories like Tyler Hamilton's and many of the others we'll explore here, it is this: *The enduring power of greatness is its ability to entice human beings to trade the good for the great.*

Your conscience for a fortune.

Your honesty for a kingdom.

Your friendship for a championship.

Your integrity for a big church.

Your soul for a chance at ministry greatness.

It's not as far-fetched as you might think. Sometimes the promise of greatness is all it takes to destroy the good in us.

GOOD TO GREAT

When Jim Collins wrote his renowned leadership manual *Good to Great*, church leaders ate it up.[4] His central thesis, "Good is the enemy of Great," contends that leaders who become satisfied with a *good* organization will cease to press toward *greatness*. Collins still headlines church leadership conferences while his books sit on the bookshelves of nearly every pastor I know. However, it seems few church leaders have ever stopped to consider whether greatness — defined by Collins as "distinctive impact" and "superior performance" — is really what we should be pursuing.

Is greatness the goal of church leadership? Is greatness good?

> Is greatness the goal of church leadership? Is greatness good?

---

4 Jim Collins, *Good to Great: Why Some Companies Make the Leap... and Others Don't* (New York: Harper Collins, 2011).

In the church leadership culture, these are not the questions typically asked. Yet I believe they are among the first and most important questions every Christian leader must ask because success has become more determinative for the church leadership conversation than faithfulness. Greatness — even for church leaders — has come to be defined more so by our culture than by a strong theological vision of the kingdom of God. We have it backward.

Authentically Christian leadership begins and ends with a conversation about Jesus' vision of the kingdom of God, not with a strategy for success. "Best practices" should be a minor side conversation in the world of Christian leadership. If we learn to think theologically about leadership at its most basic level, our vision of what greatness actually looks like will be different for churches and ministries, even for our lives.

Meanwhile, the pursuit of greatness exerts crushing pressure on the local church and produces a consuming anxiety in its leaders — especially pastors. In our pursuit of a warped vision of greatness, we have unwittingly become disconnected from goodness and virtue, embracing a leadership narrative that runs against the grain of the gospel story.

My thesis is a complete reversal of Collins's. He said that *Good is the enemy of Great*. I say that *Great is the enemy of Good in Christian leadership*. The drive to be great (read: bigger, more celebrated, and more talked about) is crowding out goodness and virtue as the central focus in Christian leadership. Christian leadership has too often become about pragmatism (what works, makes us grow, gets me predictable results, is most effective), while faithfulness has taken a backseat. Pastors have morphed into CEOs, and the worth of leaders has become intrinsically tied to the success of their congregations or ministries.

The story we are told in our society says that the measure of worth for any person is in what you can achieve. Our culture tells success-oriented leaders, "If you want to be on the stage, if you want to shape the conversation, if you want to write church leadership books and hit the speaking circuit, then you're going to need thousands of people in your congregation, millions of dollars in your budget, and some sort of success story to tell."

This is part of the reason why the church leadership conversation is so dominated by pastors of large churches. Megachurch pastors headline the conferences, write the books, and serve as the models for success. Yet the overwhelming majority of pastors in North America serve in churches of fewer than two hundred people. Just think about the irony of this concurrence. Most pastors serve in small churches. Most leadership advice comes from megachurch pastors—something is wrong with this picture.

> Most pastors serve in small churches. Most leadership advice comes from megachurch pastors — something is wrong with this picture.

I've been there many times. Small church pastors sit in the audience of the leadership conferences, and we are told to dream big. Perhaps one day we, too, will be one of the big boys. Then the small church pastors head home to cajole, poke, and prod their congregations into embracing the latest strategy. These leaders actually do their best to make their congregations feel as if something is wrong with their current situations. Then they hit their congregations with the call to action—the three-point plan—culled not from their own context but from the context of a megachurch.

It's toxic.

It's painful.

And sadly, it's common.

I've been in that audience before, and I've felt like Tyler Hamilton with his one thousand days. This is the kind of decision contemporary church leaders are facing all the time. Year one: excitement—new church planter or pastorate, just excited to be a part of something that matters. Year two: realization—the big boys are using all of these business leadership tactics; they are chasing success; they are seeing much better results than I am. Year three: clarity—if I want to be successful, I have to get this church/ministry to grow, and I will do whatever it takes to make that happen.

Doping is to professional cycling what good-to-great leadership is to ministry.

For the Christian leader, there should be only one metric that matters: *faithfulness.*

When church leaders focus on faithfulness (read: fidelity, virtue, and an active, living, breathing allegiance to the way of Christ), they have done all they are meant to do—regardless of their ministry's results. Faithfulness is our part; growth is God's part.

> For the Christian leader, there should be only one metric that matters: faithfulness.

It is my conviction that the next generation of church leaders must stop chasing the good-to-great vision and begin to focus on faithfulness instead.

This belief is based in a deep theological commitment to the vision of the kingdom that Jesus taught. The church's job is not to grow or even to survive. The church's job is to be faithful. The pastor, church leader, and church member must be trained in faithfulness above all else. Anything beyond that begins to steal the initiative from God and will cause us problems in the end.

It seems important at this point to simply acknowledge that—not unlike Clyfford Still—I'm working in a medium that is compromised. (I'm obviously not writing a book so that nobody will read it.) What if people like it and all of the sudden I'm on stage at some conference? As unlikely as that is, the moment this book is published, I'm still in danger of contradiction. I don't want to solve that tension, which is good, because I don't know how to solve it. I only know that I wish normal folks like me had more of a voice in the church leadership conversation, so I am speaking up. I have wished for a book like this so many times. I have longed to know there are others engaged in the construction of a new church leadership paradigm. Becoming a contradiction is a chance I am willing to take.

The tide may be already turning for some of us. But for many Christian leaders, what I'm describing will seem like a Clyfford Still swan dive into oblivion. You are not imagining it. That is exactly what I'm suggesting. And it all stems from this inescapable question:

Is greatness good? Is greatness—as defined by the good-to-great leadership culture—what we should be pursuing?

I MUST DECREASE

Clyfford Still isn't the only leader who ever took the plunge. In fact, Scripture is full of examples, but my favorite is John the Baptist.

John the Baptist was a legend in his own time. As far as first-century Jewish apocalyptic prophets went, John was the man; like Bono, Oprah, and Billy Graham all rolled into one. When the gospel of Mark describes John's ministry, it says that "all of Jerusalem" was coming out to see him in the wilderness. He gathered the huddled masses at the banks of the Jordan and told them it was time to change their agenda for their lives. He called them to repentance, and the crowds went crazy. The vendors were selling T-shirts, the funnel cakes were flying over the counter, and a throng of disciples followed John everywhere he went.

Then one day his cousin Jesus showed up at the banks of the Jordan. Even though Jesus was a complete nobody at the time, it seems as though John had been waiting for this day. The party was about to be over. "I'm not the one," he told his followers. "I'm just a voice crying in the wilderness—trying to keep the pathway straight. But you are about to see things your eyes won't believe. You are about to hear things your ears cannot take in." John plunged his cousin under the water, and when Jesus emerged to catch his breath, the heavens were ripped open, a dove descended on him, and his ministry was embraced and ratified by the voice of God.

Soon afterward John the Baptist's followers were wading across the Jordan River in droves to follow after Jesus. You just know John's inner circle had to be about to lose it. "I know, I know! I know you like this guy, and I know he's your cousin, but come on, John. Our bottom line is suffering. We're losing our audience. You are the man, and you are about to blow it! We've got to keep this movement heading forward."

"This is how it has to be," he responded.

"Yeah, but ..."

"No 'buts,'" John said. "I must decrease. He must increase."

Somehow John the Baptist knew that faithfulness would have to be enough for him. As more and more of his followers hustled after Jesus, John responded with faithfulness and humility, joyfully satisfied to have played his part. In the end, the size and scope of John's ministry would be determined by the will of the Father; and when he was killed by Herod, John the Baptist seemed like a failure to everyone who knew him. Yet to this day we cannot tell the story of Jesus without reminding ourselves of the faithfulness of his cousin John.

What kind of leadership can fund *this* kind of ministry?

John the Baptist is the perfect exemplar of the *Shrink* way of doing life and ministry. If we are intent on pursuing Jesus and serving the kingdom of God, we must learn how to shrink. We have to shrink, personally—we must decrease and he must increase—and we must call those around us to shrink so that Christ may become more present in our lives, living in and through us, making and remaking us in his own image, and carrying that image to the rest of the world.

PRAGMATISM

The current leadership conversation could never produce a John the Baptist or a Clyfford Still. I'm not saying that those kinds of leaders don't exist. I'm saying that the current leadership culture cannot produce them, and it certainly cannot sustain them. The reason it cannot is because the current culture is bursting at the seams with *pragmatism*.

Pragmatism is the church's kryptonite—and church leaders swallow it constantly.

> Pragmatism is the church's kryptonite – and church leaders swallow it constantly.

Take a look at books on servant leadership, books you would think recommend a different set of values, and you will find pragmatism throughout their pages. Even among those writing within the missional church conversation. If you read the books and listen to the speakers, you can bet that they will eventually end up arguing for their respective approaches as effective strategies through which one can achieve better results. Pragmatism is pervasive. Success is everyone's goal.

I know it probably sounds odd, but *I am not offering a new definition of or pathway to success. I'm saying that success is the kind of metric we simply don't know how to handle.* It's above our pay grade. We see far too little of the big picture to worry about success, so we need to talk about it much less than we do. The way of descent—which is the way Jesus taught—can never promise us success. I don't mean to alter out definition of success. I mean to reduce our focus on success to a sort of minor side conversation instead of the main thrust.

Pragmatism is just another name for the good-to-great model of leadership. I'm arguing for a leadership that is based not on pragmatism but on *faithfulness*, and the two could not be more different. Let's do a comparison:

Pragmatism focuses on getting things done, and it is the overarching goal of good-to-great leadership.

- Pragmatism asks, "What works? What is effective?"
- The building blocks of pragmatism are *strategies*, *models*, and *techniques*.
- Strategies, models, and techniques can be copied and pasted from one context to another and are meant to help us become successful or even great.
- The leader who pursues pragmatism never gets beyond the question, "What works? What is effective? What strategies, models, and techniques must I learn and execute to get the desired results?"

Faithfulness is a focus on a mode of being that conforms to the way of Jesus Christ, and it is the overarching goal of *authentically Christian* leadership.

- Faithfulness asks, "What does faithfulness look like in this context?"
- The building blocks of faithfulness are the stories and virtues rooted in the gospel and patterned on Jesus' life.
- Virtues cannot be cut and pasted from one context to another. They have to be grown out of the soil of each community's life.

- The leader who pursues faithfulness never gets beyond the question, "What does faithfulness look like right here and now? What is God's will for us in this time and place? What virtues must our community embrace to act faithfully regardless of the results?"

The current leadership conversation has to grow beyond pragmatic strategies, models, and techniques for success. Instead, the conversation needs to focus on faithfulness and the virtues that must be at work in the lives of leaders so they can act on what they know to be the faithful way.

I must interject at this point to acknowledge that the Christian leader must be constantly looking for signs of fruitfulness. Flourishing is at the center of God's heart for all creation, and the church most of all. We'll talk more about this in later chapters. However, before we can even begin to talk about fruitfulness and flourishing, we must let go of the idea of success—especially success at any cost. Otherwise we will simply make the words *fruitfulness* and *flourishing* synonymous with the cultural ideal of success.

I have often asked myself why I was so quick to buy what Jim Collins was selling. *Good to Great* was required reading for a leadership course I took, led by the pastor I worked for at the time. How could I have read that book and never questioned the premise? The first time Collins stood up in front of a group of Christians and said, "Good is the enemy of Great," why did we not immediately question it? Do we really want to say that Good is the enemy of anything?

The reason we bought what Jim Collins was selling—and what a whole host of other leadership gurus were selling as well—was that we all wanted to be great. We wanted success, and not always for a bad reason. Maybe we were chasing the social credibility that comes along with pastoring a huge church, but we also wanted the church to advance, we wanted the gospel to spread, and we wanted to change people's lives and the world in the process. Still, the fact remains that the heart of what we were chasing was bigger, better, higher, stronger, faster. We wanted success, and here was a guy telling us how we could do it. We all had our one thousand days, and many of us joined the brother- and-sisterhood of good-to-great leadership.

I know a pastor who had built a successful megachurch. He was a former evangelist who had decided to plant his own church. This pastor had been running with some pretty fast company for years—national religious and political leaders—and he had big plans for his new congregation.

As he was getting ready for the launch, he began to devise a marketing strategy. As part of the strategy, his team began collecting church directories from nearby evangelical churches and other local congregations. They also procured donor databases of local nonprofit ministries. When it came time to send out direct marketing pieces, he specifically targeted those families who were involved in—hopefully dissatisfied with—their existing churches and ministries. Thousands of members of other local congregations received materials and marketing pieces that were specifically designed to lure them away from their churches.

What that pastor did was pragmatic, and as a strategy for having a huge launch it was successful. But it was terribly unfaithful—effective, but wrong. He broke faith with every pastor of those other churches. He broke faith with the members who were left behind to pick up the pieces when their friends left for a new congregation. We could probably even say that he broke faith with Jesus by injuring the body of Christ.

This is an obvious example of how pragmatism kills faithfulness, how great becomes the enemy of good. The reason church leaders so quickly bought what Collins and others like him were selling is that most Christian leaders have been formed by a narrative of pragmatism and success instead of faithfulness and virtue. It's the same reason we can't imagine taking the Clyfford Still / John the Baptist nosedive into obscurity and why we will do nearly anything to achieve success.

If I'm completely honest, I have to admit that part of why I bought what Jim Collins was selling was because I didn't want to shrink—in the literal and symbolic sense. I didn't want to have my dreams give way to God's will. I didn't want to watch people walk away because we set the bar high on faithfulness. I didn't want to leave the results up to God; I wanted to control them myself.

Maybe we bought Collins's pragmatic leadership model because faithfulness requires *vulnerability*, and we see vulnerability as weakness. Maybe it was that we feel so *competitive* with our peers, and shrinking feels too much like losing. Maybe we bought the pragmatism because faithfulness requires *brokenness*, and it's exhausting to face our awkward issues in order to grow. Maybe we bought it because faithfulness requires *patience*, and we are tired of waiting on God to act. Maybe we bought it because faithfulness requires *fidelity*, and we could make an extra $10,000 a year if we'll leave for that job at a bigger church.

Pragmatism is what we turn to when we don't know what to do next, and we don't possess the virtue necessary to simply be faithful and still in the tension, strain, and ambiguity.

> Pragmatism is what we turn to when we don't know what to do next, and we don't possess the virtue necessary to simply be faithful and still in the tension, strain, and ambiguity.

Models are what we follow when we don't have an ecclesiology robust enough to fund the all-out pursuit of faithfulness in our own context—especially if we are not experiencing the results we desire.

Strategies are what we turn to when we don't know the stories of God's faithfulness in the past, stories that can create an imagination of a future that is still breaking into our present time through Jesus Christ.

Techniques are what we make into the essential building blocks of ministry because we do not possess the virtues necessary to act creatively and faithfully moment to moment.

Faithfulness requires the cultivation of a specific set of virtues over time—and there is no shortcut. The central Christian leadership principle is *vulnerability*—the kind of vulnerability Jesus modeled by taking on human flesh and humbling himself even to death on a cross. The hardest lesson I've had to learn as a Christian leader is this: *If I am not vulnerable, I am not leading*—at least not in the way of Jesus. It also requires virtues such as cooperation, brokenness, patience, fidelity, and the ability to live in tension and uncertainty.

The leader who has been shaped by a conversation about faithfulness, who has worked really hard to cultivate these virtues in his or her life, would instantly know that Jim Collins stole the line "Good is the enemy of Great," from the mouth of Herod and Pilate and Pharaoh. You would never hear that line from the mouth of Jesus. Jesus would never in a million years tell us "Good is the enemy of Great."

I wish I could tell you that good-to-great practices won't help you grow your organization or church. They will totally work to produce numerical growth. However, I'm not so sure they can help us make disciples. I can tell you that good-to-great practices are not trained on faithfulness, so they should be a far less important part of the conversation about what it means to be a Christian leader, if they are a part of the conversation at all.

Good-to-great practices may produce a certain kind of growth, but as I will show later, this growth is disturbing in terms of its inability to train people in faithfulness and virtue and in terms of its impact on society.

That pastor who marketed his new church to names he found in other churches' directories actually became fairly well known and was considered a great success. But he was eventually called on the carpet in a series of scathing investigative reports by a local paper. Tax problems, dubious ethical practices, and accounting issues led the bank to eventually call the church's loan and repossess their building. The congregation finally disbanded, and the pastor moved on—hero to zero, just like Tyler Hamilton.

Hamilton became a great cyclist, but in the end he lost everything: his titles, his gold medal, his wife, his friends, and even his own integrity. The quest for greatness often demands this sort of sacrifice. It systematically roots out the goodness God means for us to foster and grow.

Christian leadership cannot be all about greatness and at the same time embrace the gospel of the kingdom of God. Church leaders should be formed in the way of Jesus Christ so completely that no other leadership narrative can hold sway in our lives. Only then will we create the kind of leadership conversation it takes to produce prophets of the kingdom like John the Baptist.

SHRINK

Jesus has chosen to give the world to the powerless.

Just think about that statement for a moment. Jesus has chosen to give the world to the powerless. He has not chosen to give the world to the powerful.

What about the successful? Has Jesus chosen to give the world to the successful? I think not. It seems to me that the faithful will receive blessings that cannot be taken away from them, even when it requires them to shrink.

> Jesus has chosen to give the world to the powerless.

Pursuing faithfulness over and against success will not be easy. When I helped to plant the church I now pastor, it was founded on success-based leadership principles that worked like a charm. We grew from two families to almost two hundred families in the first three years. We planted another church in a nearby town and continued to grow. But when we decided to stop chasing success and to pursue faithfulness, we lost over 50 percent of our people. I learned through bitter tears that the *Shrink* move is not for the faint of heart.

I'm an unlikely person to write a book like this. I'm not a world-class church leader. I serve a little ragamuffin church of a couple hundred people, twenty or thirty of whom are hard-core alcoholics and addicts who live on the streets, the rest of whom are middle-class suburbanites who struggle every day with what it means to pursue the *Shrink* way of life in the midst of this world dominated by the upwardly mobile. Most of what I know comes from failure, not success.

If you pursue faithfulness in your context, if you stop chasing success, it is likely that your ministry will shrink. The way of Jesus is a narrow way. I don't mean that in an "insider/outsider" way. I mean the Jesus way is the narrow way, because you have to shrink to follow it, and few will have the courage to do so.

If pressed about my church's growth strategy, I usually say it is to *get smaller and die*. Nowadays, faithfulness — not success — is our only metric. Success is about "doing." Faithfulness is about "being." It's really hard to measure and even harder to do.

Convincing the church it does not exist merely for the benefit of its members but for the life of the world is a pretty bad church-growth strategy. It's also exactly what the church must do. I know it is a tough sell, but crucifixion seems like a losing strategy unless you believe in the resurrection. Faithfulness seems like a fool's errand unless you believe that the power of the gospel trumps our ability to come up with all the right answers to all the right questions — unless you believe Jesus has chosen to give the world to the powerless.

> Success is about "doing." Faithfulness is about "being." It's really hard to measure and even harder to do.

The call to follow in the steps of Jesus is the kind of call few will answer, but I have become convinced it is the better way. The burden of faithfulness truly is lighter than the burden of success. The call to take up our cross and follow Jesus can seem austere, harsh, and unbending, but it's nowhere near as toxic to the soul as the call to achieve ministry greatness — it just looks that way from the outside.

The *Shrink* way of ministry may have an unappealing brochure, but from the inside the experience is nothing short of amazing. The burden is lighter because the power of God funds the entire faithfulness project. To shrink means you may travel light, but you will walk with a spring in your step.

The embrace of weakness, vulnerability, and gentleness is not a strategy for success. It is simply the only way to participate in the life of Christ. In the end, following Jesus isn't separated into followers and leaders. We are all followers. Those who will humbly embody weakness and vulnerability will inherit the earth: they will see God. But we cannot expect that everyone will want to go this way. Only those with eyes to see and ears to hear will embrace Jesus' vision for ministry.

There will be times when growth does occur within the authentic

Christian leader's circle of influence. Faithful Christian leadership doesn't mean that our numbers will always shrink. However, when healthy growth occurs, it will typically be centered not on the growth of a single church, but the life of an entire community. The people in our churches listening to the message each week are the ones who will extend the kingdom to the workplace, the neighborhoods, and their friendships and families, as they embody the reality that the kingdom of God brings good news to the poor, the lame, the blind, the broken, the disturbed, the handicapped, and the sick. Their faithfulness is much more important than any perceived success.

> God save us from the successful church.

God save us from the successful church.

God give us churches who shun success and aren't afraid to face the inevitable shrinkage that comes as a result of following Jesus. God save us from church leadership strategies. After all, it takes little or no faith to follow a strategy, but extraordinary faith to pursue the kingdom of God and leave the rest in God's hands.

If I've learned anything as a pastor, it is this: *faithfulness flies in the face of pragmatism, and if you pursue it, you have to be ready to shrink.*

Chapter 3

THE FAILURE OF THE MEGACHURCH

*You've never heard of forward thrust? It is the most
central principle of American life, the necessity to
improve your lot and status at any cost, and to stay one
step ahead of the abyss that may open suddenly at your
heels. Unfortunately, forward thrust turns out not to
be helpful in the search for your true place on earth.*
—Anne Lamott

I've spent most of my professional life moving back and forth
between the disparate worlds of the small, humble neighborhood
church and the large, attractive megachurch. During the decade I
spent touring with my band, Satellite Soul, we often played concerts
for thousands at megachurches. We played just as many in small
church coffeehouses and youth groups. While planting churches I
attended many conferences put on by Willow Creek, Saddleback,
and Northpoint, and I watched scores of video conferences, events,
and meetings. Then I'd head back to the small church plant and plug
away, trying to be more like the big boys.

I'm so thankful that I spent those years bouncing back and forth
between those two contrasting environments. This forced me to
reflect on the differing dynamics working within each. In some ways,
I'm still doing this. The church I serve is fewer than 250 people. But
I've spent much of the past fifteen years planting churches in part-
nership with a Kansas City megachurch called Heartland Community Church. I have great respect and admiration for the leadership

and congregation of Heartland. These guys are my friends and have been incredibly supportive of me over the years. I love that I'm a part of the Heartland family, and I owe this church so much.

While I am going to argue that some of the negative dynamics of the megachurch model are inescapable because they are systemic, I believe Heartland has done more to mitigate those dynamics than any other megachurch I've ever encountered. They work really hard at it, and I'm proud to be one of Heartland's church planters. I love to get asked to preach there and lead worship, and I would never want anyone in that circle to think that I'm being overly critical.

Yet, if a critique of the megachurch needs to happen — and it surely does need to happen — then it should come from an ardent admirer, from somebody who has a little skin in the game, and from somebody who actually is involved with and loves a megachurch. When I critique the model, I feel like I'm doing it as at least a partial insider ... a bit like critiquing my own mother.

While planting churches, especially early on, I constantly mimicked the leadership practices of the megachurch. I lived with the intrinsic pressures, stress points, and weaknesses of the megachurch model as a whole. Yet my critique is primarily theological — it's about an ecclesiology that often becomes thinned out, ignored, or even erased in certain environments. The megachurch will always struggle to embody the gospel in a way that is truly good news for the city simply because their size limits their options, counting out certain kenotic practices that would be lethal to a church that large.

Thus the megachurch must ignore or marginalize certain essential elements of a robust ecclesiology. The fact that many of the elements of our Christian faith that are actually essential to the gospel must be subdued or ignored by the megachurch casts doubt on the wisdom of undertaking any such enterprise. So this is a theological argument first, and it doesn't mean I don't love my Heartland family or Bill Hybels, Andy Stanley, Rick Warren, and their churches. I do love you guys, and I don't want you to stop doing what you are doing.

That God uses megachurches in exceptional ways is not up for dispute. God certainly does. However, I think this is evidence that God will use whatever broken thing we give him, not that this is a particularly healthy way to be the church. Most churches in America are less than three hundred people. Sadly, many if not most of them spend their entire lives feeling bad about not being bigger. I wasted many years feeling that way. It's a terrible thing to feel. This is the culture I'm trying to change.

THE CHURCH ON STEROIDS

The art of doctoring a pitch is as old as baseball itself. A little Vaseline on the fingers makes the ball slide out of the pitcher's hand and drop like crazy. Pitchers have been known to use spray-sunscreen on their forearms and mix it with the rosin they use on the mound. This combination makes the ball stick to a pitcher's fingers like Fixodent, increasing velocity and control. Since Bruce Sutter first perfected the split-fingered fastball—a pitch that has roughly the same movement as a doctored pitch—doctoring the ball has become a bit of a lost art, but it will probably always be part of the game.

> That God uses megachurches in exceptional ways is not up for dispute.... However, I think this is evidence that God will use whatever broken thing we give him, not that this is a particularly healthy way to be the church.

One of my all-time favorite moments in professional sports came in 1987 when one of the great knuckleballers, Joe Niekro, was on the mound for the Minnesota Twins. The Twins were on the road facing the California Angels, and the score was tied 2–2 in the fourth inning. After a called strike—a dancing knuckleball that froze the batter—home plate umpire Tim Tschida walked out to the pitcher's mound and asked Niekro if he could see the ball. Soon the other umpires joined the conference asking to see Niekro's glove, his hands, and what he had in his pockets.

Neikro protested. He handed the ump his glove and a picture of his kids he always kept with him. As he turned his back pockets inside out, Niekro appeared to toss a small object casually to the side while throwing his arms up in a gesture meant to indicate, "I don't know what you're talking about." The ump leaned over and recovered an emery board and a small piece of sandpaper from the infield grass. He showed it to Tschida, who immediately tossed Niekro from the game. It was a classic moment.

The thing is, nobody got mad about it. We all thought it was funny. While serving a ten-day suspension, Niekro appeared on the *David Letterman Show*, hamming it up, wearing a tool belt with an electric sander, wire brush, and Vaseline, calling them the tools of his trade. The crowd ate it up. It wasn't like when Mark McGuire and Sammy Sosa admitted using performance-enhancing drugs. There was no public ire for Joe Niekro. It was seen as a bit of innocent fudging.

The players who have been caught using steroids and banned substances, however, receive different treatment. At the 2013 Baseball Hall of Fame induction ceremony, no living players were welcomed into the hall. The two names everyone was trying to avoid that day were Barry Bonds and Roger Clemens. Both players were thought to be first ballot shoo-ins for the Hall of Fame. After their steroid scandals, it seems unlikely that either one will make it anytime soon. As I write this, the baseball world is embroiled in another doping scandal as former MVPs Ryan Braun and Alex Rodriguez, along with a host of other players, have been suspended. These guys get no sympathy.

So, why do we laugh about Joe Niekro and rail about McGuire, Sosa, Bonds, and Clemens? Why the double standard? More importantly, why am I talking about pitchers doctoring the ball compared to players using performance-enhancing drugs in a book like this? It's weird I know, but stay with me. Most of us view doctoring the ball as a little bit of innocent tinkering, pushing the envelope, using tricks to make a pitch move. It doesn't make us mad, because we may see it as questionable but essentially harmless. Doping is an entirely different thing. For one thing, it is often a crime. For another thing, this form of cheating alters the body in ways that would not be otherwise possible. Doctoring a pitch is a skill. Doping involves *an actual change in the form and function of the human body* that gives the athlete a competitive advantage.

Here's my point: if the church is the body of Christ, then the megachurch is like a body on steroids; it involves an actual change in the form and function of the body of Christ. The problem is that we all pretend as though they are just doctoring the ball.

A megachurch is usually defined as any church with 2,000 or more people. To get a body to grow that large we must use some sort of performance enhancer. These things — typically models, strategies, and techniques gleaned not from the gospel or the Christian narrative, but from the world of business and the narrative of consumer capitalism — serve as performance enhancers that help create enormous congregations with huge facilities and hundreds of programs. The impact of these practices is akin to using performance-enhancing drugs. They actually *alter the form and function of the body*, causing real and serious long-term consequences for the church universal.

> If the church is the body of Christ, then the megachurch is like a body on steroids.

Ever watch a bodybuilding competition on ESPN? You look at these massive men and women with huge, well-defined muscles and not an ounce of body fat, and think, *That's not how a body is supposed to look. Something is wrong with this picture.* Have you ever compared pictures of Mark McGuire or Barry Bonds as a rookie with a photo taken in their last season and thought, *How did that skinny little kid turn into Andre the Giant?*

This is how I see the megachurch these days. The body is so big it looks like something is off. This didn't happen by accident. Our most celebrated church leaders have been feeding the church the equivalent of performance-enhancing drugs for decades. The rest of us treated them like they were just doctoring the ball — a little harmless gamesmanship, pushing as hard as they can to do a good thing — and we immediately asked them how they were doing it so we could try.

If anyone felt a hint of concern in those early years of the church growth movement, we easily shrugged it off because the results were so amazing. But sometimes we tend to forget the downsides.

For every megachurch that starts up, scores of smaller churches are swallowed whole.

The gift set it takes in order to be a megachurch pastor is

exceedingly rare, so churches become dependent on personalities.

The typical megachurch's size provides so much anonymity that people begin to think it's possible to follow Jesus and escape the challenges of relationship.

Megachurches have helped create a religious marketplace, where smaller churches are expected to try and compete for market share—like the mom and pop shop going up against Walmart.

These things have changed the way the church is viewed in America.

There can be no doubt that the megachurch has been an amazing laboratory in which we have tested the limits of size on the body of Christ. Maybe it is time for our megachurch leaders to teach us the most important lesson yet: *there is such a thing as too big.*

Of course, in the popular imagination the opposite is true. The megachurch has become the gold standard, the ultimate objective for all pastors. Growth has become nearly synonymous with God's blessing. I want us to think carefully about this assumption.

It is interesting to note that nearly all of the megachurches to which I have been exposed are beginning to use the language of "getting small." That is, finding a way to provide members with more connection, more friendships, more ways to feel like they are not just a cog in a huge wheel. So they form strategies, create structures, and design programs designed to create the sensation of smallness without actually having to get small. Why not just get small? Why not shrink? At least part of the reason is that shrinking brings with it a whole truckload of *vulnerabilities.*

In the megachurch narrative, vulnerability is a bad thing that is quickly mitigated. In fact, if there is anything that describes the entire megachurch phenomenon most succinctly it is this: *the megachurch is an attempt to flee vulnerability through size.* Yet, in order to be faithful, the church that follows the way of the kingdom enacted and taught by Jesus Christ must remain vulnerable at all times.

A few cracks in the megachurch armor are beginning to appear.

Financial troubles forced Rick Warren to send an anxious plea for money to his Saddleback congregation a few years ago. Recently, a Florida megachurch pastor — the son of another megachurch pastor — committed suicide after a scandal involving extramarital affairs, drugs, and guns. A Kansas City megachurch recently lost their $20 million campus to the bank. One of the country's first megachurches, the Crystal Cathedral, recently filed for bankruptcy. These stories are becoming more common, but they are just symptoms of a much deeper issue.

> The megachurch is an attempt to flee vulnerability through size.

Over the past few generations, our finest church leaders have failed us in much the same way McGuire, Sosa, Bonds, and Clemens failed baseball. Rather than facing their own vulnerabilities and limitations and waiting on God, these leaders resorted to artificial means in order to produce the fantastic outcomes they desired. To achieve success, growth, expansion, more people, dollars, and publicity, too many leaders pivoted away from the virtues of Christian leadership. They made a move to the CEO model of leadership, borrowed tactics from the world of business and entertainment, and led by example. Soon we were all chasing bigger and better.

I have to confess that I have been part of this as well. I spent over a decade chasing bigger, better, higher, faster, stronger. But as I've gotten a bit of theological perspective on that narrative and as I look back at what we've done, I can't help thinking that we were distorting the body somehow.

I don't mean to turn back the clock, and I don't mean to tear down all the megachurches. I just want us to think carefully about the ways in which the megachurch leadership techniques have radically transformed the body of Christ. We may have been able to produce big crowds, amazing programs, public popularity, and huge facilities, but I wonder if we have failed the church in important ways. The megachurch mentality isn't like doctoring a pitch; it's like taking steroids in order to alter the body permanently, so that our churches can grow without *limits*.

WHICH WE ARE WE?

There are two powerful narratives at work in every ministry leader's imagination. The first is the American narrative: a story of mass production, capital growth, entertainment, and the virtue of everything bigger, better, higher, faster, and stronger. The American story says our country was started by strong individuals who defeated the mighty British Empire, then pushed west across the frontier to settle the continent. We toppled Hitler, put a man on the moon, and won the Cold War. Americans don't like limits. We like graphs in which all lines move up and to the right.

This narrative forms the basis of American life and gives us a script for how we are to live our lives. This script says that bigger is better, more virtuous, safer, happier, and more fun. This script tells us that limits are bad and limitations are meant to be overcome. The American way is up.

If we've learned anything after 9/11 and the 2008 financial collapse, it is that this script can fail at any moment. The story of bigger, better, higher, faster, and stronger cannot make us happy, it cannot keep us safe, and it is not God's story.

Another powerful narrative is at work in the world at the same time. This narrative is called the gospel, and it was unleashed by the life, teaching, death, resurrection, and ascension of Jesus Christ. When we follow the Jesus way, our job is to *shrink*. On this, the New Testament is unambiguous: the Jesus way is down.

Jesus taught that the only way to find your life is to lose it for the sake of the gospel. He said the first must be last. If you try and keep your life, you will actually end up losing everything you were after in the first place. This teaching is so pervasive that if you attempt to remove it from the Gospels, there would be hardly any of Jesus' words left. If you attempt to remove it from his actions, then his entire life becomes unintelligible. Below are just a few of the many ways in which this theme is woven into the New Testament:

> Matthew 5:3–10: Blessed are the poor in spirit, those who
> mourn, the meek, the merciful, the peacemakers, and the
> persecuted.

Matthew 6:19–21, 25–27: Don't store up treasures on earth, don't build bigger barns.

Matthew 16:24–26: The one who seeks to save himself will lose himself; the one who lets go of herself will find herself.

Matthew 18:3: If you want to see the kingdom, you must become like a little child.

Matthew 20:16: The last will be first and the first will be last.

Matthew 20:26: If you want to be great, you have to become a servant.

Matthew 20:28: The Son of Man did not come to be served but to serve.

Matthew 23:11–12: The greatest among you will be the servant; the humble will be exalted and the exalted will be humbled.

Luke 9:23: Anyone who wants to be Jesus' disciple must deny themselves, take up their cross daily, and follow him.

Luke 17:33: If you cling to your life, you'll lose it; if you let your life go, you'll find it.

1 Corinthians 1:27: God uses the foolish things to shame the wise and chooses the weak to shame the strong.

2 Corinthians 8:9: Jesus was rich, but for our sake became poor.

2 Corinthians 12:10: We are to delight in weaknesses, insults, hardships, persecutions, and difficulties; for when we are weak, then we are strong.

Philippians 2:6–11: Jesus did not grasp his divinity, but humbled himself and emptied himself, obedient to death on the cross.

James 4:6: God opposes the proud but shows favor to the humble.

James 4:10: Humble yourself before the Lord, and he will lift you up.

These verses are just the tip of the iceberg. The New Testament is univocal: the way of Jesus is the way of descent—it's about learning to shrink.

To shrink is to experience a kind of death and resurrection. Our part is to learn how to die to ourselves and to others. God's part is to produce new life from those deaths.

This reality is woven into the nature of the universe. Life always comes from death. No matter how much you love the spring and summer, you know that fall is just around the corner. Then winter comes, and all creation looks to have died. For months the world seems barren and cold. Then it happens again. Life explodes from death and the cycle continues.

If you want to grow some grass or a garden or a tomato plant, it all starts when you take a seed and bury it in the ground and it dies. The seed must cease to be a seed in order to become a plant. We also put dead material (fertilizer, manure, etc.) on top of those things we want to grow. From death we see new life. Only after the seed dies will the plant grow into a mature organism with the ability to create more plants—sometimes hundreds or thousands of them—all from that one seed.

So when the Bible tells the story of how God is bringing new life into the world, it is telling the same story creation has told since the beginning. "Very truly I tell you," Jesus once taught, "unless a kernel of wheat falls to the ground and dies, it remains only a single seed." (John 12:24). The Christian story is about Jesus the Messiah, who is one with the Father, who became a human being, lived, taught, and died. Then God raised him again to new life. His new life, his resurrection, is the seedbed of our new life together as the church.

This new life is not just resuscitation; this is resurrection—a completely new kind of life springing forth from death. The careful observer will notice that the death and resurrection of Jesus Christ fits with the way the world has always been. Spring always follows winter; seeds die, then spring forth into new life. Life always springs from death, because it always takes a death to get a resurrection.

Here's the stunning part. In the gospel of John, right after the bit about the seed, Jesus says that this life-from-death reality isn't just about food or bodies or seasons—it's all of us. Eugene Peterson's *The Message* says it so well, "Anyone who holds on to life just as it is destroys that life. But if you let it go, reckless in your love, you'll have it forever, real and eternal" (John 12:25). Jesus isn't the only one who must enter into this process. He invites us to enter into it as well.

If you want to win, you have to learn how to lose.
If you want to keep something, you have to give it up.
If you want to live, you have to learn how to die.
If you want to lead, you have to become the servant of all.

With this one simple concept, Jesus captures the essence of the kingdom of God. If you want to live, you have to learn how to die—little by little every day—for the life of the world. Only then will you have a genuine life. If we ever truly embrace this reality as human beings, we will be transformed by it, and we will transform everything we touch.

The Jesus narrative is different from the American narrative. The American narrative teaches us that life is about growing, expanding, winning, gaining, and impressing. Our worth is connected to being faster, smarter, and better. Our value is all about being skilled, competent, and rewarded. Life is like a competition and the object is *not to die*. Our entire culture clings to a completely different reality than the one Jesus describes for us. I believe the megachurch is a better reflection of the way of our culture than the way of Jesus.

Perhaps the best example of this would be the megachurch that recently raised $5 million to build their own three-lane overpass so they could keep parking lot exit times under thirty minutes. The goal was to keep the congregation, already well over fifteen thousand people, growing bigger. It worked too. Last time I checked, this church had more than twenty-five thousand members. The $5 million overpass is a steroid, a way to attempt to grow without limits. Most people look at this and see savvy leadership. When I look at this, I see a body builder using steroids to gain just a few more pounds of muscle mass—a $5 million way to avoid to the God-given reality of *limits*.

In addition to avoiding limits, a deeper, more essential fear is at

> I believe the megachurch is a better reflection of the way of our culture than the way of Jesus.

work: the fear of being vulnerable. All of those things listed above — the last, the humble, the weak, the poor, the peacemakers, the servant, the one who loses his or her life — involve embracing our own vulnerability.

This is axiomatic for the Christian narrative: the way of Jesus is the way of vulnerability. One cannot follow Jesus without becoming completely and utterly vulnerable.

The megachurch is able, by consolidating needs and resources in much the same way a large corporation does, to flee vulnerability through size. Their congregations are younger, wealthier, and more educated. They are typically much more financially stable, despite lower levels of giving compared to all other churches.[1] The megachurch model can become an attempt to identify with the teachings of Jesus without having to actually experience the vulnerability involved with living them out.

If we are going to follow Jesus, we have to learn to switch narratives — from the American narrative of growth and expansion to the Jesus narrative of descent, humility, weakness, and vulnerability. We are going to have to shrink.

Theologian Stanley Hauerwas is fond of saying that he represents the "Tonto Principle" in Christian ethics. He's referring to the early television program in which the Lone Ranger and his sidekick, Tonto, traveled around the Old West fighting for truth and justice. Hauerwas will typically tell about the time the two were surrounded by twenty thousand Sioux in the Dakotas. The Lone Ranger turned to Tonto and said, "We're in a pretty bad fix. What do you think we ought to do?" Tonto looked at him and said, "What do you mean 'we,' white man?" Hauerwas then explains that this is the movement we all need to learn how to make — recovering the Christian "we" from the American "we." He's right. Christians need to look at America,

---

1 Scott Thumma and Warren Bird, "Not Who You Think They Are: The Real Story of People Who Attend Megachurches," Leadership Network and Hartford Institute for Religion Research, 2009. Accessed February 7, 2014: available at: http://leadnet.org/resources/not_who_you_think_they_are_real_story_of_people_attend_america_megachurches/

and American culture and say, "What do you mean 'we'? We are Christians, before we are anything else."[2]

It's time for the church to switch our primary allegiance from the narrative of American culture of bigger, better, higher, faster, more people, more programs, and no limits to the narrative of Jesus and his teachings, which will require us to embrace a whole different way of life—the way of descent.

IS THERE A PROPHET IN THE HOUSE?

Perhaps the best scriptural example of this way of thinking comes from the life of Solomon. In his classic work *The Prophetic Imagination*, Old Testament scholar Walter Brueggemann contrasts the life of Moses with the life of Solomon.[3]

Moses was the quintessential prophet, criticizing the injustice of the Egyptian regime and energizing God's people toward an alternative future. His ministry had a dismantling effect on the empire. His energizing message envisioned a new reality that did not previously exist, one where every man, woman, and child would have enough to live on. Over and over this reality was called into being not by the strength of a man, but by the power of God. Moses' entire ministry was about naming the new reality and calling his people toward it. Yet he constantly confessed that only Yahweh could make it happen and waited on God to make it so, even if that meant he wouldn't get to lead his people into the Promised Land.

Solomon took a completely different tack. He pursued the formation of an empire. Brueggemann calls this alternative narrative the "royal consciousness." The royal consciousness is a mind-set that tells us that we can generate our own existence, that by hoarding resources we can have predictable results, and that we can secure our own place in the world without needing to be vulnerable. Solomon and Pharaoh are chief exemplars of the royal consciousness. The reign of Solomon

---

2 Stanley Hauerwas, "The Tonto Principle," *Sojourners Magazine*, vol. 31, no. 1 (January–February, 2002), 30.

3 Walter Brueggemann, *The Prophetic Imagination* (Minneapolis: Fortress 2001).

can be seen as an outright rejection of the Mosaic imagination and a total change in values toward affluence, oppressive social policy, and the static religion that closed the door on God's action, thereby giving the king a complete monopoly on everything.

Think about all the things Solomon hoarded. *Sex*: he amassed a harem of a thousand wives and concubines. *Identity*: he changed the organizational structure of Israel, erasing tribal identity, reorganizing everyone into tax districts. This created citizens out of what was previously a tribe or a family. *Bureaucracy*: all power was concentrated into a system Solomon controlled. *Violence*: he created Israel's first standing army and was the first king of Israel to coerce his own people through violence. *Intellect*: Solomon collected smart and wise people, functionally controlling the information of the day. *Labor*: Solomon created his own personal labor force to build the royal palace and other projects.[4]

By the time Solomon was done, the Hebrew way of life had been radically transformed. The most dramatic impact was not found in the royal palace but in the small community. When young men looked for a woman to marry, they found Solomon had already claimed the best wives. When wise men were needed to judge local matters, they found those with the necessary gifts were tied up in King Solomon's court. People's most basic identity—tribe, clan, and family—were subverted by the tax districts and the distinctive identity found in those ties vanished forever. Solomon's royal projects sucked up all of the oxygen in their society until there was no room for the locals to improve their own communities.

When I read the story of Solomon, I can't help thinking of the megachurch. The impact Solomon's royal project had on the local community is similar to the impact of the megachurch on the small local congregation. Most of the churches in our society are small. When they look around for the resources they need to make the body of Christ beautiful, far too many are already engaged by Solomon's court.

I see three powerful threads in Brueggemann's teaching about the

---

4 Ibid., 30–31.

Solomonic kingdom, each of which seem to critique the megachurch project.

First, *God cannot become the legitimizing narrative that gives the Christian leader a rationale for any and all projects we desire.* This move functionally reverses the trajectory of God's kingdom. We join with God; God does not join with us. We will have God's blessing if and when we join in God's mission, and in the manner God has recommended. If we start talking about how big we can build this thing, or how we can make a name for ourselves, we will have God's opposition (or at least indifference). Anytime we attempt to build our own towers, our leadership has coopted God and become part of the royal consciousness.

Second, *the mission of God is not a program; it is a passion that we do not originate, but join already in progress.* This missional passion does not refer to my personal cause or the dream I have for my own life. It already has a content given by God. The Latin root of our English word *passion* is *passio*, which means *suffering.* God's passion, God's mission is about suffering, which manifests in a covenant relationship between God and God's people through which the life of the believer is continually poured out for the life of the community in which they live.

We are meant to pour out our own lives in the firm conviction that life will never run out because it is continually refreshed in God. Truly Christian leadership is not focused on accomplishing goals and meeting metrics—that's the royal consciousness. Rather, it is devoted to passionate suffering on behalf of the surrounding culture, embodying the good news by living in constant hope in the midst of the pain.

Third, *the constant covenanting required for membership in the community of the faithful is subverted by the leader who promises customer satisfaction instead of sacrifice.* Christian leadership cannot promise that your needs will be met by the church to which you belong. If leaders do this, they are promising more than the Bible seems willing to promise. Christian leadership can only promise that as you exhaust your life on behalf of the world around you, God will never let you run out of life. For every death, no matter how small, there will be a resurrection.

> Christian leadership cannot promise that your needs will be met by the church to which you belong. If leaders do this, they are promising more than the Bible seems willing to promise.

If Brueggemann is right, then we have reached a place in the life of the American church where we need to stop churning out leaders and start churning out prophets. If we are to do this, first we'll have to do a little work on what we mean when we use the word *prophet*.

PROPHETIC IMAGINATION

The contemporary notion of what it means to be a prophet bears little resemblance to the biblical one. Modern-day prophets predict the future (with little success). They attempt to tell your fortune and forecast calamitous global events. They manipulate people and gain power by claiming to possess privileged information from God concerning what will happen in the world. The prophet-as-fortune-teller paradigm is a gross misrepresentation of what the prophetic office meant to the Israelites.

In the Scriptures the prophetic office is not about telling the future. The prophetic office is a specific and essential role dedicated to the critique of the present day and how it has veered off course and to the imagination of a future that aligns more completely with the kingdom of God. The prophetic office involves these two distinct moves: *critique* and *imagination*.

Prophetic critiquing. Brueggemann says, "Criticism is not carping and denouncing. It is asserting that false claims to authority and power cannot keep their promises."[5] The prophet announces that the empire cannot keep its promises to make us safe and happy; only God can do that. No government or church can meet all of our needs; only God can. The prophet helps us to see that under the influence of the powerful, we are "pressed and urged and invited to pretend that

---

5 Ibid., 11.

things are all right" and "as long as the empire can keep the pretense alive ... there will be no serious criticism."[6] The prophet doesn't predict calamity as much as he or she simply tells the truth about where our current tack will take us.

The prophet, therefore, is concerned primarily with injustice, speaking on behalf of the little guy, the person on the margins of the culture who is suffering at the hands of the powerful. The prophet does not say, "Here's what's going to happen in the future." The prophet says, "Here is what is going on in the present day that is completely unjust. This injustice has a predictable future: it will not stand because God will not allow it."

Prophetic imagination. Brueggemann suggests three energizing dimensions of the prophetic office in which imagination is paramount.

First, the prophet energizes people to believe that a different reality is possible. Those who despair cannot see how newness can come. Those who stand with Egypt, or the empire, do so because they simply lack the imagination to pursue another way. The prophet counteracts this with an imagination of a new future. The prophet energizes a community who dares to believe and affirm that things will turn out differently than the empire has planned. Moses knew what Pharaoh didn't. Moses knew the identity of the world's true Lord.

Second, the prophet names the future reality and proclaims that God is on the side of the little guy, the person on the margins of the culture who will benefit from that future. At this point it is easy to see how closely aligned Jesus' teaching was with the message of the prophets.

Third, the worshiping community becomes the catalyst for change, the agents through which God will enact his story of human freedom from bondage (to sin, death, decay, the powers of evil, suffering, poverty, and so on). The future actually begins to break into the present through this kind of community.

Prophetic outcome. The prophetic leader doesn't tell the future so

---

6 Ibid.

much as he/she points out the natural consequences of the current actions of the group. So, the prophetic leader is the one who is able to name the anxieties of the group without participating in them. They are able to name the sins of the people without letting themselves off the hook. The prophetic leader unmasks the powers of the culture—bigger, better, higher, faster—refusing to allow those powers to claim ultimate authority and pointing to their eventual failure.

Only after we have learned to tell the truth about our own lives will God's people have a future. Once this has happened, the prophetic leader energizes a community to imagine a different future, one in which they do not fall prey to the sins of their past, one in which God reigns in the hearts and lives of God's people and in the societies of which they are a part. The prophetic leader inspires people to live toward that future—not toward the future the empire or the powers of the world wish them to live. The prophet's most powerful vision is not merely about the coming calamity that will befall the people who have been unfaithful to God. The prophet's most powerful vision is of a future where God reigns and God's people are faithful. It is this hopeful vision that actually subverts the false powers of the world.

THE TRUTH ABOUT THE MEGACHURCH

The contemporary church needs prophets who are not afraid to critique the status quo and help the church to imagine a new future based not in the American story of *up*, but on the gospel story of *down*. In our current church culture, I see no other way than for prophetic leaders to say that the narrative of empire is built into the infrastructure and narrative of the megachurch. Everywhere this narrative holds sway, the best efforts of that church will often run against the gospel story. If the prophets of our time would speak up, here are a few things they might say.

Megachurch size *insulates the body* from the natural pains and tensions that keep it healthy. Pain is good, even in the church. Pain forces a community and its leaders to grow deeper and more mature. For instance, if two families leave a small church, their leaving cannot be ignored. The small church will have to face underlying issues and learn how to heal and grow. However, if those same two families were to leave a megachurch, no one would even notice. By virtue of its size, the megachurch is insulated from so many of the naturally occurring tensions that make for a healthy body, and dysfunction is allowed to build up over time. Eventually the megachurch will become symptomatic, but by then it's usually too late. And even if the megachurch does feel the pain, it is typically derived from a threat to the institution itself and not from any inherent relational dynamic that gives dignity and importance to every single member.

I don't mean to say that the megachurch never feels any kind of pain; I know they do. I mean to say that because of its size, the megachurch has a fundamental lack of sensitivity to certain kinds of pain, especially painful feedback that might call into question the leadership, vision/direction of the church, especially regarding the *telos* of the model itself.

Megachurch size *inhibits diversity*. A great example of this phenomenon is our worship music. In 2013 superstar worship leader Chris Tomlin released a new album that debuted at number one on Billboard's top 200. As media and blogs covered the release, many picked up on a certain refrain: *Chris Tomlin is the most sung artist in history*. Reporters Eric Marrapodi and Tom Foreman ran the data in an article for CNN.com. They spoke with Howard Rachinski, the CEO of CCLI—the company that tracks what music is used in churches—who said that every Sunday in the United States, somewhere between 60,000 and 120,000 different churches are singing Tomlin's songs. That's around 20 to 30 million people every single week. At the time CNN published this story in early 2013, Tomlin had the number one most sung song, and five out of the top twenty-five songs sung in churches.[7]

Chris Tomlin is a great guy and a phenomenal songwriter to be sure, but the massive influence he has on the day-to-day worship of

---

7 Eric Marrapodi and Tom Foreman, "Chris Tomlin: King of the Sing-Along," CNN Online. Accessed December 30, 2013: http://religion.blogs.cnn.com/2013/03/09/the-most-sung-artist-on-the-planet/.

the church cannot be healthy. It's not a slam on Tomlin; it's just that no single person should have that much influence on the life of the church. Whatever holes Tomlin has in his theological game—and everybody does—we all have them now. Whatever blind spots he has in his approach to worship, we all have the same blind spots now. Worship music is healthier when it is more diverse, especially when much of the music grows from the context of people's own congregation.

The megachurch has a similar kind of influence on the diversity of church leadership. Pastors flock to megachurch conferences where we learn how to copy the latest leadership models, strategies, and techniques. After a while all of our leaders and churches begin to look and sound the same. This means that although we all have some of the same strengths, we have the same weaknesses and theological blind spots.

This lack of diversity makes us fragile—monocultures always are.

Authentically Christian leadership is always local and occasional, growing from the soil of the local neighborhood. It cannot be imported from another context, because no two contexts are alike. A friend of mine, author Tim Keel, often says copying another leader's strategy is like gluing fruit from one tree onto another tree and saying, "Look what I grew!" It is not reality. The strategy of a church and its efforts toward mission must always grow out of the context of the community in which the church lives and dies.

Megachurch size *exploits the megachurch pastor*. I've watched this happen for years, observing the toll ministry takes on the megachurch pastor. This is what I've come to believe: the megachurch pastor is like the liver of an alcoholic body. The anxiety, pressure, and stress generated by the megachurch are not shared equally but are focused primarily on the pastor. This pressure molds the pastor into something more akin to a CEO of a large corporation than a wise rabbi. Even pastors who attempt to stay healthy will end up flaming out and suffering because the systemic issues cannot be mitigated by

> The megachurch pastor is like the liver of an alcoholic body.

THE FAILURE OF THE MEGACHURCH

sound personal practices. All of the artificial means used to grow the church are filtered through the life of the pastor, and the pastor has to somehow try to cleanse the system. This is an impossible task. So the church resorts to dialysis. They give the pastor a year off to try and get healthy again. Or they do a transplant and replace the pastor altogether, only to have the problem recur some years later.

Megachurch size *impedes pastoral accountability.* Megachurch pastor Charles Stanley got a divorce from his wife and never missed a week in the pulpit. The reasons for his divorce may have been completely legitimate, but surely a few weeks off would have been appropriate. And in a recent article for the *Religion News Service,* writer Jonathan Merritt listed a few of the ill-advised remarks megachurch pastor Mark Driscoll has made:

- *Avatar* is the "most demonic, satanic film" he's ever seen.
- Stay-at-home dads are "worse than unbelievers."
- Women shouldn't hold leadership positions in the church since they are "more gullible and easier to deceive than men."
- Fallen pastor Ted Haggard's wife may be to blame for his infidelity if she didn't keep herself up.
- Biblical wives should give their husbands frequent [oral sex— he used the slang] and perhaps allow their husbands to have anal sex during menstruation.
- If a man masturbates without a woman present, it is "a form of homosexuality."[8]

If I would have written or said any one of these things publicly, I would have been confronted by our church elders. If I would have said all of them, I think I would have been fired, and rightly so. I cannot help but wonder if there would have been some sort of consequences if Driscoll were not the leader of a huge church that is dependent on his personality.

---

8 Jonathan Merritt, "Is Mark Driscoll This Generation's Pat Robertson?" *Religion News Service,* May 13, 2013. Accessed May 15, 2013, https://jonathanmerritt.religionnews.com/2013/05/13/is-mark-driscoll-this-generations-pat-robertson.

My final critique is that the megachurch *moves in the wrong direction*. This is the hardest part of my critique to write. It's hard because I know how much good megachurches have done in the world, and they have been a real lifeline for many people. It's also hard because so many of my friends are involved in these churches and I know how hard they work, how much they believe, and how much they are sacrificing for their organization.

Megachurches do some things really well. They crank out tons of leaders. Many plant a ton of churches. They are extremely visible in the community. They provide phenomenal worship events—we're talking world class music, art, and teaching every Sunday. They provide the highest quality programs and services for families. They make a space for people to remain anonymous while still worshiping with the people of God. For many people who are on the fringes of Christianity, the megachurch can make it really easy to keep investigating what it means to follow Jesus.

> The megachurch way is up. The gospel way is down. When you zoom in tight, there are some amazing things happening there. When you pan out, I'm afraid the entire project is moving in the wrong direction.

The prophetic question is: What are we communicating about God and the kingdom of God through our actions? Not with our mouths, but with our hands and feet—what gospel does the megachurch preach by virtue of its behavior, its mode of being the church? Does it preach the gospel of bigger better, higher, faster, and stronger? Or does it preach the gospel that is primarily concerned with the small things, the left out, the left behind, the vulnerable, and the weak?

The medium is the message, right? The way we go about building an organization tells us more about our beating heart than anything we could ever say. I think we need to learn to tell the truth about this. The megachurch way is up. The gospel way is down. When you zoom in tight, there are some amazing things happening there. When you pan out, I'm afraid the entire project is moving in the wrong direction.

The real friction between the Jesus narrative and the American narrative as they fight it out in the leadership culture of any church is related to the overall end in mind. What are we really about? Is it the life of the world or the growth of the church? The Jesus narrative says that the church will pattern their life on Jesus' life. For the church that is following Jesus' example, their end in mind will always be the life of the world. For the church that is following the culture's example, their end in mind will be to grow their own organization. Most megachurch resources are directed toward institutional advancement. The macro-narrative the megachurch is typically chasing is much more closely aligned with the American story. And it's important to understand that it's a macro-thing. That's why I say when you zoom in close, so many good things are happening. It's when you pan out to the big picture that we start to see the problem.

The real boots-on-the-ground crux of the problem comes when, because a church has embraced the narrative of "up," we are unable to move people past the early stages of faith to the part where we start learning how to die. Following Jesus makes some serious demands on our lives. The Jesus way requires nothing less than the death of the ego and the relinquishment of control over our lives to a God we cannot see. There's a reason Jesus' characteristic call was to take up your cross and follow him. This call has never been good at attracting huge numbers. It is, after all, a narrow way. In order to appeal to the masses, the more unappealing demands of discipleship run contrary to the needs of the organization. The result is a criticism that is so obvious that it's cliché: the megachurch is a mile wide, but an inch deep.

There's plenty of evidence for this. In 2008 Willow Creek released the results of a study of their own congregation and a couple dozen other churches following the same megachurch strategies in a book called *Reveal: Where Are You?* The study concluded that numerical growth does not equal spiritual growth, and while the megachurch can help people with the initial steps of their faith journey, it does not help people to grow toward Christian maturity. Their own critique was that the megachurch has been wonderful in its ability to make Jesus fans. It has failed in the pursuit of making Jesus followers.

Even as I write this, I'm reminded of how much love and respect

I have for megachurch pastors and leaders—some of whom I count as close friends. Still I have to confess that I believe we have *all* been part of a church leadership culture that worships success. God knows I've been guilty of this. I think that some of the past high profile leaders must bear much of the responsibility. After all, most of the current leaders of megachurches—churches over one or two thousand in attendance each week—were not the architects of the church-growth leadership culture. Most of them are second-generation leaders who have simply followed in the footsteps of their heroes.

> I have to confess that I believe we have *all* been part of a church leadership culture that worships success. God knows I've been guilty of this.

WHERE DO WE GO FROM HERE?

So what can we do? Should the megachurch leaders dismantle their churches? No, I would never argue for that. Is the goal to point fingers, blame those responsible, and string them up? No, that is not the solution either. I am not arguing that megachurches are illegitimate ministries or that they are failures. Megachurch pastors and leaders should continue to chase the kingdom where they are called to serve (not that they need any advice from me).

What I am suggesting is this: *if we want to move forward, the church leadership conversation needs to change.*

At the grassroots level, we need to stop romanticizing the megachurch, stop celebrating its growth, and stop worshiping its success. We need to stop looking to good-to-great leaders to light the way for the future of the church in America. The first step for all of us is to stop excusing our own utilization of business, CEO-style leadership models as just a little harmless gamesmanship, and recognize that it's more serious than that. The longer we chase the way up, the more difficult we make it for the run-of-the-mill church member to recognize the essential nature of the gospel, that the Jesus way is down, and this way places serious demands on our lives.

I also want to recommend that church leaders should refuse to mimic the models, strategies, and techniques of "successful" congregations for growing bigger. Church leaders have to begin to trust themselves again, use their own imaginations, and dig deep into the rich theological traditions of the church in order to learn how they should lead. We need to imagine a future that is filled not with a megachurch monoculture, but with thousands of new small churches worshiping and serving their neighborhoods in creative, organic ways.

Megachurches need to focus on church planting. They need to stop pouring their resources into creating the ultimate church experience for their congregation. Instead, they need to spend the next twenty-five years planting a dozen healthy small churches. If a congregation of three thousand wants to double in size over the next decade, then they should try to plant fifteen healthy new churches of about two hundred people each. Resource them, support them, and give your life away on their behalf.

Finally, we need to focus on the next generation of leaders. In some ways, my generation is already lost. Some of us will be able to deconstruct and deprogram, but it is a lot to ask of a normal church staff member who has a family and kids, a house, and a 401k to just up and leave the gig that makes it all work for them. I'm just being realistic. I don't think a lot of us are willing to do it. We're going to have to teach our young leaders a different way.

To the young leaders out there, this is my advice. Find a small church you can love and serve. Find a small congregation of people who want to follow Jesus and give your life to them for the next three decades. Don't chase success; chase faithfulness instead. Don't leave for a bigger church, a higher salary, or a more high profile position. Dare to do a small thing faithfully. If you do stay put, give up your dreams of greatness. Don't become caught up in the church doping scandals, and certainly don't excuse the megachurch phenomenon as a little harmless gamesmanship—doctoring the ball—when it is far more serious than that. Rope up with a small congregation of people and refuse to do anything but chase the kingdom of God with all your might.

And keep reading this book, because I'm going to try and give you my playbook for how to see the church, and your place within it, in an entirely new light.

Part 2

THREE

ESSENTIAL

TRANSITIONS

Chapter 4

FROM MODELS TO AN ECCLESIOLOGY

*What we have to learn ... is not that the church "has" a
mission, but the very reverse: that the mission of Christ
creates its own church. Mission does not come from the
church; it is from mission and in the light of mission
that the church has to be understood.*
—Jürgen Moltmann

*The church is not the kingdom but the foretaste of the
kingdom. For it is in the church that the narrative of
God is lived in a way that makes the kingdom visible.*
—Stanley Hauerwas

My first church planting job was with a new startup church in
the Kansas City suburbs. I was hired to do worship and programming. We were formed as a seeker model church and planted
from a large church nearby. Our mother church gave us a little bit
of money and a handful of people. Back then what "seeker model"
meant was that believers would suspend their church needs on Sunday morning in order to meet the needs of people who were not yet
committed to Christ. Sunday morning was geared toward these spiritual seekers, who were investigating God. Midweek services and
small groups were there to meet the needs of believers.

My job was to make sure our Sunday morning program was
excellent—music, drama, and video packages were crafted together

to augment the sermon. I spent countless hours editing videos, writing original songs, holding creative planning meetings, and doing everything I had to do to make certain our services were as good as anything we would see in the bars or theaters around town. We made annual trips to Willow Creek in Chicago to ensure we were working at the cutting edge of this model.

Our house band each week was my band, Satellite Soul. A couple of years into planting we signed a record deal with a major Christian label and started making records, touring, performing, and trying to be rock stars. I transitioned off staff into a full-time touring mode that consumed the next phase of my life.

My second church planting job was somewhat similar to the first. We planted from the same mother church with the seeker model. We told everyone that our mission was to reproduce the mother church in a different part of town. This time I was a copastor, leading worship and the programming department and much of the church's ministry life. Before we planted I met with each of the department heads from the mother church, learning their strategies so that we could reproduce them in our new congregation. Most weeks I led worship, and some weeks I preached.

I'm really proud of the work we did during those planting years at both churches. As it turns out, I had a knack for programming, and both churches had a phenomenal group of creative folks who threw themselves into the task of creating a world-class Sunday morning service. We pushed really hard, had a blast, and grew like crazy.

During our second church plant effort, I started seminary. I always knew I'd go to seminary at some point, but I had no idea how much I would love it. I started slowly at first, but was soon hooked on reading theology. Meanwhile, my professors completely broke me down. I was part of a program in which I could bypass a bunch of the practical courses and got to spend most of my ninety credit hours reading theology, church history, philosophy, and scriptural exegesis. They challenged every single assumption I had about the church and completely dismantled any commitment I previously had to the seeker model.

For the rest of our leadership team, the first cracks in the seeker model armor came in our second year as a church. We had moved to a larger location and were drawing people from the western suburbs of Kansas City, as well as from nearby Lawrence. Lawrence is a thirty-minute drive down K10 highway, and it's the home of the University of Kansas. The drive was tough for the college students, so we started doing a second service on campus each week. Our teams would travel to Lawrence Sunday evening to do the same service we had done that morning. We built parallel infrastructures, with teams covering all of the various technical aspects of a church service, as well as community structures and outreach.

What we learned was that the culture of Lawrence was drastically different from the culture of white, middle-class, suburban Johnson County. Our programming elements didn't have the same pop in both places. Packages designed to appeal to students and the more eclectic culture of Lawrence fell flat in the suburbs, and vice versa. It just wasn't going to work. So we hired a site pastor and spun them off into their own congregation over the course of the next two years, and they continue to be a wonderful church to this day.

In the third year, water started coming over the dam. Many of us were worn out from the task of programming and staffing two church services in two different communities. Portability was beginning to tax our volunteers, and the newness was beginning to wear off. Our teaching pastor went on a sabbatical that coincided with the end of our original three-year commitment to our core team. Many of them slipped away during that summer, and our attendance began to plateau. All of a sudden we were no longer growing.

Around that same time, the mother ship decided they were landlocked at their current location and needed to move in order to grow bigger. They began work on a $10 million facility just a few miles from where we were meeting. The wheels came off the cart a few months later when one of our staff members was arrested in an online sex solicitation sting and went to jail. Many disillusioned people left for other congregations or went back to Heartland.

Most of the leaders in our church were still committed to one another and to the church. To their great credit, hardly any of them decided to bail. The overwhelming majority are still serving at a high capacity in our church to this day. I know the rest of this story wouldn't be nearly as fun if it weren't for them. But for the time being, we were stuck in the doldrums for sure. What to do ...

At that time, a new model was emerging—the *organic* church. Today these are typically called missional communities. We could simply quit the seeker model, blow up our current structure, end the Sunday morning service altogether, and transition our congregation into a network of missional communities over the course of a year or two. Some wanted to go that route. But I was in a much different place after reading theology. I have since come to believe that the organic church or missional community model is simply a boutique megachurch—a way of reaping all the benefits of a megachurch with a much higher degree of control, and without having to make space for those who are in a completely different age group or socio-economic strata. I have grave doubts about any kind of church "model." What we need is an ecclesiology—to reclaim a coherent understanding of what it means to be the church.

If there is one thing I've noticed over the years of leading churches, it's that church leaders—American church leaders in particular—love models. All of the leadership training I had been a part of for the previous two decades of ministry had been based on models. We built our church based on a model, not a theology. We had no ecclesiology. (Ecclesiology is just a fancy way of saying the doctrine of the church—what is the church and what is the church for?) So when the going got tough, the first instinct was to pivot to another model—organic church, or missional communities.

This is what we default to, especially as evangelicals—we try to solve our problems by finding models of success and then copying them. When we sense trouble, we search for a model when what we need is a deep ecclesiology that will inform everything we do from top to bottom.

PICK A MODEL, ANY MODEL

Pick a model, any model: liturgical model, charismatic, or the good old Southern Baptist model. You have your seeker model and purpose-driven model, and the emerging church became a model for a while but was swallowed up for the most part by the house church model, which morphed into the missional community model. These days you can go to church consulting outfits and purchase a complete missional community franchise for between $10,000 and $20,000 up front. Who needs McDonald's?

We don't need models. We need a theological foundation, not a pragmatic one, on which to build the church. This is a question of *teleological* concern: what is our *telos*—the end toward which the church is intended? Most church "models" tell us that the *telos* is the growth of the church—not the kingdom, not faithfulness, but the growth of the church itself.

But a rich ecclesiology teaches us that the *telos* of the church is really about the growth of the world. The survival of the church is not the church's concern, nor is church growth. The spread of the gospel is not even the church's primary concern. Those things are all God's concern. *The church's job is to organize our common life together in a way that images God to all creation, bearing witness to the new reality that Jesus is Lord and that his everlasting life has broken into creation and is putting the world to rights.* That work of redemption starts in the life of the church. The church does not exist for the benefit of its members; it exists for the life of the world and the societies and cultures of the world.

The church's job is not to grow and thrive. The church's job is not even to survive. The church's job is to die for the life of the world—to literally spend itself, pour itself out in service to the world. In the words of Jürgen Moltmann, "The real point is not to spread the church but to spread the kingdom."[1]

> The church's job is to die for the life of the world – to literally spend itself, pour itself out in service to the world.

Let's take a step back and talk about the word *church* for a moment.

People think of lots of things when they think of a church. Some

---

1   Jürgen Moltmann, *The Church in the Power of the Spirit*, (New York: Harper & Row, 1977), 11.

think of a building, some of a congregation, others of an institution or denomination. To some extent those are all involved in what we mean by *church*. Some models conceive of the church almost like a rock concert—a nonparticipatory gospel presentation. Some think of church as a school, a place for religious education. Some think of church like a club, a place to become an insider. Some think of church as a kind of store or marketplace—a provider of religious goods and services. Some think of church like a hospital for the spiritually broken. There's a sense in which all of those things might be involved in church, but none of them quite get to the heart of what it means to be a church.

The Scriptures use two words for the church—*qahal*, a word of Hebrew origin that means "the assembly," and *ekklēsia*, a Greek word that also means "assembly." The problem with trying to translate the word *ekklēsia* is that there is absolutely no way that *ekklēsia* meant "church" in Paul's day in any analogical way to how we mean it today. Nobody ever would have stopped at Ephesus and asked where the *ekklēsia* was, and if they had, nobody would have sent them to a Christian fellowship. The culture had other words for church, like *thiasos* (cultic society) or synagogue (a local Jewish fellowship), but Paul didn't use those words to describe the new community of Jesus followers.

Paul used the word *ekklēsia*. The word didn't necessarily have a religious meaning—it could refer to a mob or a gathering of rabble rousers. In Acts 19 there is this great story about Paul while he was working in Ephesus. So many people were converting to Christianity that a local businessman who sold statues of the god Artemis was losing his livelihood. He rallied the other tradesmen, and they started a riot, accusing Paul and the other Christians of disrupting society. Finally, one of the civic leaders shouted everyone down, saying, "If there is anything further you want to know, it must be settled in the regular assembly" (*ennomō ekklēsia*, "lawful assembly," 19:39). So this leader dismissed the mob (*ekklēsia*, 19:41), and the people went on their way.

When we see the word *ekklēsia* in the Greek texts of the New Testament, we translate it "church." But this word does not mean to us what it meant to them. It was a sociopolitical term. The local ruling elders were the *ekklēsia*, and they would meet to discuss issues concerning the town. They would make sure the town was true to its culture, loyal to the gods, and living up to its primary confession, "Caesar is Lord."

When Paul employed the term *ekklēsia* for the new Christian assembly, he seems to have picked up on those same meanings.[2] When they gathered in the *ekklēsia*, they were expressing their intention to be loyal to the God of Israel who had come to them in the flesh and to their primary confession, "Jesus is Lord."

The word in the New Testament that we call *church* wasn't referring to a building, congregation, or institution. It was a visible body, a community of believers in Jesus Christ, whom they called Lord, and whose mission it was to be a living witness to the lordship of Jesus. They were devoted to the gospel, the good news, that Jesus was Israel's Messiah and the world's true Lord. The church is a visible assembly that expresses the lordship of Jesus Christ in their common life. As they do so, they become icons—images—of Christ in the world.

Paul also used the words *body* and *temple* to express this reality. Body had connotations of body politic as well as the human body. The church is a body in both of those senses. As a body, the church must be unified and visible. If the church is not visible, or if it is visibly disunited, it does not image God.

Temple was another word Paul used to describe the church. The temple was the one place on earth where God was always present. It was a place where heaven and earth overlapped—the veil between them almost disappeared and the realm of God and the realm of humans came together. When Jesus was born, he became the place where God was always present on the earth, the place where heaven and earth overlapped. And when he breathed his Spirit into his

---

2   It is possible that another reason Paul used the word *ekklēsia* is that this word was used to translate *qahal* in the Septuagint. Still, it is likely the political meaning, as well as some other derivations to Paul's use of the term *ekklēsia*, were in play here.

church, we became his body. We became the place on earth where God is always present, where heaven and earth overlap.

As we try to build an ecclesiology instead of a model, this is where we start. The church is a visible assembly, expressing the lordship of Jesus in their common life. The church is the body of Christ, and it is the holy temple.

That's what the church *is*.

But what is the church *for*?

What is the church's *telos*, its raison d'être?

FOR THE LIFE OF THE WORLD

Most evangelicals view the culture in which we live as a river that is flowing straight to hell. Everyone we know and love is born into this river. They think the church's job is to pull people out of the river and get them over into our stream—we call our stream the church, but it's really a Christian subculture. As evangelicals, we tell ourselves that our stream goes to heaven, while the river of culture goes to hell.

In Christian Smith's book *The Scandal of the Evangelical Con-science*, he dispenses with that myth. Smith says that in every measurable way Christian culture looks exactly like the rest of the culture. In education, socioeconomics, generosity, divorce, abortion, crime, violence—you name it—we are just like the rest of the culture. If you are measuring domestic violence, divorce rates, or racism, evangelicals actually come out worse than the culture as a whole.

In other words, the river of culture and the stream of evangelical subculture go to the exact same place. The only difference is that when you are a part of the evangelical subculture, we get to make money off you. We will sell you Christian music, Christian T-shirts, Christian books, Christian school curriculum, Christian art supplies, and even Christian mints—Testamints—which represent the Christian subculture's collective nadir. I confess, I am a part of this hypocrisy as well, assuming you paid for this book.

And to a large extent, this is how we have come to see the mission of the church: pulling people out of the river headed to hell so that we can put them into our stream. No wonder the church is in decline.

I just used the word *mission*, and there are many ways to define that word, so we need to talk about that for a moment. In church leadership circles, it's sort of assumed that any church, group, or team needs to have a mission. Churches write mission statements, vision statements, or purpose statements. They spend hundreds of hours crafting these things, teaching their congregations what they mean, and then using them to guide the entire congregation. Mission or vision statements are the language that supports a church model. It's what we say to convince church members that the way things are at this church is the way God wants them to be.

The problem with this kind of thinking is that the church does not have a mission, strictly speaking. God has a mission, and he gave that mission a church. The church's job is to humble ourselves and empty ourselves for others, and in so doing we bear witness to the lordship of Jesus Christ. The church is not primarily a place but a people—people who live faithfully under the direction of the Holy Spirit, becoming more and more like Jesus, and carrying his presence to the world as we live our day-to-day lives.

> The church does not have a mission, strictly speaking. God has a mission, and he gave that mission a church.

The best metaphor I know for how this works itself out practically is the concept of breathing. Every week God breathes his church into his lungs. It's a cosmic inhalation that draws the church together once every seven days.

What happens when the church gets breathed in is of great importance. We gather together around the Word and the Table to be shaped by God, who holds us in his lungs and empowers his people for life in the Christian colony. The people of God gather, first and foremost, around the Story of God, and they tell and retell that story in the most creative and imaginative ways possible.

Over time they begin to see themselves as living in that story, and it comes to define them over against any rival story. We say that the rival stories—individualism, consumerism, and nationalism in particular—cannot tell us who we really are. Those stories cannot really help us make sense of what we have been created to be, why we are here, and where we are going. The only story that makes sense of it all is the Story of God.

So the church bands together; we give ourselves to the Story of God and begin to organize our common life together in such a way that we can be faithful to that story. In my community we call it discipleship. Whatever you want to call it, it is the process through which God draws the church into his lungs and shapes us and forms us, enriches us and prunes us. This process is thoroughly corporate and yet always personal.

Then God exhales. He blows us out of his lungs and into the world. As little transformed agents of redemption, we are sent out into the places we always go — our homes, our schools, our work-places, our neighborhoods, our families, and so on. We go there as salt and light. We go there as people who do not walk by sight but by faith. We are transformed vessels of God's redemption sent to season all of creation. We image God.

So, when people look at us, they actually see past us and get a good look at God. Not only that, but we actually see God happening all over the place, out there in the culture. God happens as we put each other in touch with God by participating in his mission of redemption in countless small ways each and every day. We become caught up in the love of God and become transformed into the kind of people who go out into the world and image God to all creation because we're image-bearing people.

And if we participate in this breathing, an amazing thing happens in a church. The Bible calls it redemption. When redemption happens, each person begins to relate to God's creation the way God planned it from the beginning. Redemption happens in the way we relate to God, the self, other people, and to all creation. Little by little we are being transformed (i.e., switching narratives from the narratives of individualism, nationalism, and consumerism to the narrative of the Story of God) and redemption advances on creation. The Scriptures tell us that as the just begin to live by faith, the gates of hell cannot stand against the coming kingdom of God. In other words, in the end, love wins ... because God is love.

A lot of people think the pastor's job is to make a church survive or thrive or get bigger or be better, but that's not a pastor's job. Those sorts of things are best left up to God. In fact, I'd be a little wary of any pastor who thought he or she could deliver on those promises, because that's not the church's job.

Instead, the church is simply supposed to be faithful. And faithfulness takes on many forms, but most of the time it sort of looks like dying: dying to ourselves, dying to each other, dying a little bit every day for our family, friends, neighbors, coworkers, and all of humanity. But we know with death comes a resurrection. And resurrection is the great hope of our faith. That's how the church works.

> A lot of people think the pastor's job is to make a church survive or thrive or get bigger or be better, but that's not a pastor's job. Those sorts of things are best left up to God.

WHAT VANISHING CULTURES DO

So we have our ecclesiology in place. Now it is time for us to develop a model, right? Nope, and I'll tell you why, but first you have to hear a story.

> A thousand years ago, a group of Vikings led by Erik the Red set sail from Norway for the vast Arctic landmass west of Scandinavia which came to be known as Greenland. It was largely uninhabitable — a forbidding expanse of snow and ice. But along the southwestern coast there were two deep fjords protected from the harsh winds and saltwater spray of the North Atlantic Ocean, and as the Norse sailed upriver they saw grassy slopes flowering with buttercups, dandelions, and bluebells, and thick forests of willow and birch and alder. Two colonies were formed, three hundred miles apart, known as the Eastern and Western Settlements. The Norse raised sheep, goats, and cattle. They turned the grassy slopes into pastureland. They hunted seal and caribou. They built a string of parish churches and a magnificent cathedral, the remains of which are still standing. They traded actively with mainland Europe, and tithed regularly to the Roman Catholic Church. The Norse colonies in Greenland were law-abiding, economically viable, fully integrated communi-

ties, numbering at their peak five thousand people. They lasted for four hundred and fifty years—and then they vanished.[3]

That was the opening paragraph from Malcolm Gladwell's 2005 book review of Jared Diamond's *Collapse: How Societies Choose to Fail or Succeed*. Diamond argues that when societies fail, it is typically due not to some cataclysmic event or act of God but to something much simpler. Societies fail because their primary concern becomes the perpetuation of their cultural model at the expense of nearly everything else. Societies fail because they are not committed to the holistic stewardship of life, the land, the people, the animals, the environment, and the world in which they are situated; they are only committed to sustaining their model for how life should go. While attempting to preserve and perpetuate their culture, the inwardly focused society can lose sight of how their cultural model fits into the big picture. This can be a fatal mistake.

This could be what is happening in contemporary North American evangelicalism.

Evangelicals have become concerned primarily with the perpetuation of evangelical culture at the expense of nearly everything else. One of the primary examples of this is our commitment to church models. For any particular church, especially American mega-churches, the central concern is the perpetuation and survival of that particular church. Often this comes through the imposition of models on the landscape of the city and suburbs. The current state of evangelicalism in North America is this: *we are doing what vanishing cultures do.*

> The current state of evangelicalism in North America is this: *we are doing what vanishing cultures do.*

In Kansas City we have several megachurches, but one in particular is dominant, with over twenty thousand people and multiple campuses. When this church attempts to partner with other local ministries, especially those working in poverty-stricken areas, there comes an inevitable point

---

3   Malcolm Gladwell, "The Vanishing," *The New Yorker* (January 3, 2005), 70.

at which the megachurch's leadership model either wins out or they walk away. The megachurch has the money, the power, and most importantly the model. When they expand their ministry into different geographical, socioeconomic, racial, and cultural situations, they impose their model on that landscape. They do not listen to the indigenous people. They do not have to listen because they hold all of the power. They may or may not be making the right moves (often they are; often they aren't), but that does not matter because their true objective is the expansion of their ministry.

Diamond's theory is fascinating. He says the Norse met their end in Greenland because they imposed their culture on an environment that couldn't sustain it. When faced with the prospect of having to adapt Norse culture to the pressures of surviving in a harsh and (as it turns out) fragile environment, the Norse couldn't bring themselves to do it.

For example, the Vikings who originally colonized Greenland were surrounded by some of the most fertile fishing waters on the planet. Yet they nearly died of starvation. Diamond says that when archaeologists from all over the world come to dig in Greenland, they are all looking for the same thing: fish bones, which they rarely find. Why would a society that was sitting on top of the richest food source the ocean has to offer nearly starve to death?

The answer is that the Norse had a cultural taboo against eating fish. It simply wasn't done.

We think of Vikings as seafaring raiders. They thought of themselves as farmers and ranchers. The animals and crops that grew so well in their native Norway were important cultural markers for Norse society. They brought this pastoral culture to Greenland, raising cattle and crops and eating things that grew on the land. Owning and eating cattle was a status symbol. After Greenland was deforested for homes or pastureland and the fertile but thin soil was grazed into oblivion, Greenland's wind and water began to carry away the topsoil, and the Norse people began to starve.

Fishing would have been a simple and effective way to feed themselves — less labor intensive and less ecologically taxing. That one simple move would have diversified the Norse diet and would have protected Greenland's natural resources. Yet all archaeological evidence suggests that the Norse would rather starve than eat a fish.

Culturally the Norse built a society as robust as any in Western Europe. But they never learned to adapt their culture to Greenland's fragile ecosystem. They needed to learn from the native Inuit people how to harvest the sea and burn seal blubber, how to build different kinds of houses and chop down fewer trees. Most of all, they needed to learn how to fish. This was impossible for the Norse people who despised the Inuit, calling them *skraelings*, or "wretches."

In the end, the Norse vanished from Greenland because *elements of the very culture they were attempting to sustain ensured its own failure.* "The Norse were undone," Diamond says, "by the same social glue that had enabled them to master Greenland's difficulties."[4]

Could it be that this is what is happening with contemporary evangelicalism? Could it be our tribe is clinging to a set of cultural practices and values that will one day ensure our own extinction? *Could North American evangelicalism be undone by the same social glue that held it together for centuries?*

Adapting to culture is not something we evangelicals like to admit doing. But we do it all the time; we just don't like to say so out loud. Over the past twenty-five years, the church has welcomed and perfected the music of the culture, the leadership and marketing techniques of Fortune 500 companies, and the programming expertise of Broadway and television. We know how to adapt to culture.

As it turns out, though, we as evangelicals have a specific cultural agenda of our own, one that has come to dominate the essence of evangelical identity, one that we will protect at any cost. *That agenda is conversion.*

The Gospel Coalition was created in 2007 by D. A. Carson and Tim Keller, along with John Piper and other neo-Reformed theologians and pastors, to keep contemporary evangelicalism from compromising the gospel in the name of cultural relevance. Formed, at least in part, as a reaction to the rise of the emerging church, the

---

4 Jared Diamond, *Collapse: How Societies Choose to Fail or Succeed* (New York: Penguin, 2005), 275.

Gospel Coalition's website states that they are "deeply concerned about some movements within traditional evangelicalism that seem to be diminishing the church's life and leading us away from our historic beliefs and practices."[5]

Let me just say up front that I think we should all applaud this idea. The gospel is at the heart of everything we do. It matters greatly if we get this wrong. All of us, even those of us who can be critical of the Gospel Coalition at times, need to give them great credit. To lose the heart of the gospel is to lose the heart of our Christian identity. We have to get it right.

Here's the twist: the gospel that most evangelical Christians hold to is not based in Scripture, but in evangelical culture itself. The heart of the evangelical gospel has morphed into *conversion*.

Within a year of each other (2011–12), N. T. Wright and Scot McKnight, two leading voices in New Testament studies, both published books about the nature of the Christian gospel.[6] Both books serve to correct deep problems within the typical evangelical meaning of the word *gospel*.

McKnight argues that more than anything else, the common evangelical concept of the gospel has been shaped by the need to perpetuate an evangelical conversion culture. (I recommend listening to Scot McKnight's Parchman Lecture Series at Baylor's Truett Seminary titled "American Evangelicalism and the Pastor."[7])

Evangelical culture is a complex animal. Even describing what the word *evangelical* means is nearly impossible. The struggle over the meaning of the term could end up being the most important part of this discussion. The winner will likely influence denominational leaders, publishers, and editors, as well as Christian universities and

---

5 "The Gospel for All of Life: Preamble," The Gospel Coalition Website. Accessed August 2, 2013. http://thegospelcoalition.org/about/who.

6 Scot McKnight, *The King Jesus Gospel: The Original Good News Revisited* (Grand Rapids: Zondervan 2011); N. T. Wright, *How God Became King: The Forgotten Story of the Gospel* (New York: Harper One 2012).

7 You can find all of the recent Parchman Lectures at the seminary website's media page: www.baylor.edu/truett/index.php?id=84799.

seminaries. Whoever defines the word *evangelical* will, in large part, determine its future.

Many theologians and church leaders have attempted to define evangelicalism, but the most accurate, simple, and fundamental definition comes from McKnight, who says that at the heart of what it means to be an evangelical is the conversion experience itself.

Evangelicalism is known for a commitment to two words: gospel and salvation. McKnight believes that evangelicals have conflated those two ideas and have become functional "salvationists."[8] Evangelicals have what McKnight calls a salvation culture. "We ought to be called *soterians* (the saved ones) instead of evangelicals."[9] Whatever else evangelicals may be, this much we hold in common: we believe that each person must experience some kind of personal conversion to faith in Christ. The conversion experience serves as the central cultural marker for the entire evangelical tribe.

The problem is that we have equated a conversion experience, which is about the *person*, with gospel, which is about the *world*. Our primary commitment is to the gospel. The pursuit of a conversion experience has caused evangelicals and their Reformed fathers before them to exchange the gospel of New Testament for what McKnight calls a *soterian* gospel. What evangelicals wanted was a gospel that would *produce conversions* — that is, produce more evangelicals. So the gospel of the New Testament had to be adapted and reduced to produce the conversions that evangelicals desired.

> What evangelicals wanted was a gospel that would *produce conversions* — that is, produce more evangelicals.

When this happened, the evangelical church transformed from a *gospel culture* to a *salvation culture*. It is the protection of this salvation culture — not the protection of the gospel — that has inspired the neo-Reformed attack on scholars such as N. T. Wright and Scot

---

8 Scot McKnight, *The King Jesus Gospel: The Original Good News Revisited* (Grand Rapids: Zondervan, 2011), 30.

9 Ibid., 29.

McKnight, as well as pastors and more progressive church leaders such as Rob Bell.

Both Wright and McKnight stress the reality that the New Testament is devoted to a gospel characterized by the story of Jesus — his life, teaching, death, resurrection, and ascension. This gospel is about the climax and fulfillment of the story of Israel in and through Jesus Christ, who is Israel's Messiah, the Son of God, and the world's true Lord. This gospel is not merely concerned with personal conversion, but with how Jesus became King and how he is redeeming all things starting with those who follow him and call him Lord.

Most importantly, the gospel Wright and McKnight recommend is not concerned primarily with the perpetuation of evangelical culture but with the holistic stewardship of all of life, the land, the people, the animals, the environment, and the world in which we live. Their work stands in stark contrast to the typical evangelical pursuit, too often fixated on a *soterian* gospel derived not from the Scriptures but from evangelical culture itself.

Enter the church model.

The church model is concerned with perpetuating evangelical culture, with personal conversion at the center of that picture. Models are chiefly concerned with the growth of the church, not the health of the culture. Models are conformed to a *soterian* gospel that is about personal salvation and the growth of a particular congregation.

The nerdy way to say this is that any robust *ecclesiology* must include a full-bodied *soteriology*. Part of why we are so enamored with models that produce predictable growth is that we have been shaped by a *soterian* gospel. Evangelicals have been convinced that they exist for the salvation of individual people but not for the life of the world. That portrays an incomplete soteriology and a distortion of the gospel.

When we chase models and conversions meant to keep the church growing, we are doing what vanishing cultures do.

When archeologists looked through the ruins of the Western Settlement, they found plenty of the big wooden objects that were so valuable in Greenland — crucifixes, bowls, furniture, doors, roof timbers—which meant that the end came too quickly for anyone to do any scavenging. And, when the archeologists looked at the animal bones left in the debris, they found the bones of newborn calves, meaning that the Norse, in that final winter, had given up on the future. They found toe bones from cows, equal to the number of cow spaces in the barn, meaning that the Norse ate their cattle down to the hoofs, and they found the bones of dogs covered with knife marks, meaning that, in the end, they had to eat their pets. But not fish bones, of course. Right up until they starved to death, the Norse never lost sight of what they stood for.[10]

Evangelicals in America have a choice, and it's a big one. Are we going to continue to pursue the growth of the church above all else, or are we going to pursue the holistic stewardship of life, the land, the people, the animals, the environment, and the world in which we are situated? Our culture is changing rapidly, and we are not going to survive if we do not live for the life of the world, because the culture will reject us and our message out of hand. Are we going to continue to pursue and perpetuate church models, church growth, conversions, and the survival of Christian culture no matter what? Or are we going to live like Jesus lived? Are we going to embrace the cruciform life of discipleship? Are we going to continue to preach a soterian gospel meant to provide us with more "conversions"? Or are we going to lay down our lives for the sake of the world? If we do, we might find the courage and strength to begin to dive headlong into a better understanding of what the church is and what it is for.

For now, though, church models hold sway. If you have gotten nothing else from this chapter, I hope you got this: a church model is not the same as an ecclesiology. It's time for pastors and church leaders to jettison our endless devotion to church models and to grab hold of an ecclesiology rich enough to fund our devotion to the gospel that is concerned with every aspect of our lives, society, and culture.

---

10 Gladwell, "The Vanishing," 73.

Chapter 5
FROM STRATEGIES TO STORIES

What I took from Pannenberg about 19th Century
Theology, (about which he knew just about every-
thing), was: if there is one God, that God is Triune.
And the creation of that God, should that God create,
will not be a thing but a story, a narrative. And if we
are to tell that story, the meaning shall only be clear
from the end of the story. And we can only know it
because he has somehow anticipated that ending
of the story in the narrative, or in the story itself.
—Robert Jenson

I love school.

If I had the money, I'd take college courses every semester until the day I die.

One of my favorite parts is going through the syllabus on the first day. I can always tell the experienced teachers from the neophytes by their syllabi. A good syllabus tells you exactly what is expected, what books to read, when assignments are due, and what role they will play in determining your grade. A good syllabus is made up of lists, dates, expectations, and details.

What if your teacher showed up on the first day with a syllabus that contained none of those things? What if he handed you a syllabus that read, "Theology 101: Once upon a time there were three brothers who embarked on a great adventure …" and the story continued for three pages and ended without giving a list of required readings, assignments, or due dates? How would you figure out what to do?

Some situations call for a list: a trip to the grocery store, packing for a trip, and a class syllabus. Other situations call for stories: bedtime, sermons, and the dinner table.

So what kind of situation is Christian leadership?

Well, it seems as though most of those who are involved in shaping Christian leaders seem to believe that our leadership is a "list" kind of enterprise, and the list is usually comprised of one strategy after another. I think it's a story kind of enterprise.

I once attended a church leadership conference at a megachurch and heard a speaker whose main theme went something like this: "It's not the importance of your goal that will ultimately determine your success but the effectiveness of your strategy."

In a world of success-oriented people, strategy is king. Strategies are the most celebrated element of contemporary leadership. Nearly every leadership book you read will be rooted in some sort of pragmatic strategy.

> In a world of success-oriented people, strategy is king.

I'm deemphasizing strategies in my own leadership these days, for several reasons. For one thing, strategies are nearly always based in the wrong story—the American story of bigger, better, faster, and higher. For another thing, strategies are assessed by only one metric: *results*. Only secondarily are they considered in terms of their faithfulness or virtue. Strategies nearly universally address what you *do* over and above who you *are*, or who you are becoming.

Don't get me wrong. I still use strategies. But I don't revere them, and I discard or change them all the time. Strategies are like a screwdriver or a drill bit. They are simple tools. They come cheap, and I try not to feel any emotional attachment to them. Christian leaders must be able to craft and use strategies, but strategies are not things in which we should place our trust or our faith. We should not fall in love with them, and they cannot become the foundations of our leadership.

In this chapter I'm going to argue that what we need are not strategies but *stories*. I think Christian leadership is a story kind of enterprise. By stories, I'm really talking about one big story—the Story of God, or the Christian story.

A good story can bypass the major potholes that plague our use of strategies. The stories we tell in our ministry must come directly from the Christian story, not from the American story of success. Unlike strategies, a good story can actually address both what we do and who we are at the same time. A good story can recalibrate our hearts, minds, and souls better than any strategic plan could ever do.

I know this probably sounds fishy to you. How can a story tell us what we need to do in our ministries? If this is new ground for you, the answer is probably not immediately obvious. Let's see if I can convince you.

NARRATIVE: THE HEAVY LIFTING OF LEADERSHIP

When we encounter a problem at work or in our ministry, we have been trained to look for a strategy with which to solve it. But what if God doesn't want us to solve the problem at hand? What if God wants us to live with the problem for awhile? What if God is planning to use that problem to help us see the world in a new way? What if God wants us to struggle in the tension so that we can change and grow? In that case deploying a strategy and attempting to solve our problems quickly would actually work against God's purposes.

I'm not saying we should stop solving problems. I'm saying that as leaders, we need to recognize that the hard work of leadership—the heavy lifting, the heart of the matter, the central task—does not exist on the pragmatic surface with models, strategies, and techniques, but on the foundational level. There has to be something at work deep inside our soul that guides our leadership, and for this, we need stories.

I can give lots of practical reasons why I believe this to be true, but the best rationale comes from Scripture itself. The Bible is not a rule book, an owner's manual, or a strategic plan. It's not a to-do or to-don't list, nor is it a list of commands. When God decided to help guide our common life, God did not give us a syllabus. God gave us a story, because God knew a story is exactly what we would need.

Narrative is the heavy lifting of leadership. Stories are meant to operate below the frenetic surface of leadership that is always so busy with activity, details, tasks, meetings, and plans. To organize on that surface level you will need some sort of strategy. There are thousands of leadership books filled with strategies. You could pick five of them at random and find all of the strategic leadership wisdom you'll need to last a lifetime. But these strategies really only impact what pops and sizzles on the surface of the leadership world. What matters most is what lies under the surface on the story level. What provides the foundation for leadership? What is guiding the way you use those strategies and to what end? That's the true leadership question, and for this question we need stories.

My two boys are pretty close in age, so they still do a lot of playing together. One of their favorite things to play is Star Wars. They can transform any environment in which they find themselves into Lucas-World. The car becomes the Millennium Falcon, our house becomes the Death Star, their drinking straws become light sabers, and so on.

When they play, you can often hear them making corrections, commenting on one another's involvement. "No," one of them will say, "Leah is a good guy. If you want to be a bad guy, you have to be a storm trooper." Or, "Hey, somebody has to be Vader or we don't have anyone to fight." Or my favorite, "No man, Han Solo can't use the Force. He doesn't believe in it."

What's interesting is that there are no rules to playing Star Wars, no manual or instructions. The only thing that is determinative for their play is a story. The story tells them how to act. They do not follow rules per se. Instead, they immerse themselves in the narrative by watching movies or cartoons, they talk about it with their friends, and they faithfully act out the story in their own way with the materials available to them.

This is how it works with Christian leadership and the Story of God. Christian leadership—really, any involvement in ministry—is not first and foremost about developing and using strategies. Chris-

> Narrative is the heavy lifting of leadership.

tian leadership is about immersing ourselves in the Story of God and then living faithfully within that narrative as it is still unfolding. Ministry leaders today need to spend far more time immersing themselves in the story and less time learning and implementing success-determined strategies.

A SHARED STORY

What we need is not just a story, but a *shared* story.

When my oldest son was about five years old, we all sat down to watch the movie *Sandlot*—the ultimate friendship movie. At one point in the movie the main character, Scotty Smalls, asks a question about "the beast" (the mysterious dog who steals their baseballs). Instead of answering Smalls's question right there, the boys shout in unison, "Campout!" They reconvene after dark at their tree house for a campout so they can tell the story of the beast to the new kid. It was as though the boys knew they needed a better environment through which to convey the power of the story that guided their play. Telling the story wasn't just about the transfer of information, it was about a common experience. Everyone in their group needed to be *initiated* into the telling of their foundational story together. They needed to experience the power of the story together so that it would have the same meaning for the whole group. It's actually a good look at why we worship together weekly as Christians.

> What we need is not just a story, but a *shared* story.

Stories do something important to us. They aren't just for entertainment; they work on us; they shape and form us. The corporate telling of those stories is indispensible for the life of the church.

Imagine yourself a little Jewish boy or girl two or three thousand years ago. It is summertime in Palestine—cool in the evenings—so you and your whole family are sitting around the fire in the dark under an amazing sky: grandmas, grandpas, aunts and uncles, moms and dads, brothers and sisters—the whole family is there. There's no TV or radio, no internet or video games, not a written word of any kind.

What do you do while you sit around the fire?

You tell stories.

What stories do you tell?

You tell about Father Abraham and how while no one else on the planet was listening, he heard the voice of the Lord. You look up at the sky and say, "Those stars ... the Lord is making Abraham's children like the stars. One of those stars shines for our family." You tell about Isaac and the ram caught in the thicket. You tell about Jacob and Esau and how God chose the shrewd trickster to lead his people, and the story leads you.

You tell about Joseph and the ornate robe his father gave him. You tell about his brothers' jealousy and how they sold him into slavery. You tell of Potiphar's wife, Joseph's ability to interpret dreams, and how Pharaoh put him in charge of the whole country. You tell of how God used Joseph to save his family and to keep Abraham's dream alive, and the story leads you.

You tell about King David and his mighty men, and how Saul killed his thousands but David his tens of thousands; how David slew Goliath and how his scandal with Bathsheba developed. You tell how he repented and was forgiven. You tell about how God took care of the people while David was their leader because David, while human and broken, was still a faithful king, and the story leads you.

Night after night, year after year, you'd tell these stories, sing the psalms, recite the Scriptures. And after a while, you would realize these stories are not just a form of entertainment. The stories are telling you who you are. They teach you your own identity and form your imagination for what it means to be a part of the people of God. These stories shape the way you see yourself, your family, your people, the world, and the God of Abraham, Isaac, and Jacob whom you serve.

Stories make mental maps for us, maps of our own lives. They tell us who we are and help us make sense of the world around us. Stories help us to learn the difference between right and wrong, between good and evil. They help us to define and embody the virtues of our culture. Stories help us to locate ourselves within the grand narrative of the Story of God. Even if the world around us feels chaotic and dark, stories can give our lives meaning and purpose.

A bad story can have the opposite effect. Bad stories can confuse us, miscalibrate our brains, obscure our sense of virtue, depress and discourage us. A bad story can cause us to feel completely lost with no means of being found again.

All stories function in this way. All stories attempt to reset our internal compass. Stories work to recalibrate our brains. This is true of good stories and bad stories alike.

> Stories make mental maps for us, maps of our own lives. They tell us who we are and help us make sense of the world around us.

When my friend Tim Keel teaches on leadership, he sometimes explains that there's actually a part of the brain that specializes in making mental maps. It's called the *hippocampus*. When you walk into a room or an environment for the first time, the hippocampus makes and stores a mental map of the place. The more times you frequent that place, the more detailed the map becomes. Our minds are constantly mapping and remapping our environment. That's the job of the hippocampus. Here's the weird part. In times of stress, the hippocampus stops working at optimal levels. It stops making accurate mental maps. Stress arrests our body's ability to locate ourselves in the world.

Now, get this: when the hippocampus shuts down in times of stress, another part of the brain kicks in, a part called the *amygdala*. The amygdala controls, among other things, the secretion of adrenaline. Adrenaline makes our hearts beat faster and gives us an intense bias for action. Adrenaline makes us need to move, to do something, to make something happen.

So, when we are in a period of intense stress, the amygdala kicks in, floods the body with adrenaline, and gives us a sense of urgency that we need to move and do something, while at the same time the hippocampus — the part of the body that helps us to locate ourselves in the world — shuts down.

This means that when we face stressful situations — problems in our ministry or relationships, issues with our work, challenges to our leadership, and so on—we're actually dealing with a powerful physiological response: an irresistible impulse toward movement coupled with an inability to recognize where we are. It's what Daniel Goleman calls an emotional hijacking.[1] This actually gives new meaning to the phrase, "We don't know where we're going, but we're making good time." In reality, stress hinders our ability to map our surroundings while boosting our bias toward action. This is a troubling situation, especially when we consider the fact that most leaders operate in an environment of chronic stress.

Stories serve to reorient our lives in times of stress. Stories are like the artificial horizon for a pilot flying through dense cloud cover.

Yet we live in a culture that tells some pretty bad stories. It's getting harder to tell the good guys from the bad guys these days. The stories of our culture are typically violent, cynical, and despairing, or else they are sappy and sentimental. The stories our culture tells us cannot teach us who we are and where we are, and so they end up making us feel stressed out, vulnerable, and lost. It's not surprising, then, that when we hit problems or challenges, the *hippocampus* shuts down, the *amygdala* shoots adrenaline into the system, and we run and run without any direction, purpose, or sense of where we are going.

> Stories serve to reorient our lives in times of stress.

The Christian story—the story of the people of God down through history until the present day—can recalibrate our brains. The Story of God can make a mental map for us that tells us not only *where* we are, but *who* we are even in times of great stress. The Story of God can locate us at all times, whether we are wandering in the wilderness or standing in the Holy of Holies, and it can tell us what it means to be a human being in the world.

No other story can do that.

The Story of God is different from all other stories because at the heart of it, at its center, we find peace instead of violence. We find

---

1 For an in-depth discussion of the neural physiology of this phenomenon, see Daniel Goleman, *Emotional Intelligence* (New York: Bantam, 2006), 13–14 (also chapter 2 and appendix C).

hope instead of despair. We find meaning and purpose instead of a list of things we have to accomplish. We find not a list of ways to get to God, but a God who came for us. The Christian story advances not because the people who champion it are powerful or successful. The Christian story advances because the people who live within it seem to understand *who they are and where history is headed.*

When we hear the Christian story, it resets our compass just as all stories do, but with this story all of a sudden we realize in the deepest part of our heart and soul that our compass has found its true north, that this story makes sense of our lives, that this story brings a sense of peace. When we follow this story we begin to understand who we are and where we are going.

> The Christian story advances because the people who live within it seem to understand *who they are and where history is headed.*

In a recent issue of *Parade* magazine that dealt with the happiness of the family, the writer said that psychologists who measured children's resilience have discovered that the kids who are best able to handle *stress* are the ones who know the most about their family's *history*. The article said, "The more children know about their family's history, the stronger their sense of control over their lives and the higher their self-esteem. The reason: these children have a strong sense of 'intergenerational self' — they understand that they belong to something bigger than themselves, and that families naturally experience both highs and lows."[2]

Human beings are hardwired to respond to stories.

STORY AS A VEHICLE FOR MEANING

Over the past few decades, the memoir has become one of the best-selling forms of contemporary literature. Memoirs dominate the *New York Times* nonfiction bestseller list.

I'll admit that I'm kind of a memoir junky. My top five memoirs in order are: *Cash* by Johnny Cash, *Night* by Elie Weisel, *Hannah's Child* by Stanley Hauerwas, *Telling Secrets* by Frederick Buechner,

---

2 Bruce Feiler, "The Secrets to a Happy Family" *Parade*, February 14, 2013.

and last but not least, *Everyone Poops* by Taro Gomi. (Okay, that last one is not a memoir, but it's still a handy book.) You might want to include *Grace in the Maybe*, by my friend Katie Savage, or *Confessions* by Augustine—written around AD 397—perhaps the world's best-known memoir, if not one of the first.

Ever stop and think about why memoir is so popular today? Some people say it is because our culture is narcissistic. We can't stop talking about ourselves, and everybody thinks their own story is interesting. Others say it is because we no longer have any discretion. Things that should really be left unsaid are now featured on the back cover of our tell-all memoir.

I read a brilliant article in the *New Yorker* by Daniel Mendelsohn about the history of the memoir, in which he said, "Memoir, for much of its modern history, has been the black sheep of the literary family. Like a drunken guest at a wedding, it is constantly mortifying its soberer relatives (philosophy, history, literary fiction)—spilling family secrets, embarrassing old friends—motivated, it would seem, by an overpowering need to be the center of attention."[3] Maybe he's right to an extent. Maybe we are all narcissists with little personal discretion, but I think there's more going on.

One of the more interesting memoirs is Andre Agassi's *Open*. When the book came out, it made a splash in part because Agassi admitted that he did crystal meth while on the tour. It also had some salacious details about his marriage to Brooke Shields. Sex and drugs—solid gold book-selling material.

The book begins with Agassi at his last U.S. Open, in 2006. During the tournament he was helping himself relax by reading a memoir called *The Tender Bar* by Pulitzer Prize winner J. R. Moehringer. Agassi loved the book and started thinking about what it would be like to write his own memoir. So he called Moehringer up to ask him to be his ghost-writer ... which is what you do if you are Andre Agassi. Want to write a book? Call a Pulitzer Prize winner.

When Agassi tells the story in the acknowledgments of the

---

3 Daniel Mendelsohn, "But Enough about Me," *The New Yorker* (January 25, 2010), 68.

memoir, he says, "I asked him to show me my life through a Pulitzer Prize-winner's lens,"[4] which is a really interesting thing to say. That's narcissism, right? How many of us would have the thought, *I want to know what my life would look like through the lens of a Pulitzer Prize winner?*

After some begging on Agassi's part, Moehringer said yes, and when the book was published, Agassi spoke with NPR radio host Teri Gross about what it was like to work with the author.[5] "I knew the stories of my life," he said, "but didn't know what they meant ... what the truths were I'd been searching for about my life."

Agassi's statement gives us a key as to why we love memoirs so much. For many people in our culture, we know the stories of our lives, but we don't know what they mean. We all have an innate desire to know what our stories mean, and more than that, we want to know the truth toward which our lives drive us, the truth about what it means to be a human being in this world.

This is part of why memoir is so huge in our culture. We're all looking for a story that will make sense of our story. And although our culture can tell us what to wear, what to watch, how to talk, where to go on vacation, what to eat, what to drink, and what to drive, the one thing our culture cannot tell us with any sort of truthfulness is what our lives mean.

> We love memoir, at least in part, because it is one person's attempt to make some sense out of their own story, to find a story that makes sense of all of their other stories.

We love memoir, at least in part, because it is one person's attempt to make some sense out of their own story, to find a story that makes sense of all of their other stories. We love reading a memoir because we are all trying to make sense of our own lives and hearing other people's stories can help us.

One of my favorite books of the Bible is a memoir. The story

---

4 Andre Agassi and J. R. Moehringer, *Open: An Autobiography* (New York: Knopf, 2009).

5 NPR, *Fresh Air*, November 11, 2009.

comes at a vulnerable point in Israel's history. Somewhere around the year 1300 BC, Moses led the people out of Egypt into the wilderness. Forty years later they emerged and began to inhabit the Promised Land. Israel reached its zenith about three hundred years later under the rule of King David. Then they entered into a long, slow descent. First they had a schism, dividing into the northern and southern kingdoms. The northern kingdom fell to Assyria in 722 BC, and then the southern kingdom fell to Babylon about a hundred fifty years later. By the year 587 BC, Israel was pretty much finished as a nation until 1948.

When the Babylonians sacked Jerusalem, they took most of the wealthy and educated leaders back to Babylon when they left. Instead of killing or enslaving the wealthy and talented Israelites, the Babylonians forced Israel's best and brightest to enter Babylonian society. Their thinking was that if the Israelites were busy making money in Babylon, they couldn't be back in Jerusalem raising an army.

A short time later, Babylon itself was conquered by the armies of Persia. The Persian approach to the Hebrew people was a bit different. After a while, Artaxerxes, the Persian king, allowed some of the exiled Jews to return to Jerusalem under the leadership of Ezra the priest. He wanted them to rebuild Jerusalem and exist as a vassal state. Things did not go well at first, until a little-known government official named Nehemiah stepped in. The book of Nehemiah is the memoir of the Persian king's cupbearer and how he helped to save Jerusalem.

Being a cupbearer sounds like grunt work to us, but in those days it was a place of high esteem. The cupbearer didn't just hold the king's dishes; it was his job to taste the wine before it was presented to the king, both to make sure the wine hadn't turned to vinegar and to make sure that it hadn't been poisoned. The king trusted the cupbearer with his life.

Nehemiah was a trusted adviser and friend to King Artaxerxes, the Persian ruler. He had the king's ear. One day Nehemiah learned that things were not going well with Ezra and the rebuilding of Jerusalem. The pilgrims who had returned were not faring well. The city was still in ruins, disgraced and uninhabited. The story upset

Nehemiah so much so that he couldn't hide his feelings in the presence of the king.

So King Artaxerxes asked Nehemiah why he was so sad, and Nehemiah told him the truth. Nehemiah's ancestral city was in ruins, and it was breaking his heart. Would the king allow him to return and rebuild the walls and restore his city? To everyone's surprise, the king said yes.

The book of Nehemiah is a *memoir* of Nehemiah's return to Jerusalem and how he led the people to restore the walls. It's actually the only true memoir in the entire Bible and one of the oldest in world history.

When the walls were restored in Jerusalem, Nehemiah planned a huge celebration in the city square—it's a stunning scene. The people had completed the walls, they were moving back in, and they called to their priest, Ezra, to come lead them in celebration and teach them from the Hebrew Scriptures. This was the first time in several centuries that the word of God had been publicly proclaimed in Jerusalem. It was a scene of great emotion and passion. Everyone listened with a lump in their throat.

Ezra read to them from the Law, or the Torah—he read *their story*. He stood on a platform high above the people in the city square to read, and as they listened, the people began to weep. Why did they weep? This is a key to understanding Nehemiah's memoir. You have to understand why they were weeping.

MIND THE GAP

When Andre Agassi's memoir came out, the key revelation of the book was this: Andre Agassi—a former number one ranked player in the world, winner of eight grand slams and millions of dollars—hated tennis. Listen to this:

> I hate tennis. I hate it with a dark, secret passion and always have....
> I hate tennis, hate it with all my heart, and still I keep playing, keep
> hitting all morning and all afternoon, because I have no choice.
> No matter how much I want to stop, I don't. I keep begging myself
> to stop, and still I keep playing, and this gap, this contradiction

between what I want to do and what I actually do, feels like the core of my life.[6]

How many people read Andre Agassi's story and thought to themselves, "I feel that gap in my own life." Often when we hear stories like Agassi's, we begin to give ourselves permission to say, "I hate what I do for a living and I'm going to make a change," or "I have to get out of this situation I'm in so I'm going to do something about it." That's the power of story. That's the power that must be unleashed by leaders.

Story—not strategy—is the real catalyst to change.

> Story – not strategy – is the real catalyst to change.

Story has incredible reorienting power. When Ezra read aloud to the people, the story of God began to call into question the way they were living their lives. They realized there was this gap between God's vision for his people and the way his people were actually living. The story caused so much tension that they resolved to change the way they were living.

Stories convey a sense of meaning and truth that can shape our imaginations for what our lives should be like. Some of the stories we tell shape our imaginations in illegitimate ways. Every time you watch a movie or a television show, you are bombarded with stories that constantly shape your imagination, and many of them are terrible stories.

For example, what story does our culture tell us about the female body? What kind of story do we tell about beauty? Where does beauty stop for a woman? Size six? Size eight? Size ten? What a load of garbage that is. How early on do our little girls pick up on this story? How does that false truth shape their lives?

What story do we tell little boys about what it means to be a man, especially in terms of violence, sexuality, vocation, and achievement? Most movies and television shows tell one of two main stories: either you are the action hero who wins by violence, or you are the harmless

---

6 Agassi and Moehringer, *Open*, 25.

buffoon who is constantly outsmarted by his wife. How early on do our little boys pick up on this story? How does that false truth shape their lives?

We tell a lot of mixed-up stories in our culture. It's no wonder so many people are living such terrible stories.

Yet the deepest Christian conviction is that there is only one story that can tell us what it means to be a human being, a man, or a woman. The story that Ezra the priest read to the people of God in the city square, and its fulfillment in the life of Jesus, is the only story that makes sense of all of our other stories. When we encounter this story, it begins to recalibrate our hearts and minds; it becomes the story that sets our identity, and we become aware of this gap between God's vision for us and for the world, and the reality of how we are living—*and this gap can feel like the core of our lives.* Then the story leads us back to obedience. It resets our internal compass to its true north.

This is what we do when we worship together as a church. We tell the story of God's vision for the world and look at the way the world really is—the way we really are—and we talk about the difference.

You see, there is this grand story—a narrative arc—called the Story of God. It has a history. I'm talking about real people, places, things, actions, events, and ideas and how they have intersected with the living God over time. This story is moving down through time like a river. It has a flow, a mass, a trajectory. When we flow with it, we are carried by its energy and it brings us life. When we fight against it, it will grind us into dust. Many of the stories we are living end up going against the flow of the Story of God. Not only is it painful to go against the narrative arc of the Story of God, but doing so can actually destroy us.

> Our lives have to move in concert with the story that makes sense of all other stories.

If we want to move in harmony with God, our lives have to come into sync with the Story of God. Our lives have to move in concert with the story that makes sense of all other stories.

THIS STORY IS STILL HAPPENING

Back to Nehemiah. So the people began to weep when they heard the story read to them by Ezra the priest, and this is what happened next: the leaders told the people to stop crying. Nehemiah told them, "Go your way. Eat the fat and drink sweet wine and send portions to anyone who has nothing ready, for this day is holy to our Lord. And do not be grieved, for the joy of the LORD is your strength" (Neh. 8:10 ESV).

Something about the story Ezra read convinced Nehemiah and the leaders that the appropriate response of the people should be joy and feasting. What did he hear in God's Story that could have convinced him of that?

Well, Ezra was reading the Torah, or the first five books of the Bible; the stories of creation, fall, covenant, and redemption; the stories of Abraham, Isaac, Jacob, Joseph, and so on. Ezra was reading the same stories the people of God had recited by their campfires for centuries. These were the stories that told them who they were and where they were headed.

Here's the twist. As the people began thinking about their ancestors, they remembered how they had so often been unfaithful while God had always been faithful. They also remembered all of the pain of the past two hundred years, and how their fathers and grandfathers had failed and been driven into exile. Something clicked. They realized that in the past fifty-two days, God was at work again. God was redeeming them, just as he had done in the stories of old. Nehemiah was helping them to read their current story through that old story. And as they viewed their current story through the lens of the Torah, they realized, "The story is still going on. We're living in this story right now. I see it in our past, how we've failed time and time again, and yet our God never fails. Our God never gives up on us. This thing that is happening to us right now . . . this is God's doing!"

I hope you'll see this as profoundly good news for all of us, because the Story of God is our story too. The story is still going on all around us. As we look at God's vision for the world and then look at our own lives, we are forced to struggle with the gap between them. The good news, the gospel, is that God doesn't leave us here to struggle all alone.

That's why Nehemiah said that this wasn't a day for weeping. The people rejoiced because they realized that the story they were living was a story of redemption, a story about the God who never gives up on his people. That's good news. No matter how far you have strayed from the story, God will never give up on you. That's the story in which you are living. We are promised to a God whose love for us will never end, a God who will chase us down no matter how far we run.

This story of redemption is the story that should fund church leadership, but sadly it does not. The story we follow is the story of success and its oppressive syllabus of bigger, better, stronger, higher, faster. It's time to change stories.

> This story of redemption is the story that should fund church leadership, but sadly it does not. The story we follow is the story of success and its oppressive syllabus of bigger, better, stronger, higher, faster.

MY STORY OF REDEMPTION

A few years back, my church had just raised about a million dollars to buy a building and renovate it. That we could do this was pretty stunning given the fact that we were just a small church of maybe fifty families who routinely gave to the church. We went through a capital campaign, procured a loan, bought a building, and renovated it. The day we moved in was a day of such utter joy, I'll never forget it. Then real life hit us. The next year was really about our proving to ourselves that we could handle this new responsibility. During the third year something strange began to happen. Everybody came up for air and started asking, "What's next?"

I began to ask around to other leaders, "What do you think should be next?" Every single leader I asked who is part of the good-to-great Christian leadership conversation gave me the same advice: do another capital campaign. I looked to my colleagues and mentors at other churches in which I've served; all of them were on their third consecutive capital campaign.

I couldn't do it. I didn't want a strategy; I wanted a story.

So I picked the story of Nehemiah and the return from exile. I read books about it and listened to talks and sermons. I spent nine weeks preaching through the book of Nehemiah with our congregation and the impact was amazing. Nehemiah reminded us all what kind of story we were living in. The story taught us about mission, leadership, faithfulness, and waiting on God. It became the seedbed not for success-driven leadership but for plain old ordinary faithfulness and how to resist the impulse to reach for a strategy that would produce a little heat.

Next, I started looking for a story from another strong leader who could help me find perspective. This, I found, is an important step. Leaders must be humble enough to remember that we are not the first ones to try to lead the church, read the Scriptures, and follow Jesus. We have to look to our traditions and find a way to give the past a vote in our present lives. I knew I needed a story from more recent church history that could help me find perspective.

I found it in Eugene Peterson's memoir, *Pastor*. Peterson tells a story much like the story of my church. He had planted his congregation in a similar fashion, starting with just a few people. As they grew, slowly over time, they decided to try to raise the funds to build a church. The campaign worked, and they hired an architect. They went through the construction phase and then learned how to faithfully inhabit a building. A few months later, Peterson noticed everyone looking at him as if to say, "What's next?"

He asked his mentors at the denomination, and they told him the same thing I was told: start another capital campaign. Peterson refused, and the months that followed were sometimes painful and disorienting. He named this time of disorientation *the badlands*. He told his church there was no "what's next." There was just *a long obedience in the same direction*.

Peterson's story was incredibly orienting for me. I could finally name what we were experiencing: we were in the badlands. I could feel it happening, and everyone around me could sense it as well. I could resist the desire to launch us into a new strategic plan or capital campaign in order to calm the anxieties of the group. When I was tempted to do so, I could think back to Eugene Peterson and to the story of Nehemiah, and I knew that all we needed to do was simply wait on God and pursue faithfulness—our own long obedience in the same direction.

What I learned over the ensuing months was that God would use this season in powerful ways. God would expose some of our deep blind spots as a church. God would use the slow pace to help new folks and younger believers catch up. God would weed out a few people who were interested only in steady progress and obvious results. This would become a season of deep and significant growth, nearly all of it deep below the surface of our community life.

Those two stories—Nehemiah's and Eugene Peterson's—have sustained me through one of the toughest seasons of my ministry life. I can relax because I know that God is shaping our imagination for what is next through the stories of Scripture. I don't have to have a strategic plan so much as a story of redemption that helps me to locate myself in the world and tells me what my job is. I know that God must want us living in this liminal space for a while, and I trust him, so I can relax and just decide to be okay with that.

I know that some leaders will be getting a little twitchy just reading that account. You want me to get off my duff and find a strategy, cast a vision, recruit good leaders, equip and train them, and get to work. All I can say is that impulse comes from the wrong story—certainly not the story in which we are living. My church is now living in a better story—one where strategies are not king and where we rest in the notion that God will be faithful to us just as he has since the beginning of time.

Chapter 6

FROM TECHNIQUES TO VIRTUES

Power, success, happiness, as the world knows them,
are his who will fight for them hard enough,
but peace, love, joy are only from God.
—Frederick Buechner, *The Magnificent Defeat*

RATIONALIZING SUCCESS

Behavioral scientist and Duke professor Dan Ariely did a massive study to try and understand why some people lie, cheat, and steal.[1] In this study, Ariely and his team went to college campuses and offered students ten dollars to participate in a ten-minute research project. During the project, researchers passed out a worksheet with twenty math puzzles on it to a class full of students and told them they would be paid a dollar for every puzzle they could solve in five minutes. At the end of the five minutes, the students were asked to grade their own papers, walk them to a shredder in the back of the room, and destroy them. Then the students would stand in line to report their number of solved puzzles to the proctor, who would pay them an extra dollar for every right answer.

What the students didn't know was that the shredder was rigged. It looked and sounded as though it was shredding their papers, but it

---

1 Dan Ariely, *The Honest Truth about Dishonesty: How We Lie to Everyone—Especially Ourselves* (New York: HarperCollins, 2013).

was really preserving their answers so researchers could check to see if the participants were telling the truth.

This is what they found: on average, students reported solving six problems, when in fact they solved only four.

Over the course of their research, Ariely's team tested about thirty thousand people. Of those thirty thousand people, they found only twelve big cheaters, compared to eighteen thousand small cheaters. The big cheaters stole a total of $150, while the small cheaters stole around $36,000—just one or two dollars at a time. Ariely did this research project all over the world—in the United States, Western Europe, Turkey, Israel, China, and many other countries—and the results were always roughly the same.

Ariely believes this is an accurate snapshot of how human behavior impacts society. Yes, there are some big cheaters in the world, but on the whole there are few of them, and they make little impact. Most dishonesty happens among ordinary people who think of themselves as basically honest. When all this dishonesty is added together, it has a tremendous impact on culture. Most of the problems faced by the human race are not rooted in the lives of outliers and psychopaths—life's big cheaters. Our problems are rooted in the lives of typical, ordinary people who find ways to *rationalize* their own bad behavior.

Ariely's research shows that rationalization lives at the heart of our problem. He says most people want to be able to do two things at once: we want to be able to think of ourselves as honest people, and we want to enjoy the benefits of dishonesty every now and then. The way we pull this off is that we find a way to rationalize our bad behavior, finding a reason to justify what we are doing. That way we can still feel good about ourselves.

Ariely tells about an experiment in which researchers put two people who didn't know each other in a room together and asked them to have a conversation for ten minutes. After the conversation, researchers asked participants if they had told any lies during the ten minutes. They all said no. After participants reviewed a video of the conversation, however, they admitted lying an average of three times in ten minutes.[2] According to a 2011 study published in *Psychology Today*, most people in our society lie on average 1.65 times a day.[3] Yet when asked, most people claim to be honest at all times. How do we do it? Ariely says that the answer is *rationalization*.[4]

The ability to rationalize bad behavior is like an evil superpower. Think of any comic book story villain, and at the root of their criminal behavior you will find some ability to rationalize what they are doing. They find a reason that allows them to justify their actions. Rationalization allows us to lie but not see ourselves as liars, to cheat but not see ourselves as cheaters, to break small laws but not see ourselves as criminals.

> The ability to rationalize bad behavior is like an evil superpower.

How do good people do bad things?

We rationalize our behavior.

If you put a dollar bill and a can of soda in a college dorm room fridge, which one will disappear first? Ariely tested this in dorm rooms all over the campus of MIT. Every soda can disappeared, but none of the money.[5] Stealing cash feels too much like real crime. We can't rationalize that behavior. But taking a soda isn't really a theft. It's more like preemptive hospitality. That's the power of rationalization, and culturally it has much more of an impact than all the pathological liars, professional thieves, and psychotic killers combined.

Why am I talking about Ariely's research on cheating and ratio-

---

2 This example was cited by Dan Ariely in a speech he gave to the Royal Society for the Encouragement of Arts on July 10, 2012. The audio and video for this speech can be found at thersa.org.

3 Gad Saad, "The Pinocchio Effect: Lying in Daily Life," *Psychology Today*. Online, published November 30, 2011. Accessed March 13, 2014: www.psychologytoday.com/blog/homo-consumericus/201111/how-often-do-people-lie-in-their-daily-lives. Original research published by Kim B. Serota, Timothy R. Levine, and J. Franklin, "The Prevalence of Lying in America: Three Studies of Self-Reported Lies," *Human Communication Research* 36, no. 1 (January 2010): 2–25.

4 Ariely, *The Honest Truth*, 53.

5 Ibid., 32.

nalization? Because Christian leaders working in the context of ministry have a remarkable ability to rationalize any technique that will produce the desired results. Christian leaders seem all too willing to exchange the *virtues* of the kingdom of God for the *techniques* of business leadership that will help us control outcomes. Our passion for the gospel provides all the urgency we need in order to rationalize this exchange. Just as in Ariely's research, I think the small compromises and mundane rationalizations of day-to-day activities subvert the church's impact on the world. In this chapter I want to explore why and how Christian leaders do this, and why virtue is so much more central to the task of leadership than is technique.

FASCINATION WITH TECHNIQUE

Techniques are technical skills, specialized procedures, and methods learned and used as a way of accomplishing a desired result. Techniques are repeatable skill sets meant to help us to control outcomes. A golfer's swing is a technique. Professional golfers hit tens of thousands of golf balls from the practice range and spend seven or eight hours a day working on their technique until it is flawless. Then they can control the outcomes of nearly every shot.

Techniques are the rudiments of contemporary church leadership. Nearly every single leadership book I've ever read is filled with techniques. They are easy to spot: *7 Habits of Highly Effective People*, or *The 21 Irrefutable Laws of Leadership*. Techniques come from the "how to" genre. When faced with a challenge, leaders can reach into their bag of tricks, find a suitable technique, and control the outcomes, right?

The problem is that the kingdom of God is not that kind of a venture. We are not in control of outcomes. When we attempt to control the outcomes, we actually co-opt the mission of God.

When George Steinbrenner bought the New York Yankees from CBS in 1972, he paid a net of $8.8 million for the struggling franchise. At the time of his death in 2010, the Yankee Empire was worth an estimated $3.4 billion. How did he do it?

The answer is, he didn't do it, not really. Cable television did.

For the first decade Steinbrenner owned the Yankees, the team's on-field results improved notably. In that ten-year stretch, they had an average finish of 2.4 with two World Series Championships, compared to 4.7 and no championships over the previous decade.[6] But they were still not a profitable franchise.[7]

Then came the advent of local cable television channels. In 1988 Madison Square Garden Sports offered Steinbrenner and the Yankees $486 million for the rights to broadcast all of their games on local New York television. From that moment on the Yankees were profitable, and their on-field performance got even better. In the nearly two and a half decades since they signed the deal with MSG, the Yankees' average finish is around second place. They have finished in first place a record fourteen times while winning five World Series titles. They consistently have among the highest payrolls in baseball.

In 1972 Steinbrenner could have never foreseen the impact cable television would one day have on professional baseball. Before he signed the deal, Steinbrenner had no control over cable TV, no financial interests in that sector, and no part in its development. What made Steinbrenner, *Steinbrenner* was his personality and leadership style. What made Steinbrenner an astounding success was cable television—a variable completely out of his control.

The church is like that. The results are out of our control. We have no idea what God is up to at any given time. We have no idea what will make for our success or struggle. When we serve the kingdom of God, we are not serving in the realm of predictable results. We cannot control outcomes.

The world of business wants every chart to run up and to the right—no downturns. But healthy things don't work like that. Healthy things don't go in a straight line. A flat line on an EKG does, but that means you are dead. Healthy things have rhythms, cycles, ups and downs. This is breathing, a heartbeat, the tides, the seasons, and all of life that ebbs and flows. There is evening and

---

6   www.baseball-reference.com/teams/NYY/.

7   Joe Nocera, "Was Steinbrenner Just Lucky?" *The New York Times*, July 16, 2010.

there is morning, and that's what the day is like. It's not a day without a season of moving up, and a season of moving down. When we attempt to force a constant upward motion, we are fighting against nature. Ministry life has its ups and downs, and we usually cannot tell at any given time whether God has us all in an upturn or downturn, especially when it comes to the macrolevel and the church universal. We cannot control outcomes in God's kingdom. It's simply arrogant and above our pay grade.

The kingdom of God is always a surprise. It always comes to those who least expect it, and usually to those who are down to their last nickel. Any attempts to bottle success, replicate it, or conjure it through leadership techniques will ultimately pale in their impact compared to the will of God. God is going to do with the church what God wants to do. The moment we think we can control the results of our ministry, we have stepped outside the Christian story.

The problem is that leaving the results in God's hands can be a pretty vulnerable feeling. It's hard to practice faithfulness when growth does not materialize, especially for a church leader whose congregation is clamoring for predictable outcomes and charts that go up and to the right.

During the early days of the church growth movement, church leaders began to believe they could game the system. The entire church growth movement is an experiment in controlling the outcomes of the kingdom. Leaders began to borrow techniques from the world of business leadership to get the results they desired without having to wait on God. They rationalized the utilization of nearly anything that would make the church grow.

Just as in Ariely's experiment, it is never the big cheaters who make the biggest impact. Most folks who joined this movement—and remember that I'm one of those folks—didn't compromise the gospel, water down their message, or openly compete with other congregations. They just made thousands of tiny compromises, attempting to produce consistent success. Those choices have had a phenomenal influence on subsequent generations of church and ministry leaders.

While Dan Ariely was doing his research on rationalizing

behavior, he interviewed the staff of waiters at restaurants to tell him the best way to "dine and dash" (eat a meal and leave without paying). Almost without exception, servers had good ideas on how to pull this off. Go to the bathroom and sneak out the back. Leave while your server is in the kitchen. They also said that it hardly ever happens.[8] For some reason people *cannot* rationalize this behavior.

> Most folks who joined this movement ... didn't compromise the gospel, water down their message, or openly compete with other congregations. They just made thousands of tiny compromises, attempting to produce consistent success.

Ariely also found that nearly every college-aged student he spoke with had some form of illegally downloaded music or movies on their computer. One young man said he didn't even think it was wrong. Musicians want their music to be heard. Record labels are evil and shouldn't be supported. He wasn't going to buy the music anyway. It's not hurting anybody, and everybody does it, so what's the harm? After hearing his rationale, one would think the student wasn't illegally downloading music but was fighting for freedom.[9] For some reason people *can* easily rationalize this behavior.

The rationalization that works for illegal music downloads doesn't work for the dine-and-dash scenario. Why? Well, one would never say that a chef just wants his food to be eaten, and the restaurant is owned by an evil corporation, and everybody is doing it, so it is okay. What Ariely learned by comparing these scenarios is that *some things lend themselves to rationalization* more than others.

The gospel is one of those things; the gospel lends itself to rationalization.

It's easy to rationalize the use of nearly any leadership technique — no matter how foreign it might be to the world Jesus envisioned — in order to further the reach of the faith.

---

8 Ariely, *The Honest Truth*, 255–56.
9 Ibid.

It's called the Robin Hood syndrome: do a little harm for a greater good. Such is the contemporary leadership technique in the hands of a pastor. Here's how our rationalization pitch goes. It's the gospel we're talking about, right? We're engaged in a battle against real evil and eternity is at stake. So what if we spend thousands of dollars on church marketing? So what if we fire employees when they don't produce results? So what if I push my volunteers to the point of exhaustion and my wife to the brink of divorce? So what if I turned reverent worship into a Vegas sideshow. So what if hundreds of people in our churches do not become involved in the life of the church in any meaningful way? They are hearing the gospel, right? The stakes are high.

It's easy to rationalize the use of pragmatic, results-driven leadership techniques. The truth is that leadership techniques can produce a certain kind of result, mostly numerical growth. But the gospel isn't about reaching numbers; the gospel is about participating in God's redemption of the cosmos, and most church leaders would agree — today's church growth strategies are not producing fully committed followers of Christ. They are making church *fans*. Church growth techniques tend to produce people who attend church because they can hear a comforting message, check off the religion box, contribute just a little bit financially, and leave feeling good about themselves without ever having to change the basic disposition of their lives — and everybody's happy.

I know this is controversial, but as I speak with church leaders and listen to their frustrations, I'm convinced that it is true. Leadership techniques do not contribute nearly as much as we think to the overall health of the church. Yet techniques live at the foundation of our existing church leadership culture. They dominate church leadership culture.

While doing his research, sometimes Ariely would put an actor in the front row of the class as he was testing a group of participants to see if they would cheat for money. About thirty seconds after the instructor told everyone to begin, the actor would raise his hand and say, "I finished all twenty problems. What do I do?" The rest of the students were still on the first problem, so they knew this person was cheating. They all stopped to see what would happen.

The researcher would say, "Shred your paper and come get your $20." The actor would shred his paper, collect his money, and leave. What the team found was that cheating went up in that circumstance. When someone from their own social group cheated, it became easier for the rest to rationalize their own behavior.

Then the researchers introduced another variable. This time they dressed the actor up in a hat and sweatshirt from a rival college. For example, if they would have been on the Ohio State campus, they'd put the actor in Michigan gear. What they found in that instance was that cheating went down. One had to feel a sense of social affinity with the cheater in order to rationalize one's own behavior.

Megachurch pastors and highly successful leaders are wearing our team colors. We look up to them. We feel a strong affinity with leadership gurus who teach ministry techniques and promise consistent results. The example set by megachurch pastors and leadership consultants makes it so much easier for us to rationalize the use of success-driven ministry techniques in our own context. It doesn't even feel like rationalizing; it feels like common sense.

> If the language of contemporary church leadership is *success*, then the grammar of the technically proficient church leader is the *technique*.

The use of techniques in ministry has even changed the nature of how we define the word *pastor*. Pastors are no longer content to pray, study, preach, and shepherd a small congregation for the rest of their lives. Pastors now must be technically proficient leaders who design programs, cast vision, recruit and train leaders, and engineer an organization capable of growth no matter the external environment or the will of God. They've change the definition of what it means to be a pastor and have adapted it to our culture of bigger, better, higher, faster, stronger.

If the language of contemporary church leadership is *success*, then the grammar of the technically proficient church leader is the *technique*.

THE LONG-TERM IMPACT OF THE SHORT-TERM

My suggestion is that church leaders — really, anyone engaged in the life of the church — should begin to pursue *virtues* instead of techniques. If the language of Christian leadership is about faithfulness, then the grammar — the basic building blocks — of truly Christian leadership is *virtue*.

Before Dan Ariely's research, the leading theory concerning rationalizing human behavior held that most people make decisions about their own behavior on the basis of a crude cost-benefit analysis. Let's say I'm short on cash and I need to pay some bills or my electricity is going to be shut off. I happen to know that my next-door neighbor keeps a roll of twenties buried in his backyard under a rock. I can quickly analyze the benefit of stealing the twenties versus the likelihood that I'll get caught, factor in the punishment I would receive if that were to happen, and weigh the cost-benefit. The analysis will help me decide whether I will rip off my neighbor in order to pay my bills.

If I think I'm not likely to be caught, I might go ahead and do it. If I think I'm likely to get caught but I don't really care what my neighbor thinks of me and I know he wouldn't call the police, I might go ahead and do it. If I'm sure I'll get caught or can't stand the thought of going to jail, I might try a different option.

This is the simple model of rational crime (SMORC), and nearly everybody assumes that this is how the world works. That's why in our society the only variables we adjust in order to reduce crime are increasing the magnitude of punishment (higher prison terms) and the likelihood that criminals will be caught (more police officers and surveillance cameras).

But Ariely's data shows a different story. Remember that the big cheaters had little impact on his research. The real impact was made by the eighteen thousand participants who stole just a few dollars each. These participants only cheated a little bit because they could rationalize their own behavior. It wasn't even really like cheating; it was more like *fudging*. They would only cheat by one or two questions — enough that they could still feel as though they were basically honest people. If they stole too much, they could no longer rationalize their behavior — no longer think of themselves as honest. That's why there were so few big cheaters.

Ariely explains that the reason the simple model of rational behavior doesn't hold up under scrutiny is that people do not typically think about the long-term effects of their behavior. They only think about how they feel in the moment. We all know this is true; otherwise nobody would ever smoke cigarettes or eat Big Macs. People don't typically think about the long-term impact of their short-term behavior. The only question is: Can I rationalize this behavior right now? If they will end up feeling like a criminal, liar, or a cheater right there at that specific point in time, they will usually refrain from stealing, lying, or cheating. But if they can rationalize their behavior in some way, do a little wrong without feeling like a criminal, liar, or cheater, then they might end up doing all three. My argument in this chapter is that the only thing that stands in the way of the Christian leader pivoting to any technique that will help us to be successful — no matter how foreign to the gospel — is the knowledge and practice of *virtue*.

> People do not typically think about the long-term effects of their behavior. They only think about how they feel in the moment.

When Ariely interviewed criminals who had been involved in decade-long patterns of criminal behavior, he found that none of them thought of the whole sequence of events that would transpire or the net effect of their actions. They only thought about the first step. I need some money. I'm in big trouble if I don't get it. I'm not really stealing so much as solving a huge problem. That's how we rationalize. The long-term effects do not generally enter in.[10]

We do this in ministry all the time. I'm not misleading. I'm just embellishing a story for effect. I'm not selling out. I'm just doing what everybody else is doing. I am not manipulating. I'm leading.

As I was reading Ariely's research, I wondered whether my thesis

10 Ariely, Speech to the RSA.

was true that a deep sense of and practice of virtue might impact a person's ability to rationalize his or her own behavior, especially in ministry. Is a strong sense of virtue powerful enough to overcome our tendency to rationalize our behavior? As it turns out, Ariely tested for this. His team did a study on the UCLA campus in which he asked the students to try and name all of the Ten Commandments before they took the test and had the opportunity to cheat. What they found was stunning. Nobody cheated. Not a single person.

That's the power of virtue.

Here's the thing. Techniques are fine. You can hop online and read the first dozen leadership books you find and learn enough techniques to last a lifetime. The truth is that it's impossible to do leadership in nearly any context *without* using some sort of leadership techniques. They are like tools in a toolbox, right? You can use a hammer to drive a nail or to break into a store to rob it. What guides the technique is the virtue. Too much of the church leadership conversation is focused on technique, and not nearly enough is focused on virtue.

The church doesn't need technically proficient leaders. *The church needs virtuous leaders.* You see, when the going gets tough, virtue is the only thing that will keep us from rationalizing whatever decision will produce the desired outcomes.

> The church doesn't need technically proficient leaders. *The church needs virtuous leaders.*

When we lead in the context of the church, we know beyond a shadow of a doubt that we will find ourselves in tough situations, facing heart-wrenching decisions, often wishing for a quick and easy way out. We will face the prospect of years of effort with not a lot to show for it, and we will long for tangible results. We will constantly be faced with opportunities to rationalize almost any leadership technique or decision that we know will produce results. The only thing powerful enough to stop it will be a commitment to virtue.

Techniques are built for the short run. They work well in solving immediate tension, and they will often tempt us to rationalize anything that will work in the short-term. Virtues are built for the long haul. Virtues are the guard rails that will keep us from damaging the long-term health of the church for short-term gains. Virtues are about behaving in ways that are consistent with the life and teachings of Jesus Christ even when the immediate tensions make that seem difficult or impractical.

All human beings are responsible for what we put out into the world; ministry leaders even more so, since we are actively working to create culture. Christianity isn't a belief system; it's a new mode of being patterned on the life of Jesus. The church is supposed to have a completely different mode of being than the rest of our society. We are meant to be a little colony of heaven in the midst of a world that is sometimes broken and dark. The world is watching how we live, how we organize ourselves as the people of God. When we exhibit a wholesale acceptance of the techniques and methods of the wider culture, we lose all contrast. We fade into the background of the culture and cease to image God. Our mode of being should be peculiar and distinct, richly committed to the virtues that will sustain God's people precisely when the entire culture goes another way.

> We shouldn't be looking at our techniques and wondering if they produce the right results; we should be looking at our lives and wondering if they image God to the world around us.

Often when I question a church leadership technique, I am opposed by those who say, "Yeah, but it works." When I reply, "I don't care about results, I care about faithfulness," I often feel as though I'm speaking a foreign language. We want to grow; we want to succeed, and success provides the ultimate rationale for any behavior, especially when it comes to spreading the gospel. But we shouldn't be looking at our techniques and wondering if they produce the right results; we should be looking at our lives and wondering if they image God to the world around us.

THE DYNAMICS OF VIRTUE

For the Greeks the concept of virtue (*aretē*) referred to that which caused a thing to perform its intended function well. The virtue of an eye was in seeing. The virtue of a knife was cutting. A human virtue is anything that helps a human being become fully human as God intended humans to be.

In his book *A Community of Character*, Stanley Hauerwas argues that the virtues cannot be established in some static or universal sense. We cannot simply say the virtue of honesty is in being honest. Any account of what honesty might mean will be dictated by the guiding narratives and stories of the community. Few people in our society would think being an honest person requires an honest answer to the question, "Honey, does this dress make me look fat?" Virtues are always "context-dependent."[11]

Those two aspects of virtue combine in the Christian narrative to help form a powerful picture of Christian virtue. Christian virtue is not a possession of the individual. Virtues are instilled in us as we learn how to be a part of the people of God. Virtue is about learning how to be a part of the community of people who have organized their lives around the worship of the God of Israel and Jesus. Christian virtues are imbedded in and transmitted by the Christian story and community, in accordance with the Scriptures and the traditions of the church. What it means to practice virtues will ultimately come to us from our community and from the context in which we are making choices about what it means to be a human being in a given situation.

Training in virtue is not something that is often a part of the leadership conversation, but it should be. The dynamics of how virtue is formed, nurtured, and transmitted are an extremely important part of learning how to lead. The rest of this chapter is devoted to understanding a few of the dynamics of some Christian virtues as they relate to the life of the church.

Virtues Are Imbedded in Communities and Cultures

Virtues live in communities as much or more than they live in individual persons. The community to which a person belongs has a tremendous power to shape the imagination of its members. Its members tell stories, enact customs, and produce art, songs, and liturgies

---

11 Stanley Hauerwas, *A Community of Character* (South Bend, IN: University of Notre Dame Press, 1981), 112.

that serve to maintain and extend the community's virtues to all of its members. Virtues become embodied in a group of people who live together over time.

In Kansas we have a number of Mennonite and Anabaptist communities. Many of the young Anabaptist men relocated to Topeka during the Vietnam War because they were conscientious objectors. They were brought in to work in the State Industrial School for Boys or Topeka State Hospital, and after the war many stayed to raise their families.

Nonviolence is a great example of how a virtue actually lives in and among a community. Nonviolence is an important virtue for the Anabaptist people, but it does not exist to any great degree in the wider culture. To those who consider themselves part of the Anabaptist community, it is hard to imagine another way of seeing the world. You can learn about nonviolence from books, and you can take classes and seminars that will help you understand it. But if you want to begin to embody nonviolence in any deep and lasting sense, at some point you will have to spend some time among the Anabaptists. They have struggled for centuries with how to live nonviolently in a world that is committed to violence, and to possess deep wisdom that is not available in books — the kind of wisdom necessary to sustain this virtue.

Apart from a few political science departments and possibly a few religious orders, it's possible that the virtue of nonviolence could disappear completely from American society if the Anabaptists were to suddenly disappear. In order for the virtue of nonviolence to survive, these people must survive because virtues are imbedded in communities and cultures. Part of what it means to lead a church is to help that community preserve its essential virtues, each of which is derived from the gospel and not from the story of the wider culture. Our ability to lead in the way of Christ is fully dependent upon our being initiated into a community of virtue — one whose life is rooted not in the cultural narratives but in the Christian narrative.

Virtues Are Not Taught; They Are Caught
There's an old joke about a child who is sent home from school with a note saying he stole a pencil from a student in his class. The boy's

father is furious and lectures the boy on the virtue of honesty. "I'm very disappointed in you," the father says. "Besides, if you needed a pencil, you could have just asked me. I can bring home dozens of pencils from the office." What virtue is the child learning from his father?

Virtues are not taught; they are caught.

When researcher and storyteller Brené Brown talks about parenting, she says that parents shouldn't put too much trust in techniques. In fact, her research shows that when it comes to imparting the most important gifts we have to give to our children—things such as courage, compassion, and connection that will allow our kids to feel a deep sense that they are worthy of love and belonging in their own lives—no technique can help us. The only way to pass those things on to our children is if we are experiencing them ourselves.

Learning a virtue is like learning a trade. The only way to become a master is to become apprenticed to a master and to allow them to pass on to you the wisdom they have accrued over time. This is one of the chief differences between techniques and virtues. Techniques can be transferred without any direct contact. To learn a virtue, you must be in a relationship with a person who has learned to master that virtue. This is one of the reasons I love the parish church model, in which an associate pastor serves under the leadership of a senior pastor for a period of years.

There's a story that is often told by people who are part of Alcoholics Anonymous. A guy falls into a hole and can't get himself out. A doctor passes by, and the man yells for help. The doctor writes him a prescription, throws it down into the hole, and walks on by. Then a priest walks by and the man yells to him for help. The priest says a prayer for the man and walks on by. Then his friend walks by. "Hey, Joe! It's me. I'm stuck down here in this hole. Can you help me out?" Joe

> This is one of the chief differences between techniques and virtues. Techniques can be transferred without any direct contact. To learn a virtue, you must be in a relationship with a person who has learned to master that virtue.

jumps down into the hole. His friend says, "What are you doing, Joe? Now we're both stuck down here."

Joe says in reply, "Yeah, but I've been down here before, and I know the way out."

If you jump into the hole with someone who is in trouble, and you do not know the way out, you are certain to make things worse. In the same way, if you try to learn virtues from a person who has not yet been formed in them, it will never work, and you'll both be worse off for having tried. We cannot pass on that which we do not have. Virtues are not taught; they are caught. The hard work of leadership is first and foremost about *being*, not doing. Our primary task as leaders must be to be trained to practice a particular set of Christian virtues.

Virtues Are Not Possessions; They Are Practices

I'm trying to teach my sons how to whistle, and it's not going well. Whistling is a skill you can develop with certain techniques. Once you master the techniques, you are officially a whistler. Whether you actually whistle every day doesn't really matter; the fact is you know how to whistle. If you haven't whistled for years, you can pretty much pick it up again whenever you like.

Virtues *aren't* like whistling. You can't learn the techniques of hope, practice them a few times, and then say, "Okay, I'm a hopeful person." Hopeful people are not the world's foremost authorities on the subject of hope. They are hopers. Hopeful people hope. Loving people love people. Caring people care. This is how virtue works. You can't understand the virtue of love by reading books, listening to songs, or reciting poems. If you want to understand love, you have to take a risk and actually love somebody.

Virtues are not possessions; they are practices.

That they are practices will mean that virtues have a short shelf life. I can be quite loving toward my wife one day, and the next day... not so much. To be a loving person, one must continue practicing love. There is no other way. In this sense, virtues spoil quickly. You have to wake up every morning and decide to embody them, or you'll find yourself unable to do so.

There Are No Shortcuts to Virtue

My youngest son has a rare form of dyslexia. He is really smart, so it took us awhile to figure it out. Since he's been diagnosed, we've learned that one of the things he struggles with is working memory. For instance, he knows each of the sounds that the letters T-A-B-L-E make, but when he's sounding out the word, he has to work really hard to access each individual letter's sound. So, by the time he gets to the E at the end of the word, it's possible that he has forgotten what the earlier sounds in the progression were.

When we first started seeing signs that something might be wrong, we kept being thrown off by how well he was doing on things like spelling. If you asked him to spell the word *table*, he could do it. However, if he ran into the word *table* in a reading assignment, he usually didn't recognize it. So how was he passing his spelling tests?

What we discovered was that he had simply been memorizing letter sequences and assigning them to words. If we would have told him that you spell the word *table* "E-J-6-yellow-14," he simply would have committed that sequence to memory and regurgitated it for the test. It's really quite stunning when you think about it. He taught himself—without any help or instruction from us—how to game the system. It worked for awhile, but then we moved from ten spelling words to twenty, and then thirty. By that point his memory couldn't keep up. When it was time to really start reading, we realized we were facing a whole different challenge.

> Virtues are like this: they come slowly over time, there are no shortcuts, and you can never game the system.

If my son were to continue relying on his technique involving memory, he would never learn how to read, write, spell, or use language with any sort of freedom or fluency. There are no shortcuts for reading. Fluency is a difficult thing to master, and those who have dyslexia have to work even harder.

Virtues are like this: they come slowly over time, there are no shortcuts, and you can never game the system.

Virtues Are Nurtured and Sustained by a Common Story

Dirk Willems was an Anabaptist church leader in the Netherlands during the sixteenth century. He was part of a group of Christians who resisted the state church that engaged in violence in the name of Christ. Willems and other Anabaptists practiced nonviolence, which made them easy pickings for the authorities.

During the harsh rule of the Duke of Alva, Willems was arrested and imprisoned. While in jail, he escaped by making a rope out of knotted rags and lowering himself to the ground. One of the guards saw him attempting to escape and pursued him. Willems ran for all he was worth until he came to the edge of a frozen pond. Malnourished from his prison rations, Willems weighed little and easily made it to the other side on the thin layer of ice. The officer who was pursuing him was apparently well fed, because he broke through the ice and began to drown in the icy water.

Willems felt it would go against his commitment to nonviolence to leave the officer to die, so he ran back onto the pond and pulled him out, saving his life. The officer immediately seized Willems, rearrested him, and took him back to jail, where he was eventually executed.

If you had been raised in an Anabaptist community, you would have heard this story, and scores of others just like it, from the time you were young. This story would have seeded your imagination for what it meant to practice nonviolence. It would have empowered you to stay true to this virtue even if it meant suffering a great injustice in the process. It would have told you about the attitude many other people have toward nonviolence. It would have been gathered with many other stories about the price and pain of nonviolence and repeated time and again. The story of Dirk Willems functions to nurture and sustain the virtue of nonviolence among the Anabaptist people.

All societies and cultures tell stories that enforce the virtues of their people. Many of us were weaned on the story of George Washington and the cherry tree. This story reinforced the virtue of honesty. We were told stories about patriots like Patrick Henry, whose bold proclamation, "Give me liberty or give me death," taught us the virtue of courage and conviction. The virtues of any society are sustained by common stories.

Techniques are nurtured by stories as well. But they are nearly always nurtured by the American story of bigger, better, farther, higher, and faster. Techniques that do not produce relevant results are not protected, and they often fall by the wayside and are no longer practiced.

Stories make sure that the virtues of the community will continue to be embodied, practiced, and passed on to successive generations regardless of the short-term results. For the Christian leader, we must begin to do this in more intentional ways.

When It Comes to Virtue, Failure Is as Important as Success

A few weeks ago, I was in the midst of trying to finish this manuscript, writing a sermon, pushing through an important initiative at church, and trying to meet another writing deadline. I was working at home one afternoon, and my wife said she needed to run to the store—could I watch the kids? I'll admit that it always bothers me a little bit when my wife asks me to watch the kids while I'm working at home. I think to myself, I am actually *working*; I am not sitting at my desk playing video games. So I was already cooking a little bit when my kids started arguing about the game they were playing. I asked them to keep it down and put on my noise-blocking headphones. Next thing I know, my oldest comes down to my office sobbing with a big red welt on his head. Let's just say I didn't handle myself with a great amount of virtue.

I started scolding them, but just a few seconds in, I stopped in midsentence. I sat there silent for a moment, thinking about how they are just kids and how I have a short fuse because of my own choices, not theirs. I cracked a little smile, and so did they. I apologized to them and told them I was stressed out about other stuff, and it wasn't their fault. They forgave me, and I took a quick break to help them settle their dispute.

I can't tell you how many times I've apologized to my own kids. In our house, my wife and I *look* for reasons to apologize and admit our own failures. Not only does it teach our children the virtues of forgiveness and long-suffering, but it models virtues like contrition and seeking forgiveness even when it's hard.

Nobody gets it right all of the time, which is how virtues like forgiveness, self-compassion, patience, and fidelity become imbedded in a particular community. How will we learn forgiveness if nobody messes up? When it comes to being formed in virtue, even failure is important. Much of what we describe as virtue will only come through failure.

The only way to learn patience is to be a part of community where people are really annoying. The only way to learn forgiveness is to experience the pain of having been wronged in some way. Virtues such as perseverance, tolerance, honesty, compassion, sensitivity, justice, mercy, awareness, assertiveness, kindness, self-restraint—just to name a few—presuppose the existence of some sort of conflict or tension.

The Process of Developing and Practicing Virtue Is Open-Ended

When it comes to developing virtue, you never get to cross the goal line, spike the ball, and do your touchdown dance. The pursuit of virtue is a lifelong commitment.

> The pursuit of virtue is a lifelong commitment.

Often virtues that served us well in the first half of our lives no longer seem to function in the same way that they used to. Some of the virtues like ambition, hard work, industriousness, responsibility, tenacity, and resilience that are needed so desperately on our way up will be replaced by virtues that seem to align more closely with the second half of life. When we are finally ready to travel the Jesus way of descent, virtues such as acceptance, mindfulness, restraint, openness, awareness, and discernment will become indispensible to us.

Anyone who is in a relationship with an aging parent or grandparent knows that one of two things usually happens as people age. Either they begin to have a more fixed mind-set—closed off and rigid, ceasing to grow and learn—or they develop a whole new set of virtues that cultivate an openness to an increasingly foreign and often scary new set of cultural dynamics. The process of developing and practicing virtue is like that: it is always open-ended.

Virtue Is Its Own Reward

Mrs. Jeffers, one of the teachers at my son's school, is somewhat of a teaching Jedi. She's been doing the classroom teaching thing for a long time, and she's seen just about everything there is to see. She's a demanding teacher who sets high expectations, but she makes it tons of fun. She's catching kids at that point in their education when it's time for them to start taking more responsibility for their work, and she has this ability to help them do far more than they ever dreamed they could.

The kids love this teacher.

The parents, predictably, tend to struggle at first.

The turn toward taking responsibility for their own education—homework assignments, reports, doing their own work without a parent looking over their shoulder—it's not a skill set that comes automatically for our children. The kids struggle quite a bit over the first nine weeks. Parents, however, are used to results. They want to see performance—the same performance they have come to expect. Parents want success, they want As, and they can become a bit impatient when their kids don't meet those expectations.

Every year the parents start grumbling pretty early on. Their kids are not making the kinds of grades they are used to, so the work load must be too high. Or if we could only check our children's work before it is handed in. Mrs. Jeffers refuses. She patiently explains that she needs to be able to see each student's mistakes. She has to understand what each one of them struggles with so that she can work on those concepts with them. How will she understand what they still need to learn if the parents have already fixed their mistakes?

The kids do difficult assignments every week that involve their vocabulary words and grammar lessons, combined with the use of certain assigned parts of speech and different sentence structures and forms. This is tough stuff. I've written several books and I can't do all of these assignments. One parent lobbied to be able to proofread the sentences before they were turned in; that way the student could get a better grade. The teacher stood her ground, asking the question that wise teachers everywhere have learned to ask impatient parents: "Do you want your child to get straight A's or do you want them to learn? I'm trying to help them to learn. The grades will come later on."

The parents have been nurtured in a story of success and achievement. Mrs. Evans has been nurtured in a story of learning and education. She knows that in the fourth grade getting straight A's is not important. What's important is learning how to take responsibility for your own learning process. She has been formed by the virtues that live within the community of good school teachers, and she practices those virtues with great fidelity. When social pressures are exerted on her, she instinctively knows when to give a little and when it's important to hold her ground. Over the course of the year, she almost always wins over the entire group of parents.

That's the power of virtue. When the going gets rough, when we are not getting the results we like, when we are pressured, criticized, and tempted to rationalize the use of techniques that are foreign to the gospel and the church, only a deep commitment to the practice of certain virtues will keep us from bartering away our birthright for a bowl of beans.

We need church leaders who are so formed in the virtues of Christian leadership, and whose allegiance is not to success but to faithfulness, that they instinctively know when they should resist the path of the culture, even if by doing so they could get some short-term gains or make everyone around them happy.

The following six chapters are an exploration of some of the little-celebrated virtues of Christian leadership. These six virtues probably don't make the top-ten list for most leaders of any stripe, but they are absolutely essential: vulnerability, cooperation, brokenness, patience, and fidelity. These are the virtues that live at the heart of truly Christian leadership. They are more fundamental to our leadership that any list of techniques could ever be.

Part 3

GROWING

IN

VIRTUE

Chapter 7

VULNERABILITY – THE CARDINAL VIRTUE OF CHRISTIAN LEADERSHIP

*I am deeply convinced that the Christian leader of the
future is called to be completely irrelevant and to stand
in this world with nothing to offer but his or her own
vulnerable self. That is the way Jesus came to reveal
God's love. The great message we have to carry, as
ministers of God's word and followers of Jesus, is that
God loves us not because of what we do or accomplish,
but because God has created and redeemed us in love
and has chosen us to proclaim that love as the true
source of all human life.*
—Henri Nouwen, *In the Name of Jesus*

Dietrich Bonhoeffer is considered one of the greatest Christian leaders of the twentieth century. When the National Socialist Party first gained power in Germany, they naturally sought the support of the German church. One would assume the church would have resisted, but when Hitler first came to power, few suspected that he was a genocidal lunatic. The German church was at an all-time low, having lost influence and the respect of the people over the years. Many church leaders thought supporting the National Socialists could return the church to its former glory.

Others disagreed. Some, like Bonhoeffer, believed that supporting Hitler's vision of the Third Reich compromised their faithfulness to Christ, especially in regard to the Nazi treatment of the Jews. These disagreements fractured the German church.

After years of struggle and conflict, Bonhoeffer joined several other clergy in signing the Barmen Declaration—a formal denouncement of Hitler's attempts to influence the church. The declaration was written by one of the great theologians of the century, Karl Barth, and it stated clearly that Christ was the head of the church, not Hitler. Hitler's handpicked church leaders were not amused. Although Bonhoeffer and his friends fought valiantly to save the German church, they were eventually pushed out of all leadership positions.

These exiled Christian leaders started their own church, which they called the "Confessing Church." Bonhoeffer continued to work against the Hitler regime's takeover of the German church by training church leaders in an underground seminary. The Gestapo was always after him and eventually shut down the seminary, arresting Bonhoeffer and many other leaders of the Confessing Church. Hitler's government intimidated, harassed, and interrogated Bonhoeffer, while abasing the church he loved. Bonhoeffer saw his share of suffering, but he was undeterred in his opposition to Hitler. He, along with others in the Confessing Church, believed that opposition to the German Christians and the Nazi regime was what faithfulness meant, even if it didn't lead to immediate change.

Eventually it became clear that Bonhoeffer was either going to have to join with Hitler's army and fight, or continue to oppose Hitler and be imprisoned. His friends in the Confessing Church believed that the best course of action was for him to flee the country and wait out the war. So they arranged for a student visa and snuck him to America by way of Switzerland and Great Britain.

It was not Bonhoeffer's first trip to America. Earlier in his life, he had spent a year teaching at Union Theological Seminary in the United States. During that year he grew somewhat disenchanted with American Christianity. Bonhoeffer believed that American Christians had been raised on a narrative that skewed their view of the church and the gospel. American Christians were taught from a young age that America had been established by Christians fleeing religious persecution in Europe. The narrative had a clear message:

faithful Christians didn't stay and suffer; instead, they traveled to the new world to find freedom.

Bonhoeffer thought that this narrative had deceived American Christians into believing that it was possible to follow Jesus and forego the final step in Christian life: suffering for the gospel. He believed that staying and suffering—not an escape to freedom—was the necessary step for those who follow Jesus in the midst of a fallen world. For Bonhoeffer, those who believed they could follow Jesus without experiencing Christ's suffering had not rightly understood what it means to be a Christian.

And yet here he was, fleeing his own suffering by running to America.

He was miserable.

Bonhoeffer could not escape the feeling that he was running away. Back in Germany his colleagues were being rounded up by the Gestapo and imprisoned or forced into military service. Leaders of the Confessing Church had asked him to come to America so he could help rebuild the German church after the war. But he found this assignment incompatible with the call to faithfulness. He wrote:

> I have made a mistake in coming to America. I must live through this difficult period of our national history with the Christian people of Germany. I shall have no right to participate in the reconstruction of Christian life in Germany after the war if I do not share the trials of this time with my people. My brothers in the Confessing Synod wanted me to go. They may have been right in urging me to do so, but I was wrong in going.... Christians in Germany will face the terrible alternative of either willing the defeat of their nation in order that Christian civilization may survive, or willing the victory of their nation and thereby destroying our civilization. I know which of these alternatives I must choose [the defeat of his own nation], but I cannot make that choice in security.[1]

Bonhoeffer understood something that many leaders miss—the necessity of *vulnerability* in following Christ. Bonhoeffer knew that

---

1 Dietrich Bonhoeffer, quoted by Eberhard Bethge, *Dietrich Bonhoeffer: A Biography* (Minneapolis: Fortress, 2000), 655.

to lead, he would need to share in the vulnerability of his people. There was no way that he could participate in the body of Christ, much less help to lead it, while remaining in a position of safety and security. If the church was suffering, he needed to suffer with them.

One month after arriving in New York, Bonhoeffer sailed back to Germany. He became part of the Abwehr and the underground resistance to Hitler. Four years later he was killed by the SS—a mere three weeks before Hitler committed suicide.

> We cannot lead from a position of safety. We must lead from a position of vulnerability.

I've often thought about that month Bonhoeffer spent in New York City—heartsick at the thought of his friends being killed and imprisoned. No doubt he was somewhat reluctant to return to Germany, but Bonhoeffer understood a crucial aspect of Christian leadership: we cannot lead from a position of safety. We must lead from a position of vulnerability.

Most people think that leadership is the exercise of power, but it is not. Leadership that has been informed and transformed by Christ is about learning to embrace vulnerability, leveraging it in ways that will inspire faithfulness in the lives of others.

WORTHINESS AND VULNERABILITY

Brené Brown is a researcher on the topic of shame. She has spent a dozen years trying to understand the things that keep us from experiencing a deep sense of love and belonging in our lives. After all her years of education and research, Brown is sure of one thing: "Connection is why we are here. We are hardwired to connect with others; it's what gives purpose and meaning to our lives, and without it there is suffering."[2]

I was initially drawn to Brown's research because of this great phrase: *connection is why we are here.* My first book, *An Evangelical Social Gospel*,[3] was my attempt to explain theologically this universal

---

2 Brené Brown, *Daring Greatly* (New York: Gotham, 2012), 7.
3 Tim Suttle, *An Evangelical Social Gospel* (Eugene, OR: Cascade, 2011).

need for connection, by connecting it to the gospel message itself. The gospel is not just personal, it is social as well. I found deep resonances between the work Brené Brown was doing and the Christian story.

After doing thousands of hours of interviews with thousands of people, Brown concluded that the world can be roughly divided into two groups: those who experience a healthy sense of love and belonging and those who don't. If you examine those two groups, what you will find is that in most ways they are identical. Age, gender, sexuality, hopes, dreams, successes, failures, addictions, tragedies, education, socioeconomics—you name it—the two groups are identical in every way except one. Those who experience a healthy sense of love and belonging believe that they are *worthy* of those things. Those who do not experience a healthy sense of love and belonging do *not* believe they are worthy.

Worthiness—that's the difference.

At this point, bells should be going off in our minds as we think about all of the time and effort Jesus spent trying to get the lost, the left out, and the left behind to believe that they were precious children of God. Deep down, what it means to follow Jesus is knowing and believing that his love has made us worthy of being called the children of God.

> Perhaps the most revolutionary change Jesus made to the Jewish faith was that he taught his followers to call God "Father."

Perhaps the most revolutionary change Jesus made to the Jewish faith was that he taught his followers to call God "Father." We do not have to achieve some status in order to receive God's love. God is our Father, and we are the precious children of God and are worthy of love and belonging because God's love makes us so. The problem is that far too many of us do not experience this as a reality in our lives—especially those who are involved in ministry.

One of the main reasons we do not experience love and belonging can be traced to the complex relationship between vulnerability and shame. Brown defines *shame* as "the intensely painful feeling or experience of believing that we are flawed and therefore unworthy of love and belonging."[4] The experience of shame is highly correlated with much of what we are trying to avoid in our lives and in the lives of our loved ones: anger, aggression, violence, addiction, depression, eating disorders, teen pregnancy, bullying, and so on.[5]

Brown defines *vulnerability* as "uncertainty, risk, and emotional exposure."[6] Vulnerability is the willingness to show up and allow oneself to be seen even when that is scary or uncertain. Vulnerability is a posture in which we let down our guard and allow others to see our true colors, hear our true story. Being vulnerable brings the possibility that we can be wounded. Yet Brown says that her research shows that vulnerability is the birthplace of all of the good things we want for our lives and our loved ones: love, belonging, joy, courage, empathy, hope, accountability, and authenticity.

Which of those lists do you think we need to draw from as we engage in ministry? Do we need more violence, anger, aggression, and depression? Or do we need more love, belonging, joy, courage, empathy, accountability, and authenticity?

Vulnerability is an inescapable part of the human experience, so I'm not arguing here that we need to find a way to *become* more vulnerable. We already are vulnerable. The question is how are we handling our vulnerability. Are we masking it? Numbing it? Do we power up and avoid it? Do we shrink back and hide or let ourselves be manipulated and controlled?

We are vulnerable people. Yet we will go to nearly any lengths to keep ourselves from feeling vulnerability. We don't do vulnerability well as Americans. We do strength and victory. We do fight and scratch to the top. We do "win at any cost." We don't do vulnerability— it sounds too much like weakness and failure to us.

One of the most important lessons I've learned from Brown's research is that vulnerability feels like weakness, but it looks like raw courage. It takes an extraordinary amount of courage to stand up

---

4   Brené Brown, *The Gifts of Imperfection* (Center City, MN: Hazeldon, 2010), 39.

5   Brown, *Daring Greatly*, 73.

6   Ibid., 34.

and let yourself be seen. In her book *The Gifts of Imperfection*, Brown notes that the root of the word *courage* is the Latin *cor*—which means "heart." She says the earliest form of the word *courage* meant, "to speak one's mind by telling all one's heart."[7] Vulnerability is about having the courage to speak your mind by revealing your true heart, even though you might be wounded in the process.

> Vulnerability feels like weakness, but it looks like raw courage.

Here we hit another deep resonance with the Christian story. Embracing weakness is at the heart of what it means to follow Jesus. The vulnerability of Jesus was essential to his life and ministry (see chapter 3). When Jesus taught about the kingdom of God, he said that people can only find their lives by losing them. That's vulnerability: learning how to die—little by little every day—for life of the world.

When my oldest child went to kindergarten for the first time, it felt as if something inside me was dying. I couldn't accept that this was happening. It felt like only an hour ago I was changing his diaper and teaching him to walk. Now, here I was, walking him into a building with a bunch of other wide-eyed newbies and handing him over to a teacher I hardly knew. How did this happen?

Two years later I did the same walk with my younger son, and it felt exactly the same—as if something inside me was dying. It was a small death, I suppose, but it still *felt* like death. I sensed my own vulnerability in that moment.

And yet, in that moment of death and letting go of the past, a whole new life was suddenly possible for my sons. If I would have refused, holding onto the present, I would have put my children's lives in jeopardy. Nothing says "let it die" more than a sixth-grade boy whose dad still cuts his food for him. When I see parents today fighting their adolescent (or worse, young adult) children's battles for them and cleaning up their messes, something wants to say, "I get it. I know how you feel. But you have to let it go. You have to let this thing die so that your child can grow into what's next for them."

---

7 Brown, *Gifts of Imperfection*, 12.

Often, the fear of death is what keeps us from experiencing life.

And the fear of vulnerability is what keeps us from love, joy, courage, empathy, creativity, hope, and authenticity.

The other day I was going through some old boxes, and I found a stack of Satellite Soul CDs. Satellite Soul was the band I was in for a decade after college. After I graduated from college I couldn't find a good job, so I did what I had always wanted to do—I started a band. Before I knew what was happening, we had signed with one of the major Christian record labels and were touring all over the country. I had the time of my life. And yet, as amazing as that time was, it was also often dark and painful.

Looking at our old records, I read some of the song titles and lyrics: "Wash My Fears Away," "I Will Be a Fool," "Still Looking for the Pieces," "I'm Not as Good as I Say I Am," "Maybe," "Everything around Me It Is Passing Away," "Broken Again," "Song for a Lonely Person," "Crazy," "Gone," "Ruin Me," "Bury Me," "Saddest Happy Ending." I suddenly realized that most of the songs I had written and recorded were about weakness, brokenness, and pain.

We played around a thousand shows as a band. In all those years of touring, nearly every single night I would recite the same passage from 2 Corinthians 12:9–10: "'My grace is sufficient for you, for my power is made perfect in weakness.' Therefore I will boast all the more gladly of my weaknesses, so that the power of Christ may rest on me. That is why, for Christ's sake, I delight in weaknesses, in insults, in hardships, in persecutions, in difficulties. For when I am weak, then I am strong." In those years, I learned that our weakness is the heart of God's strength in our lives. Knowing our own weakness is at the heart of what it means to follow Jesus. And it's at the heart of Christian leadership as well.

Brown's research suggests something I find stunning. She says that while our experience of vulnerability *feels* like weakness, to the outside observer it *looks* like strength. Brown says that vulnerability is the first thing we look for in other people, even though it is the last thing we want to feel ourselves. We long to experience the vulnerability of others, but our own experience of it can be excruciating. So we go to great lengths to avoid it.

VULNERABILITY DEFENSE MECHANISMS

Leaders have to learn how to become vulnerable if they want to lead in the way of Jesus. Yet, by the time most of us are working on establishing a career, we have developed a long list of defense mechanisms that protect us from feeling vulnerable. It takes time and effort to learn to recognize and overcome them. I'm convinced this is an important part of what it means to grow as a mature follower of Jesus. You can't do ministry without embracing your own vulnerability, and yet we have years of practice in avoidance of vulnerability. We have built up some pretty great defense mechanisms. What are these defenses, these barriers to vulnerability?

Numbing

Most commonly, Brown says, we *numb* ourselves. She writes, "We are the most in debt, obese, addicted, and medicated adult cohort in U.S. history."[8] These things are all means of numbing our hearts, our desires, our emotions and feelings. The experience of vulnerability can so overwhelm us that to protect ourselves, to avoid it, we reach for something that numbs the pain. The problem with numbing, she explains, is that you cannot selectively numb emotion. You cannot numb shame, fear, grief, and regret without also numbing joy, gratitude, love, happiness, creativity, hope, and all of the beautiful things about our lives.

> Vulnerability is the first thing we look for in other people, even though it is the last thing we want to feel ourselves.

Brown's research suggests that "vulnerability is the core of all emotions and feelings. To feel is to be vulnerable."[9] In other words, vulnerability lives at the heart of every other emotion we can feel. To feel anything at all is to be vulnerable. So numbing our sense of vulnerability numbs the root of our sensitivity, what makes all feeling possible.

---

8   This quote comes from Brown's first TED talk, from TEDxHouston, "The Power of Vulnerability" (given June 12, 2010).

9   Brown, *Daring Greatly*, 33.

Sadly, Christian leaders are not immune to this. Addictions to alcohol, drugs, and pornography are not uncommon. Many leaders numb in less obvious ways by hiding out in their office, refusing to engage with others. Even healthy things like medicine, friendships, books, and movies can become a means of numbing, distractions that keep us from ever addressing the root emotional problems that are the source of pain, fear, and shame in our lives.

Not only do individual leaders have these struggles, but the culture of the church places many demands on its leaders. What will it take for churches to give pastors and leaders the kind of time and space away from the daily demands of ministry to heal from past hurts and the pains of life? If we cannot numb our sense of vulnerability, we will have to deal with it somehow. The trouble comes when our productivity falls off as we get help and embrace periods of healing. We will need some space to get healthy. Are churches ready to make this kind of a commitment to their leaders' health?

Perfectionism

Perfectionism is another way we avoid vulnerability, and it also happens to be my favorite sin. I say this because I'm an achiever, which means that I spend an inordinate amount of energy trying to do things perfectly. I often attempt to avoid vulnerability through perfectionism. I tell myself that if I do it perfectly every time, then no one can critique me, and I don't have to feel vulnerable.

> If I do it perfectly every time, then no one can critique me, and I don't have to feel vulnerable.

I notice this often when I'm writing. I will have an article ready to go at one o'clock in the afternoon and then spend the next ten hours obsessing over one or two words or phrases that might offend somebody. I struggle just to show up and say what I think and feel. I tell myself that I can say what I think and feel so perfectly that it will be impossible for others to find fault with it. Of course, when I say it out loud I realize this is completely unrealistic.

I also do this with my own kids. This past baseball season my oldest son was having trouble hitting the ball. For most of the season he either walked or struck out. Game after game he would go without a single hit. Every kid goes through times when he or she struggles, but this was really getting to him, and to me. Every time he stepped up to the plate, I felt so vulnerable. I hated to watch him walk back to the dugout after striking out, trying unsuccessfully to hide his tears.

One evening, on the way home from a game, we talked about his repeated strikeouts. I said to him, "You know what I think? I think you show way more courage when you strike out than when you get a hit. Anybody can stand up there when they know that they can get a hit every time. You stand up there swinging, and it makes me feel really proud." Something changed for both of us that night. It was like we had discovered that he was playing a much bigger game.

Watching those we love experience emotional pain is a reminder of our own vulnerability. As a perfectionist, my tendency is to try working harder—practice hitting, hire a coach, go to the batting cages every day after school—all so that I don't have to feel vulnerable watching them strike out. But that's not love. Instead, I need to show up, have some courage, and be there for him, both when he hits the ball and when he doesn't. That's the real game we are playing.

Certitude

Making the *uncertain certain* is another way we try to avoid feeling vulnerable. Often, as church leaders, we do this by taking an aspect of our faith that is meant to inspire wonder, awe, and mystery and reduce it into a set of beliefs and doctrines that are either right or wrong. That's just one way we make the uncertain certain. For most of the history of Christianity, worship was meant to cultivate a sense of the mystery, awe, and wonder of God. The heart of worship was about reveling in a position of reverence and humility while corporately contemplating the mystery of faith.

Worship today, however, is different. It's about accumulating information, about knowing facts with certitude. The church today no longer says, "Come sit with us at the feet of the cross as we gaze in complete awe and wonder at the mystery that is our salvation in

Christ." What the world hears from us today is far different: "We are right. You are wrong. Turn or burn."

Our ability to embody Jesus in any significant way has little to do with a sense of certitude or the accumulation of information. It has everything to do, however, with doubt, weakness, unknowing, mystery, wonder, awe, and reverence—in other words, *faith*.

One of the most powerful tools in my leadership toolbox has been the words "I don't know." Once while our church was facing a crisis, I confessed to the congregation that I really didn't know what we should do. I can't tell you how many people found me after that confession to tell me how much they appreciated my vulnerability. I actually gained leadership credibility through my vulnerability that day—which was an interesting experience, given that it felt like I was failing my church at the time. Certitude does not inspire people; vulnerability does.

> Certitude does not inspire people; vulnerability does.

Cynicism

When we engage in ministry, we expose ourselves to all kinds of criticism. How do you, as a leader, respond to criticism? It is easy to allow ourselves to grow cynical and jaded—too cool to really care that deeply about what really happens. This is yet another way of avoiding vulnerability. Similar to numbing, we refuse to embrace that place of vulnerability and we act as if we simply don't care.

When my son was struggling with hitting the baseball that summer, I noticed that after a few strikeouts he didn't seem as affected. I asked him about it, and his answer was cynical: "I'm never going to hit the ball, so I don't care anymore." He stopped trying. When I heard him say this, that's when we started hitting the batting cages—not to flee vulnerability, but to encourage it. This is the danger of cynicism: it kills healthy striving.

I realize there is a "cool" factor in being a skeptic, a cynic, or a doubter. Some of this is healthy, but today it has reached near-canonical status. Dallas Willard once said, "We live in a culture that has, for centuries now, cultivated the idea that the *skeptical* person is always smarter than one who believes. You can almost be as stupid as a cabbage as long as you *doubt*."[10] The truth is that it doesn't take much work to be a cynic. The path of doubting is always easier than the decision to open our hearts and our lives up to others, to walk in faith. It is so much easier to be a cynic or a skeptic than to actually admit that we care about something.

> This is the danger of cynicism: it kills healthy striving.

VULNERABILITY IS A SUPERPOWER

Recently, I had an experience that reminded me of my own vulnerability. I was hired by a publisher to write the book portion of a small group curriculum based on a set of videos by a well-known New Testament scholar. I was really excited about this project. The scholar was someone I respected who had profoundly influenced my own thinking. I accepted the job, wrote my six chapters, turned them in, and didn't think much about it.

A couple of months later, I woke up to an email and learned that the scholar in question had not been aware of what I had done. He wanted an explanation. *Ugh.* Soon, others learned of the book, and there were several blog and Facebook posts suggesting the entire project was a scam. Some called me a rip-off artist, others a liar. Even *Christianity Today* picked up the story and soon it was everywhere.

I was crushed.

As it turns out, the entire thing was a misunderstanding, a lesson in the importance of good communication. The author had indeed signed a contract allowing the project but was so busy he had forgotten about it. When he did see it, he wasn't comfortable with the way it was being marketed. In the end, the publishers decided to pull the entire project. I had agreed to write a few chapters. I had no control over the way the project was marketed, and yet I felt as if I was being shamed for something I had not done.

I recalled from reading Brené Brown the importance of recognizing the physical manifestations of our shame. For me it was a stomach

---

10 Dallas Willard, *Hearing God* (Downers Grove: IL, InterVarsity Press, 1999), 218.

ache, sweaty armpits, and a flood of nervous energy accompanied by a paralyzing impulse to hide. The whole situation was made worse by the fact that I was stuck in a house at the time with my entire extended family, twenty-two of us gathered together to celebrate my dad's seventieth birthday. All of my family-of-origin shame triggers were front and center as well.

The calls, emails, texts, and messages kept flowing in. I literally hid out in one of the bedrooms. Finally, I called one of my trusted friends, a pastor who knows me well. He helped me to process what I was feeling and see my way through. He encouraged me to speak out and tell my story. Since writing is a helpful outlet for me, I wrote a blog post in order to try and show up in my own shame-storm and to let myself be seen. Here's some of what I said:

> I confess that I feel terribly exposed and vulnerable today. I was really excited about a writing project that I put my heart and soul into doing. I thought it represented some of my best pastoral writing. Now it's being completely slammed, and I'm being treated like a joke, and the whole thing may fall through. Last time I looked, a blog post ripping me had nearly a thousand shares. If you know anything about page-views, a share is worth about ten page-views.... I'm guessing 10–15 thousand people today were told I'm a big fraud. That's a pretty awful feeling.
>
> I'm sure God is teaching me through this.... Shame triggers two ubiquitous tapes in our minds which play over and over in situations like this. They tell us: "You are not good enough," and "Who do you think you are?" Those tapes are on repeat for me today.
>
> So, I confess that I will summon the courage to say I'm really proud of the work I did. I'm doing my best to learn how to be a better writer and to do something with my life and my gifts that serves the church. I am dented and smarting, but ultimately undeterred.

Once I typed those words and hit POST, I immediately felt better. I felt empowered. I felt as though I had done all I could do, and I was actually content to let the chips fall. I later exchanged some good emails with the author, and the publishers of the project thanked me for not throwing them under the bus. Most of the critical blog posts were taken down or amended.

To my surprise, I began receiving a flood of messages responding to my confession post. I've never had more phone calls or emails from a single post I've written. Scores of people from all over the world wrote me to say that they respected that I had shown up and allowed myself to be seen. They told me stories about similar things that had happened in their own lives. It was good and rich and healing.

I now understand what Brené Brown means when she says *vulnerability is a superpower.*

We all have a choice when we are hurt, wounded, afraid, doubting, or uncertain. When we are faced with something that triggers shame, that makes us worried, that leaves us feeling vulnerable and weak, we can choose to respond with numbing, perfectionism, certitude, and cynicism. Or we can choose to respond with authenticity and acknowledge our own vulnerability. Christian leadership is about choosing the latter.

Your goal as a leader can be to win the approval of others, to get them to like you, or to fit in. If you succeed in doing that, you will feel fine. But if you fail, you will feel shame. On the other hand, your goal can be simply to show up and let yourself be seen, to say what you really believe, and to be your authentic self. If you succeed, you will feel fine. If you fail, you will feel disappointment, sadness, frustration, maybe even anger—but you will not feel shame.

How do you try to hide your own vulnerability? Do you numb your emotions? Do you avoid them? Do you cut off that sense of deep connection before it starts so that you don't have to feel disappointed? Do you try to control your environment? Do you resort to perfectionism to keep from feeling the vulnerability of honest critique?

WHOLEHEARTED

On a typical Sunday morning I get up really early, maybe 5:30 a.m. I head to the office and work on my message until about 8:30 or so. I take preaching seriously, and I work hard at it. Those last three hours on Sunday morning are when the week's study and writing comes together for the last time. Over the course of the morning, my sense of vulnerability undergoes a subtle shift. At first I'm feeling vulnerable about the message. After I work on it and practice it several times, I usually start to feel much better about it. Then I pray, and that's where the real lesson in vulnerability begins.

At my church, there are usually only about 120 people in the seats during the message. On any given Sunday, twenty or twenty-five of them are homeless friends from all over the city. We send a couple of vans out each week to pick them up and bring them to church, where they can get a hot shower and enjoy some coffee and doughnuts before we worship together. Often we will share a meal together as a church, right after the service. We eat picnic-style and spend some time in conversation.

All of this makes us feel incredibly vulnerable.

The folks from our congregation who live on the streets are the hardcore homeless. Most can't or won't come into the shelters because they are still using drugs and alcohol. When you are in relationship with them, there is a lot of disorder, lying, violence, disease, drug abuse, alcohol abuse, mental illness, arrest warrants—not to mention the fact that these people live outside the social norms of our society.

About 8:30 each Sunday morning, the reality that I am exposing myself to people with these sorts of problems hits home, and I start to feel intensely vulnerable. It finally struck me one morning when I was praying how absurd my prayers sounded: "God, don't let anyone die at church today. Don't let the rival camps get into a knife fight and play stinking Sharks and Jets in the parking lot. I pray that nobody will have to call the police, that nobody pukes during the message or gets stoned in the van on the way to church. Don't let our van drivers get arrested for harboring felons, or for transporting them across state lines carrying God-knows-what sort of substances in their backpacks. Don't let anyone get hold of one of our little kids and drag them into a broom closet or empty classroom to abuse them. Keep us safe. Keep us alive."

These were not normal prayers, especially not the pre-worship kind of prayers.

We all know the kind of world in which we are living. It only takes one incident—one thing that goes wrong and makes it on the news, one abduction or murder, one fight or stabbing—and we are toast, done.

I feel *so* vulnerable.

I know the stakes are high. Our church has made itself vulnerable, and we feel it every Sunday when we gather to worship. It causes me and the other leaders no small level of anxiety, but we show up. We tell the truth. We let ourselves be seen. We confess our own weakness and trust that God knows what God is doing with us.

Earlier this year we held an all-church meeting to talk about how we should organize our common life so that everyone could feel welcome and everyone could feel safe, and so worship could be rightly ordered. People shared some pretty raw concerns. A mom told me that she doesn't let her girls go to the bathroom unless she goes with them. A dad said that he sometimes drives to our parking lot, then leaves to go to another church because it's just too much for him to feel vulnerable that day.

And yet something amazing is happening as well. God is using our church in ways I never could have planned or imagined.

Brené Brown has a name for people who choose to live vulnerable lives. She calls them "wholehearted." I want to be wholehearted. Leading a church demands that we chase after wholehearted living.

The truth is that when you peel back the surface, our church is a beautiful, fragile, and wonderful mess ... ragamuffins to the core. But because we are vulnerable, we are free to be wholehearted. Wholehearted people are not perfect people; they are people who have experienced God's grace, the unconditional love of Christ, and they know they are worthy.

Only those who know and *feel* loved are able to love others in return. Only those people who feel forgiven are able to truly forgive. Only those people who allow themselves to be seen for who they are can know the freedom and power that comes in being vulnerable.

The church needs wholehearted leaders—vulnerable leaders who have the courage to let others see who they are. Whatever faithfulness looks like in your context, it begins with the vulnerability that leads to love. The wholehearted believe that they are worthy of love because God's love makes them so.

Chapter 8

COOPERATION AND THE MYTHIC FAILURE OF COMPETITION

I love winning, man.... You hear what I'm saying?
It's like better than losing.
—Nuke LaLoosh, character in *Bull Durham*

Ever since I was a little boy, I have loved to watch the Olympic Games, especially the Winter Olympics. For a kid from small-town Kansas, this glimpse into a world of snowy peaks and strange sports like bobsledding, alpine skiing, and luge was both thrilling and bizarre. I have fond memories of watching Jim McKay and Curt Gowdy teaching the rules of curling and the biathlon.

Today, the Olympic Games don't have quite the same mystique for me. We now face the never-ending series of steroids scandals and soap opera–style dramas (remember Nancy Kerrigan and Tonya Harding?). Athletes are no longer amateurs. As much as I love the Olympic Games, they don't have that sense of innocence and purity that I remember from my youth.

The Olympic experience is undoubtedly an amazing spectacle, but when I consider all that world-class athletes have to go through just to compete, I wouldn't wish that for anyone I care about. I look at millionaire swimmers and twelve-year-old gymnasts and weight-lifters who look as though their knees are going to explode, and it all seems off to me. Are the extremes to which these athletes push themselves physically, mentally, and emotionally really worth it? The chief prerequisite to becoming an Olympian is the willingness to live completely out of balance. It can all seem a bit *excessive*. But that's the nature of competition. The Olympic motto is, after all, *"Citius, Altius, Fortius"* — "Faster, Higher, Stronger."

> That's the power of first place. It can turn winning a silver medal at the Olympic Games into a complete failure.

Researchers have analyzed the emotional responses of medal winners at the Olympic Games. What they found was that gold medal winners were obviously the most pleased with their performance. One would think the silver would be next, right? But they found bronze medalists were much more pleased with their performance than those who won the silver. The reason, the researchers discovered, was that the only thing bronze medalists could think about was how close they came to winning no medal at all. All the silver medalists could think of was how close they came to winning the gold.[1] They were tormented by what might have been.

That's the power of first place. It can turn winning a silver medal at the Olympic Games into a complete failure. The difference between, "I almost didn't get a medal at all," and "I almost got first place," is a world of hurt, because we live in a society that loves first place. And this love affair with winning causes us major problems.

COMPETITION IS EVERYWHERE

Much of American culture involves some sort of competition. We are all on a quest to win in some way. Educational guru Alfie Kohn says, "Life for us has become an endless succession of contests.... This is our posture at work and at school, on the playing field and back at home. It is the common denominator of American life."[2] From youth soccer to the NBA, from Billboard's charts to Nielson

---

1   Victoria Husted Medvec, Scott E. Madey, Thomas Gilovich, "When Less Is More: Counterfactual Thinking and Satisfaction among Olympic Medalists," *Journal of Personality and Social Psychology* 69 (October 1995): 603–10.

2   Alfie Kohn, *No Contest: The Case against Competition* (New York: Houghton Mifflin, 1986), 1.

ratings, from *American Idol* to the New York Stock Exchange, competition is a cultural obsession.

How does all this competition affect our lives? For all of the airtime given to drug scandals, gambling, doping, and cheating in sports, little is said about the drive we have to beat and defeat others. People will gladly offer their thoughts on instant replay or the designated hitter, but I never hear anyone reflecting critically on the nature of competition itself. What sort of world do we have when my success requires your failure?

Competition is the basis for our economy: the free markets. Competition influences our government: elections are contests. It defines our educational system: admission, scholarships, grants, and funding are decided competitively. Competition shapes the way we define beauty and how we rate brilliance. We give out awards for literature—Pulitzer Prizes and National Book Awards, as well as Nobel Prizes for Physics, Chemistry, Literature, Medicine, Economics, and Peace.

We give out Grammys for music, Emmys for television, Oscars for movies, Tonys for Broadway, and ESPYs for athletes. We give away Golden Globes, Critics' Choice Awards, People's Choice Awards, Image Awards, Independent Spirit Awards, and Screen Actors Guild Awards. Nickelodeon holds the annual Kids Choice Awards. MTV holds the Video Music Awards. Country Music has its night to rock with the CMA Awards. And Christians are not immune either. The Gospel Music Association holds their annual Dove Awards, hailing it as contemporary Christian music's biggest night. And in none of those award shows do they give out an award for second place.

On a recent trip to the grocery store, I drove to the parking lot and had a little race with two other cars to see who could get the prized parking spot closest to the entrance. As I navigated the store, I realized I was competing with myself to see if I could take the shortest and most efficient route through the store to collect my items. Throughout the store I noticed signs for competitive pricing, telling me to compare and save and guaranteeing the lowest prices.

Then there is the ultimate competition: the checkout line—the medal round, my specialty. To win at this game, you have to consider both the length of the line and the relative competency of the checker. I laugh when the amateur next to me chooses the short line—sucker. Then two guys who look like they came to play cut in front of me in the fast-checker's line. I start to panic. Then I remember my secret weapon. I blast past the two and pay for my three items at the customer service line, bypassing lines altogether. "Eat my dust, nerds! You just got second place," I say to myself on my way out the door. Lord, have mercy—I have a sickness.

This pervasive competitive atmosphere shapes us, teaching us to compare ourselves to others, training us to care about winners and losers and to celebrate people for no reason other than the fact that they know how to throw a ball into a hoop or eat sixty-eight hot dogs in ten minutes. We are constantly reinforcing a belief that winning is everything. I've coached enough youth baseball and football teams to know that with some parents, losing is not an option.

We suspend our value judgments to cheer for the winner. We will ignore the fact that someone is cruel and conceited if they know how to win. Why? Because we like winners. We will cheer on and pull for the most awful people—because winning is everything.

And just as much as we love winning, we hate losing. What is Tiger Woods's famous line? "Second place is really just the first loser."

When my kids were really young, we started playing board games. Any parent knows that when you play games with your young children, it's a pretty good idea to assess their emotional capacity in the moment. Sometimes you can play the game straight up. Sometimes you will need to throw it and let them win just to keep the peace.

On one particular occasion, it had been a long day, and my oldest son was going straight to bed after a quick game of Stratego. I sensed that I would probably need to lose in order for my little guy to be okay. In my defense, I was trying to lose. I did everything wrong: I gave hints; I let my best pieces get captured; I left my flag completely unprotected. Nevertheless, I stumbled onto his flag and the game was over. Instant tears—big alligator tears—and inconsolable sadness ensued, all because he lost a game. "Come on, buddy," I said. "You gotta learn how to do this. You can't get this upset. Losing is just a part of life."

He pushed back off my chest and looked me right in the eye and in anguish said, "Yeah, it's the worst part of life."

At eight years of age, he has already decided that losing is the worst part of life. This is our culture. This is the narrative in which we are all living:

Competition is everywhere.
Winning is everything.
Losing is the worst part of life.

Let's think about this.

WHAT ARE THE OPTIONS?

In Mark 9:33–37 Jesus confronted this narrative. "What were you arguing about on the road?" Jesus asked them.

> But they kept quiet, becauase on the way they had argued about who was the greatest.
>
> Sitting down, Jesus called the Twelve and said, "Anyone who wants to be first must be the very last, and the servant of all."
>
> He took a little child whom he placed among them. Taking the child in his arms, he said to them, "Whoever welcomes one of these little children in my name welcomes me; and whoever welcomes me does not welcome me but the one who sent me."

To really understand this story, we need a bit of context. When you think about Jews in Palestine under the Roman Empire, think of the French people under the Nazi regime during World War II. They were in their own land, but they were not free. They were all waiting for the Messiah to come, raise an army, kick the Romans out, and restore the Jewish worship and rule. The disciples were starting to believe that Jesus was the one, the Messiah. So on their way down to Capernaum, they started comparing résumés. They were trying to figure out who'll get to be Vice-Messiah, Jesus' second in charge.

Jesus waits until they are all sitting together that night before he decides to confront them. "So," he asks, "what were you guys talking about back there on the road?" Crickets ... nobody wanted to talk, because they'd been fighting about which one of them was the greatest. So Jesus sits them down to teach them why the impulse to win was drastically missing the point. "Whoever wants to be first must be last of all and servant of all," he said.

One of the real tragic things about living in our competition-crazed culture is that it's nearly impossible for us to hear this short teaching and understand it. Most of us have no idea what he's talking about. I call it tragic because nearly everything that Jesus taught can be summed up with this one idea, this reversal of last and first things. You take this theme away from his teaching and you have hardly anything left, and what you are left with will not make any sense at all.

> Nearly everything that Jesus taught can be summed up with this one idea, this reversal of last and first things.

He taught on this same concept over and over. Matthew 5: all eight Beatitudes argue for powerlessness over the competition for power. Matthew 6:14–15: if you forgive others, God will forgive you. Forgiveness is the refusal to exploit another's brokenness in order to win out over them. Matthew 6:1–18: give alms, pray, and fast secretly, so you won't be tempted to use religion as a way to keep score. Matthew 20: the Son of Man came not to be served, but to serve. Matthew 23 is full of this reversal imagery: don't build monuments to God, because they'll just end up being monuments to how cool you think you are, and how you're the greatest in the kingdom of God. The greatest will be the servant; the exalted will be humbled.

So when Jesus sits his followers down in Mark 9 and says, "What were you talking about back there on the road," he's trying to get them to see their own cultural assumptions. It was hard for them. It's hard for us as well.

I think Jesus means to ask all of us these same kinds of questions. Why am I always trying so hard to get first place? Why do I spend so much energy trying to stay ahead of the game? Why do I celebrate those who fight and scratch their way to the top?

Anytime I bring up competition's impact on the church, I know that I'm messing with a cultural sacred cow. We will immediately have these visceral objections. I have them, too.

The first push-back is always that competition is a natural, inescapable part of life. There are always winners and there are always losers. We can't hide from reality. Like many, I've uncritically accepted this for most of my life. Human beings have an inborn instinct to compete for survival, right? We have been hardwired to compete.

Stuart Brown is a psychiatrist who has spent years researching and writing about the essential nature of play in human development. Brown began studying alongside scientists such as Jane Goodall to understand how play works in nature. Brown says that contest is often a part of play in the animal kingdom. Animals play, chase, and wrestle. But Brown says that they do so without the necessity of domination. They don't want winners and losers.

If two primates are playing chase and the bigger, stronger one catches the smaller, slower one, he might tackle and pin him to the ground. At this point, humans would yell, "I win," and do a touchdown dance. In the animal kingdom, the bigger primate would let the smaller slower primate up, smack him on the nose, turn around, and then take off running. Immediately, the chaser becomes the chase-ee and the game continues. Brown says that the difference between the animal world and the human world is that animals will handicap themselves to keep the game going. The object is not to dominate. The object is to extend play.[3]

Evolutionary biologists have long noted that natural selection is not, strictly speaking, the same as the competition we see in contemporary American culture. In 1975 famed Harvard evolutionary biologist E. O. Wilson published *Sociobiology*, a book that became perhaps the most revolutionary refinement of evolutionary thought since Darwin's *Origin of the Species*.[4] In it Wilson argued convincingly that for any highly evolved species, part of the secret to their survival is altruism. Wilson's view successfully controverted Darwin's more

---

3   This comes from an interview Stuart Brown did with Krista Tippett that I highly recommend. Her show is called *On Being*, and the episode "Play, Spirit, and Character," aired on July 2, 2009.

4   E.O. Wilson, *Sociobiology* (Cambridge, MA: Harvard University Press, 1975.

brutal perspective on the necessity of competition for survival. More recently Wilson updated his research, asserting again that "a group of altruists will beat a society of selfish individuals every time. Group selection favors biological traits like communication and cooperation that are needed for the group to remain cohesive."[5] Nature rewards species that maintain the social structures necessary for cooperation.

So while elements of play are innate to human behavior, competition is not an inherent part of the natural order. My winning does not always require your losing. In their book *Winning Is Everything and Other American Myths*, pioneering sport psychologists Thomas Tutko and William Bruns tell us that "competition is a learned phenomenon, that people are not born with a motivation to win or to be competitive.... The will to win comes through training and influences of one's family and environment."[6] In other words, competition is *learned* behavior.

Another common objection is that competition will produce the best results. We need competition in order to push us to get things done, right? This is one of those things that nearly everyone believes is true, but it is really hard to prove. Those who shape the narratives of business, politics, and power constantly preach competition as the best way to get results. But among those who actually study outcomes, hardly anyone believes it is true.

In his classic book *No Contest: The Case against Competition*, Alfie Kohn suggests that there are actually three options available to us as we approach any task or goal. We can use a competitive, cooperative, or an independent approach.

Competitive. In a competitive environment, the goal is not just to complete a task, but to beat others in certain metrics like time or height. Often a competitive environment is constructed so that one person's success requires another person's failure, as in pole vaulting or a spelling bee. Sometimes one person's success is directly tied to

---

5 Pamela Weintraub, "E.O. Wilson's Theory of Altruism Shakes Up Understanding of Evolution," *Discover* 32, no. 1 (January/February 2011): 20–22.

6 Thomas A. Tutko and William Bruns, *Winning Is Everything and Other American Myths* (New York: Macmillan, 1976), 53.

their ability to force another person's failure, as in tennis or fencing. Or there can be more than one winner, like in a competitive college admissions process. Sometimes there are no winners, as is often the case in a state lottery. Most competitions, however, end with a single winner or group of winners—everybody else loses.

Cooperative. In a cooperative environment, the goal is to work together as a team or group. The main goal is not to beat others, but to reach the objective in the most efficient or effective way. Many different cooperative environments may occur, but the chief characteristic is that participants work with each other, not against each other. Cooperation involves the sharing of resources, outcomes, and rewards.

Independent. The third option is an independent environment where participants work neither against each other nor with each other. Instead, they work *apart* from each other, on their own without assistance from other participants.

So, which approach is the most effective?

Kohn presents study after study that proves the winner is cooperation. Citing research from the fields of education and industry, Kohn shows that competition consistently loses to cooperative efforts in tasks ranging from learning math facts to manufacturing widgets. In fact, the evidence is overwhelmingly consistent: "Superior performance not only does not require competition; it usually seems to require its absence."[7]

Much of what we consider successful has nothing to do with competition. You can be a great mom without someone else needing to be a terrible mother. You grill the perfect steak without someone else having to burn theirs. Many of the things we care most about in life seem to grow and thrive in the absence of competition.

Kohn presents a century's worth of research on the relative ineffectiveness of competition, especially in comparison to cooperation. In one study, students were tested to see if they could solve anagrams faster working cooperatively or in a competition—cooperation was

---

7 Kohn, *No Contest*, 47.

faster. In another study, high school students were tested using a card game—again, competition trailed cooperation.

Famed professor and social psychologist Morton Deutsch (MIT and Columbia University) is one of the pioneers of conflict resolution research. His famous 1948 study, "Resolution of Conflict," was one of the first to show how cooperation typically outperforms competition. His theories have been tested and reconfirmed throughout the past half century. In everything from decoding Japanese poetry to guessing the number of jellybeans in a jar, cooperation outperforms competition every time.[8]

They studied manufacturing, holding production contests linked to pay. They found that production went up, but quality went down. It was net loss. They studied white collar workers and found that the more competitive the environment, the lower the overall achievement. There might be one or two winners who thrived in the competitive environment. They would perform way above the norm, but when you consider the impact of competition on the whole group, overall achievement went down.

They've studied airline pilots, scholars, educators, researchers, adults, and children. The results are always the same: the more competitive the environment, the lower the overall achievement.

The reason competition loses out to cooperation is because competition makes us selfish. In an intense competitive environment, people started hoarding resources. In a competitive environment, workers hoard information that might give them a competitive advantage, even though its usefulness to everyone could help the company. Salespeople hoard leads, managers hoard talent, and executives hoard power and influence. Competitive environments that pit us against each other make us selfish. But when we cooperate with one another, we become unselfish, and this is always a better way.

> The reason competition loses out to cooperation is because competition makes us selfish.

8 Ibid., 49.

Not only does the research show that cooperation gives better results, but it also shows that competition can be a source of many problems. One study considered the impact of competition on the field of journalism. They found that when competition for a story was fierce, reporters would distort their findings. When the competition was to be first, reporters were inaccurate. Not only that, but they would tend to leave out certain facts in order to hype a story, shifting the whole enterprise toward sensationalism. Researchers concluded that inaccuracy and distortions were greater in a system in which news outlets competed for a story, greater than they would be if news outlets worked together to bring the news to the public.[9]

Another study tested the impact of competition on creativity. The researchers took a group of seven- to eleven-year-old girls and split them into two groups. The girls in each group were asked to make silly collages. One group was told that they would be judged for prizes, the other group was not. Researchers worked with seven artists who independently rated the collages according to twenty-three different criteria. The result was that the children in the competitive group produced works that were "significantly less creative than those made by children in the control group."[10] The works were considered "less spontaneous, less complex, and less varied."[11]

There was one thing, however, that the research showed that competition consistently did a much better job with: *causing anxiety*. Competition increases anxiety and inhibits performance. Cooperation lowers anxiety and increases performance, and yet most of us believe that competition is natural and is the best way to get things done.[12]

When Jesus pulls his disciples aside and tells them that whoever wants to be first has to become last and become the servant of all, he's not just giving them a new social ethic. He's trying to wake them up to reality. He's saying that they have missed the way that God has

9 Ibid., 54–55.

10 Ibid., 54.

11 Ibid.

12 Ibid., 55.

created the world to be and created humans to function. Jesus knew that we are at our best when we are thinking about the common good, not when we're thinking about how to get ahead. When we are constantly thinking about how to win, it can become destructive to our souls.

THE AMERICAN CHURCH COMPETITION

Churches are clearly not immune to the pressures of competition that exist in our culture. Churches today have become vendors of religious goods and services. They amass huge pools of talent and put on world-class programs, market their product using the latest advertising techniques, and shape their image to encourage brand loyalty. Church in America has become a marketplace, competing with other institutions for time, money, influence, and attention.

Parishioners are treated like customers with a shopping list of expectations and needs, which gives them great power. People want certain types of programs and a particular kind of experience, and if a church does not meet the customer's needs, they quickly move to another vendor. For true discipleship—which is always about learning the way of descent—this situation is a disaster.

The competitive landscape of American Christianity has turned pastors into executives and managers. Today, the job of a pastor is not to simply preach the Word of God; a pastor needs to be world-class, impressive, and polished. Pastors must cultivate their skills and try to be the perfect combination of CEO, prophet, and talk show host. If they fail, people will leave for another congregation with a more engaging speaker or teacher. On top of this pressure, pastors are also responsible for understanding the felt needs of the congregation and meeting those needs with world-class programs, facilities, and staff. They must attract and inspire a staff of professionals (middle management) who are smartly engaged in the production of religious goods and services. If the parishioner is the one who controls the demand side of this social contract, the pastor is the one who is in charge of *production*.

Members are now called *volunteers*—the unpaid labor force

engaged in the meeting of these felt needs. Volunteers are highly invested in increasing production because they are stockholders in the corporation. They are also engaged in competition with other volunteers to produce for their leaders. Those who produce on a regular basis are promoted to bigger and better leadership posts and may eventually move into a paid staff position (a jump from labor to management). But at the heart of it all is one basic reality—the praise and attention volunteers receive is directly connected to their ability to produce.

All of this has led churches to become corporations busy creating and maintaining brands that will compete in the religious marketplace. The goal of the church is clear: increase market share and create brand loyalty. The net effect of all this is that the American church has become a competitive culture, one modeled on the consumer-producer marketplace system. Those who win market share are celebrated—they make the annual *Outreach* magazine list of the top 100 fastest-growing churches and top 100 largest churches. Competition shapes how we judge the success of a church, far more than most church leaders realize.

I'm convinced that competition is toxic to the soul of the church.

When I think about our culture, this is what I see: competition is everywhere, winning is everything, and losing is the worst part of life. When I think about Jesus' vision for his people—whoever wants to be first must learn to be the last of all and the servant of all—it seems painfully clear those two narratives couldn't be more different. This is the exact same tension that Jesus builds with his own followers in Mark 9. They've been having an argument about who is the greatest, and he has just told them that the kingdom of God is built on a completely different set of assumptions. They had to feel the same tension I am feeling.

This is one of those instances when we can see what a naturally brilliant teacher Jesus was, because his next move is stunning. After he has built all of this tension and his disciples are speechless, his way of marking the moment was to plop a little child down right in front of them with these words: "Whoever welcomes one of these little children in my name welcomes me; and whoever welcomes me does not welcome me but the one who sent me" (Mark 9:37). What an interesting thing to do. How would the disciples have understood this move?

It's hard for us to really get the subversive undertones of Jesus in that moment, because we view children so differently now than they did back then. We see childhood as a romantic and sentimental time of innocence and purity. Childhood is a privileged time, and we make sure children have rights. The child in Jesus' time did not have any rights. They were essentially nonpersons until they were granted personhood by their parents and community through rites of passage. There was a sense in which they did represent the future, but for the time being they were a liability, not an asset. They were often sick, were much more susceptible to accidents, and much more likely to die. They used resources without contributing much. In terms of power, they were completely on the outside. They were more like property than persons. In fact, they had more in common with slaves than anyone else in the household of antiquity.

So when Jesus plops a child down in the midst of his followers, he is saying, in effect, "Until you learn how to welcome the most vulnerable people in our society, you'll never get what I'm doing. Until you learn how to welcome the people who are always in last place, you'll never know what it means to love me or my Father."

I was presenting in a breakout session at a conference recently and got to sit in on one of the main sessions in which Andy Crouch from *Christianity Today* was speaking. Crouch said something I'll never forget. He was talking about what God is really after in the world, particularly in terms of the big picture. What does God really want? Crouch's answer was simple and dramatic. He said that what God really wants is *flourishing*. God is somewhat like Athey Keith from *Jayber Crow*: everywhere God looks God wants to see things flourishing.

> So when Jesus plops a child down in the midst of his followers, he is saying, in effect, "Until you learn how to welcome the most vulnerable people in our society, you'll never get what I'm doing.

When Crouch began to unpack more about what he meant by flourishing, he said that flourishing is to be *magnificently oneself.* That's it. What God is really after, in the end, is for you to get to be you, for me to get to be me, for all of us to fulfill our God-given purpose, to find meaningful and redemptive work to do with our hands, to live in splendid interdependence, and to help create a world in which everyone else, and every other thing, is flourishing as well.

Jesus seemed to understand that the world of competition is always hardest on the weak, the vulnerable, the people who are always at the bottom of the pile — in his world, these were the children. So he places a child right in front of his ambitious disciples. And he took the child in his arms, pulling the kid up close to his chest ... this symbol of all things weak and vulnerable. Then he says, "You have to learn how to welcome this child. If all you know how to do is fight and scratch your way to first place, you'll forget to care for this child, and my kingdom is all about this vulnerable one."

> Jesus seemed to understand that the world of competition is always hardest on the weak, and the vulnerable, and the people who are always at the bottom of the pile.

This word *welcome*, which Jesus uses, is essential. It conjures up images of making space for a visitor, the other, the one who's not like you, caring for the traveler, and making sure they have everything they need to flourish. It's a word that points to a kind of hospitality that is the antithesis of competition. That's the life Jesus pointed toward — a life of hospitality, not a life of competition.

As Crouch mused on what flourishing should look like, I felt myself growing sad about the state of the American church and how fixated we all have been on growth, to the point where we really do exist in a state of all-out competition for market share, all the while ignoring the most vulnerable in our communities. Then Crouch said one more stunning thing: in a world like ours — to which I would add, in a *competitive* world like ours — *the flourishing of the vulnerable depends on the vulnerability of the flourishing.* What a thing to say. I've had to repeat it to myself a thousand times since that day. If the weak and wounded, the sick and sore, are going to flourish once again, it will be because those of us who are flourishing decide to somehow take their vulnerability upon ourselves.

God's vision for his world is not a bunch of strong people who scratch and claw their way to the top, then do nice things for the vulnerable. Throwing the poor a few crumbs now and then doesn't cut it. God's vision is for a bunch of strong people who actually become vulnerable themselves. That's the *Shrink* move. God's solution to the problem of our world was to form a community of people who would stop trying to win everything. Instead, they would just go stand with all of the losers, left out, and left behind. His plan was to form a community of reckless lovers who would make the weakness of the marginalized their own.

This is a life of essential *cooperation*, a constant joining together with the weakest. The Jesus way of life has nothing to do with the endless competitions of American life. The Jesus way of life has everything to do with the strong cooperating with the weak.

In theological terms, this is the essence of the incarnation—that time when the all-powerful God, the maker and sustainer of the universe, became a vulnerable child. Can you think of anything more completely vulnerable than a newborn baby? He took our weakness and made it his own. He took on our brokenness, our vulnerability, and made them his own, because that is the way to redemption. For us, it is the only way to be human as human is meant to be; we must learn to somehow take on the weakness of Christ, and there's no way to do this without becoming vulnerable ourselves.

> To become vulnerable is to bear some of the pain of the world. It is going to hurt, and there's no way around that.

The kingdom of God is a kingdom not of competition, but of cooperation.

To welcome the little children of our world is to virtually assume last position, to choose to lose instead of trying to win. That is the Jesus way. The problem for most of us, at least for me, is that this choice to become weak, to be last, to be vulnerable carries with it a truckload of pain. To welcome the vulnerable is to become vulnerable ourselves. To become vulnerable is to bear some of the pain of the world. It is going to hurt, and there's no way around that.

This means that, as Barbara Brown Taylor has taught me to say, we will somehow have to learn how to live our lives without the benefit of anesthesia. We will have to learn to live without the crutches we use to prop up our fragile egos and emotional instability. We will have to live without the artificial fillers we use to fill the void in our hearts that only God can fill. We will have to live without the spiritual pacifiers that cannot nourish us, but can only keep us quiet. Somehow, following Jesus means learning to live without those things. We will have to undergo life without the benefit of anesthesia. We're going to feel everything.[13]

I'm embarrassed to think of the many years of ministry when I thought I was so clever. I would constantly compare myself to others, trying to climb the ladder of success. Even though I was doing ministry in the church, competition was my primary mode of existence. I was no better than the disciples—climbing my way to the top and proving my worth.

> Competition robs the church of its ability to image Christ, because Christ chose to sit in last place.

Competition robs the church of its ability to image Christ, because Christ chose to sit in last place. When we allow competitive dynamics to pervade our ethos, we cease to image Jesus and begin to image a culture that cheers the person who has learned how to fight and scratch and claw their way into first place.

Is this dynamic at work in your ministry? In your church community? Most pastors with whom I have discussed this nearly universally say, "We don't have that mind-set at our church," or "That's just not the way I think." My response is that we cannot help but think that way. Competition is the water in which we swim. Unless we are constantly fighting it, unless we are constantly cooperating with those on the margins, we remain blind to our own cultural biases.

---

13 Barbara Brown Taylor, *Home by Another Way* (Lanham, MD: Cowley, 1999), 66–67.

This is where the *Shrink* mentality becomes so important. It's not enough to say, "We're not trying to compete or get big." We have to consciously choose the way down. The only sure way to reject the culture of competition is to commit to staying small as we cooperate with the vulnerable.

In our church, we have a plan in place to avoid becoming too big. Studies have demonstrated that when a church reaches four hundred members, the dynamics of the community fundamentally change. Leaders begin to switch from a parish church mind-set to a mega-church mind-set. So we have planned that if we ever reach four hundred, we will immediately seek to identify a leader and spawn a new congregation. Rather than grow, we will multiply, asking at least 120 to 150 people to leave to start a new church. We haven't been tested, so I'm not sure if I will have the courage — and faithfulness — to follow through if we actually reach that point. I know I'll be tempted to find reasons to justify continued growth. But I know growth is not the ultimate goal. As a leader, I need to shape my heart and the culture of our church in such a way that when the time comes, we are ready to remain faithful.

If planning to remain small is not possible for you right now, an intermediate step might be to stop counting numbers. Stop taking attendance. Stop focusing on the question "How many people are in your church?" Stop using numbers to motivate people. Change your rhetoric, forget about the numbers for five years, and see what happens.

Another option is to reject the competitive culture of the marketplace by encouraging people to return to churches they are in the midst of leaving. When people show up at our church stinging and bruised, if not disillusioned and sad about the state of their previous churches, we take them in and help them heal. But when people show up to our church pious and disgruntled about their previous church, I always encourage them to return to the church from which they came. Most of the time, they leave our church as well. I usually hear that they have ended up somewhere else, but at least I know they didn't stay with us — which means that we didn't participate in the church marketplace.

Occasionally, a person needs to get away from a toxic situation or a relational problem. But when people come to our church upset about their old church, filled with complaints, I tell them to go back to practice fidelity, voice their concerns, and stick around to see the conflict through. Again, it's just one small way in which we can refuse to compete.

You may also want to involve your church and its leaders in other congregations and include the leaders of other churches in your ministry. On Monday evenings at our church we have an ESL (English as Second Language) program that serves immigrant families in our neighborhood. We have volunteers from four or five area churches serving together in our building—some of them are even staff members from other churches.

As a pastor, I'm involved in the Associated Ministerial Order, a group of pastors who meet for soul care, retreats, theological conversation, and ordination. These pastors speak at our church routinely. They are thought leaders in our congregation, even though they serve at other churches. Every single week I meet with two of my closest friends who are both in ministry in other parts of the city. My life is tethered to their lives in ways that keep me from ever competing with them.

There's a lot riding on our ability to dispense with the competitive church environment.

I heard a story once about a couple of churches in a large Texas city. Between the two largest congregations in the city there was an unspoken competition. The two congregations would often try to outdo one another when it came to holding spectacular events. The ultimate competitive occasion each year was the Easter pageant.

One of the churches decided to pull out all the stops and put on the greatest Easter pageant in the history of Texas. The performance included hundreds of actors, stage hands, world class sound and lighting, a flying (ascending) Jesus, and a menagerie of live animals, including a live camel (which expired backstage during one of the performances).

On the final night, the centurions were playing an intense game of cards in the back room when they heard their call to the stage. It was the scene where one of them was supposed to pierce the side of Jesus. In their hurry to put down their cards and get to the stage, the two centurions accidentally switched spears. The spear with the collapsing blade ended up in the wrong hands, so when that centurion stabbed Jesus, he actually *stabbed Jesus*. The blade sunk into the chest of the actor, and the audience watched in horror as Jesus screamed, "Ooooouch! What the bleep? You stabbed me!"

They had to pull him off the cross, call an ambulance, and take Jesus to the hospital.

Once they got the crowd settled back down, they put the understudy Jesus back on the cross and continued the pageant. However, when they got to the ascension scene, nobody realized that they hadn't thought to change the weights in the counter-balance mechanism that would raise Jesus into heaven. Understudy-Jesus was a good sixty-five pounds lighter than the Jesus who was on his way to the hospital. So when they cut Jesus loose for his big ascension scene, he shot up into the ceiling like a rubber band, bounced out of his harness, and fell thirty feet to the ground, breaking his leg. They finally relented, said their amens, and adjourned.

Two people playing Jesus carried to the hospital in one performance, all in the name of having the best Easter pageant in the state of Texas. Maybe it's an absurd example, but this is where competition will take us, and it's not that far off. The sad thing is considering how many financial and human resources were poured into the pageant, and what a difference all of those efforts could have made if they would have been matched up with those who live on the margins of our society—the vulnerable, the weak, the poor.

So, is there any hope for the church? Can we change and reject the competitive mind-set that is all too common today? I don't know what you think, but I will always believe in the church. However, I don't have a model, technique, or strategy that will help you foster cooperation. There are no transferable principles for me to offer, nor are there steps to cooperation you can implement right away in your church. Even if I could give you something like that, it would probably not work for long. The competitive environment of your church will likely destroy feeble attempts at change.

What I can say is that if you commit consistently, relentlessly, honestly, and ruthlessly to root out competition from your culture, resisting it where you see it in your community, you will begin to see a culture of cooperation develop and grow. There is no magic formula here, and the paths to cooperation will be as varied as the number of churches who chase after it. You will have to find ways to cooperate and work together that fit your own context. But you will need to begin by resisting the draw of first place.

Letting go of competition is possible, but the first step is to admit that you have bought into the lie that competition is the path to success. This is going to be hard. It's tough to force ourselves to admit the subtle ways in which we play the competitive game. I've been working at it for years, and I am still surprised at the insidious ways in which I still keep score.

How often do we resort to sensationalism and hype? How often do we hoard resources? And what about the impact of competition on our creativity? Are we generating art born of a fertile imagination, or just copying the culture?

Confronting the competitive culture forces us to ask: What is my true motivation—faithfulness or market share? Is my self-esteem tethered to the size of my congregation? These questions will always sting. We have breathed the air of competition for so long we don't even notice how deeply marked by it we are. We can no longer effectively image God in our society because we simply look like everyone else. We must respond to God's call to change, and change starts by naming our own sins.

Chapter 9

THE POWER OF BROKENNESS

When the poor and weak are present, they prevent us
from falling into the trap of power—even the power
to do good—of thinking that it is we who are the good
ones, who must save the Savior and his church.
—Jean Vanier

BOB

When I first met my friend Bob Starkey, I felt like I was getting a peek into the life of the prodigal son while he was still in the far country. I'm not kidding: Bob had squandered his father's wealth and was slopping the pigs; he was all the way down.

Bob lived in a tent back in the woods in a part of Kansas City that most people don't even know exists. It is a homeless camp where the vagabonds and misfits aggregate around each other in makeshift settlements. They try to camp close enough to provide some protection but far enough away from one another that there will be minimal friction when drunkenness turns to belligerence.

Bob had a terribly hard life, and he experienced a lot of pain and death as he was growing up. As a young man, he served in the military and was deployed overseas in Somalia and Iraq, seeing his fair share of the horrors of war—bodies exploding, flying limbs, buddies blown to bits right in front of his eyes. As a result of those traumatic experiences, Bob struggled with PTSD and a deep inner sadness. For the previous ten or fifteen years of his life, Bob's way of coping was to drink himself into a coma every day. He lost his job and his family and wound up living on the streets, drinking away every penny he could get his hands on.

Bob became my friend because two members of my church, Jim and Jennifer, started visiting him to feed him and a number of other homeless people twice a week. They work with an organization in Kansas City called Uplift. Uplift takes food and provisions to the hardcore homeless. These are the people who really can't come into the shelters or take part in typical relief programs. Some of them are drunk or high every day of their lives, and many are singularly committed to terribly self-destructive patterns of life. My friends joined with Uplift to take food, clothing, and some of the basic necessities of life out to these people who are living off the grid.

Over several years, Jim and Jennifer became friends with Bob. They would visit with him and pray for him when he asked for prayer, and often they ended up in conversations about God. Bob really loved Jesus. His alcoholism never tempered that. I know it's hard to believe this, but I believe that even while Bob was in the throes of his intense, active alcohol addiction, he was still in relationship with God. He was even being used by God in the camps.

Bob started asking Jim and Jennifer if they would bring him to their church. So one Sunday they drove down to his camp, picked him up, and brought him to Redemption Church. Pretty soon there were a few others who wanted to go, so they brought them too. Each week Jim or Jennifer or someone else from our church would go get Bob and a few of his friends and bring them to worship.

During the first few months that Bob was at our church, he drew quite a bit of attention. Most people never get to speak to a homeless person for any extended period of time. Our people took to it, took to Bob actually. He would tell us his stories over and over, and those of us who took the time to listen began to care about him. We grew to love Bob. Every week or so, a different member of the church would show up with a new sleeping bag or a coat or a few books to give to him. People really started to watch out for him and care for him and his friends.

One day Bob just stopped drinking. He just stopped. He showed up sober and said he hadn't had a drink all week. Nobody asked him to stop or even really talked to him about it. He just quit on his own—cold turkey. As far as I know, he never had another drink. Once he was sober I couldn't believe how different he looked. He seemed ten years younger. His face was a different color, eyes no longer distant and hollow. Bob was fully present with us—for perhaps the first time ever.

As I started to get to know the sober Bob, I realized that I had always assumed his underlying problem was the alcohol. Bob was fun to be with—even as a drunk. He was a good conversationalist, well read, funny, and kind. I imagined that when he finally sobered up, he would be able to get a job and begin to rebuild his life and resume a normal role in society. But I was wrong. It soon became clear there was a lot more going on under the surface in Bob's life.

I learned that even when a guy like Bob can get clean and sober, he finds himself back at square one with all of the same problems, dysfunctions, issues, and challenges that led them to live on the streets in the first place. The only difference is that they must now *feel* them and live with them—without the numbing assistance of alcohol.

I never knew just how deeply broken Bob was until he showed up sober that Sunday morning. As we began to talk, he told me that he was not really looking forward to heading back down to his camp. He was learning how tough it was to live sober in an alcoholic culture. He spent more and more time by himself in his tent reading books, trying to keep on the straight and narrow, and facing up to his own brokenness. We knew immediately that if we hoped to help Bob stay sober, we needed to get him out of there.

The pastor of a church close to where Bob was camping found a way to get him into a small, run-down apartment. Bob filed for Social Security benefits and started receiving a monthly check. The apartment didn't work out though. It was too close to his old stomping grounds, and friends from the woods started using his place as a crash pad, bringing with them all of the drugs and alcohol he was hoping to avoid. He was still about thirty minutes from our church, which made it hard for us to be involved in his life during the week. We knew we needed a better solution.

A member of our church told us that she managed some property that was owned by her grandmother, and she would be happy to rent Bob a tiny two-bedroom house. If he would pay her the $125 a month she owed in property taxes, he could stay there rent-free. It was the perfect solution. A group of people from our church came and fixed the place up as best we could, giving Bob furniture and household items. It was a little hot in the summer and cold in the winter, but Bob was off the streets and much closer to our church family. For the first time, he could easily make it to nearly every event or meeting we had.

For the last two years of his life, I would drive to pick Bob up every Sunday morning and take him to church. It was one of my favorite Sunday rituals. On the way, we'd stop at the QuickTrip for a Coke (Bob drank more Coca-Cola than any person I've ever met), and then we'd head to the church. It was a short time in the car, usually just ten or fifteen minutes, but it happened nearly every Sunday, and I grew used to our times together.

Bob had this nagging question about why he was still alive. He told me that he should have died many times, if not in war, then when he was drunk and doing crazy things. He had been in lots of fights. One fight had landed him in the hospital for weeks and left him with permanent brain injuries. After all he had been through, Bob believed that if God hadn't let him die yet, then God must still have a purpose for him to fulfill.

"I've been through so much stuff in my life, pastor," he would say. "You have no idea. I've seen so many things and done so many things and smoked so many things"—at this point he would nearly die laughing—"I can't figure out why I'm still alive. But I am. I've always believed God was with me. I know he's with me now, but I just can't figure out what he wants me to do with the rest of my life." This really bothered Bob. I would receive these odd text messages from him. The most common was, "Pastor, can you tell me why I'm here?" The blunt, raw question was always startling to me. "Pastor, why am I still alive? The Lord has told me I have a purpose. Can you tell me what it is?"

Bob's PTSD and his brain injury, as well as several other physical issues, made it impossible for Bob to land a job. So our church tried to provide him with some meaningful work to do. He helped greet at the front door, and he would come over to the church every few weeks and spend a few hours washing windows. He helped out when we were renovating our new facility and would just happen by the office from time to time for a chat. Most weeks he would walk ten blocks to a nearby soup kitchen to help serve a community meal. Many of the people he served were homeless—the irony of that was never lost on Bob.

Yet all of this was never enough for him. Bob was restless and dissatisfied, and sometimes he grew a little angry. He would call me and text me at all hours of the day or night. I would often have to step aside from a family meal or my duties at the church to try and talk him down when he was out on the ledge. "Pastor, can you tell me why I'm still here? What God has for me to do?"

None of the answers we gave him were ever good enough. But it really challenged me to try and find a way to communicate what I believed to be true about Bob's life. As I was trying to articulate this, I stumbled into the power of brokenness.

BROKENNESS HAS SAVED US

When we first planted our little church, I wanted to believe that we would change the world for the better. I wanted to believe that we were on the right track. Even before our public launch, though, I began to notice this unsettled, nagging feeling in my heart that something was fundamentally wrong with what we were doing. I couldn't quite put my finger on it, but something seemed off.

At first I tried to identify problems we encountered and solve them. I helped create structures and teams that addressed issues that needed correction or ministries that needed development. I kept waiting for that uneasy feeling to go away, but it didn't. Something always felt like it wasn't quite right. It was as if there was something fundamental missing, some essential component that we had left out when we put the church together. The problem was that I had no idea what it was. This nagging feeling was always there, just under the surface.

When I first met Bob, he was so lost, so desperate—the prodigal son far from home. As his journey unfolded, our little church got to see the return of the prodigal son happen in real time, right before our eyes. We watched as he approached God warily, full of shame and self-disgust. We saw the Father run to meet him. There's nothing quite like watching someone look up from their knees, literally covered in dirt and brokenness and shame, and seeing God pull them to their feet, kiss their cheek, and slip his ring on their finger and his robe around their shoulders. I never tire of seeing God welcome his prodigals home.

When Bob became a part of our ragamuffin church, it was a sight to behold. I've never seen a man more grateful to be found. He was a miracle, and he knew it. Bob lived with a fundamental brokenness: physical pain from years of hard living, psychological pain from PTSD and memories of war, emotional pain from the loss of loved ones and estrangement from family. He bore the scars of a hard life, and he wore them on his sleeve. Bob never hid his brokenness from us.

And it completely changed our church. From the moment Bob and the rest of the homeless showed up, I had a sense that we had finally found what we'd been missing. That nagging feeling went away, and it has never come back.

When Bob would call me and ask me to tell him why he was still here, I would say to him: "There used to be something wrong with our church, Bob. I always felt it, but I could never quite put my finger on it. Something was wrong. Something was missing. The day you showed up it disappeared. You made our church a holy place. I can't explain it, but I know it happened. Just by becoming a part of our community, you helped to restore what was missing. You have helped us follow Christ because you had the courage to come and show us your broken self. You are so important to our church. You are having a deep and lasting impact on this ministry, and we need you. You are doing good work, Bob. Keep it up."

One Sunday morning I called Bob and he didn't answer. I sent him a text message, but no response came back. I went to his house and knocked on the door, but it looked like he wasn't home. It was a cold day with ten inches of snow on the ground, and he had shoveled his walk. I didn't think he would have tried to walk all the way to church, but I traced the route he would have taken and didn't see him. I looked for him until just before our service started and he still hadn't shown up. I told my friend Jim that Bob wasn't responding, and Jim went over to Bob's place to see if he could get in. He peeked through the bathroom window and saw Bob lying lifeless on the floor.

Bob's death was a serious blow to our church. It turns out that our mostly white, suburban, middle-class evangelical church was heartbroken because our homeless friend Bob had died. His ministry at our church wasn't complicated. It involved sitting around talking to people, asking us for help, and being our friend. But it was profound.

We held his funeral after church the next Sunday, and there was hardly room for everyone to fit in our sanctuary. We told stories about Bob, and we marveled at the ministry he had. Our congregation took a turn down a new path that day Bob showed up, and we have never looked back.

What was it that made Bob so special to so many? I think it was his utter brokenness, his willingness to be vulnerable, his awareness that he was a man who needed God's help, who wasn't afraid to share his struggles and tell us that he needed us in his life. Bob wasn't afraid to let us see how broken he was. If he was having a problem, he'd just start telling people until somebody talked him through how he should fix it. If his meds were off, he'd tell you about it. If he needed a ride to the doctor, he'd start asking. If he was out of money and needed groceries, he'd walk around asking until someone volunteered to help. He never acted as if he had his life together. He wore his broken and battered heart on his sleeve.

Bob forced us to see beyond our self-concern. I sometimes felt startled by Bob's cries for help, like he was waking me out of a deep sleep. Completely consumed by the maintenance of my middle-class suburban life, I would get a call from Bob, and it was if he screamed,

"Help! I am so broken! I need you!" It took so much courage for him to admit how much he needed other people.

The cry of the broken has immense power. It saved my life, and it is at work today, saving me still.

A PRODIGAL PROBLEM

One man, more than anyone else, has taught me how to reflect on the power of brokenness. His name is Jean Vanier. Vanier was born in Switzerland where his father, a Canadian diplomat, served as part of the Canadian Foreign Service. At the tender age of thirteen, Vanier went alone to England to join the Royal Navy College and train as a naval officer. That was 1942, when the war with Nazi Germany was at a fever pitch. Vanier looked to have a promising naval career in front of him but served for only eight years and left naval service in 1950 for college in Paris. He stayed in Paris until he finished his PhD in philosophy, writing on Aristotle.

Vanier began pursuing an academic career, one that appeared to have the same promise as his run in the navy did. Again, Vanier shunned the fast track, leaving academia while his star was still on the rise.

In 1964 Jean Vanier decided that he wanted to be nearer to his friend and mentor, Father Thomas, who had become the chaplain at a small institution that served people with mental disabilities in France. So Vanier moved to a little village north of Paris and bought a small house, still not knowing quite why God had led him there.

Through the influence of Father Thomas, Vanier began to spend more and more time with people who suffered from various kinds of mental disabilities. He was disturbed by how society treated these "men and women who had been put aside, looked down upon, sometimes laughed at or scorned." He would later write, "They were seen as misfits of nature, not as human beings."[1]

In particular, Vanier befriended two men with disabilities who had been locked away in a terrible institution. Vanier invited them

1 Jean Vanier, *Becoming Human* (Toronto: House of Anansi Press, 2008), 1.

to come live with him in his home. The two men, Philippe Seux and Raphael Simi, were both severely disabled and had no parents or family who could care for them. Vanier took them in, christened his house L'Arche (the ark), and began to share his life with them. Thus was born the first L'Arche community.

Almost as though appearing from thin air, people began to show up and help Vanier and his friends. Within six months he was asked to take over at the facility where Father Thomas was chaplain. Five years later he was asked to go to India, where the second L'Arche community was begun. Today there are 134 such communities in thirty-five countries around the world. Most of them are still small homes and communities where the boundaries between "patients" and "professionals" have been completely erased. Residents live and work together in mutuality and love regardless of their relative health.

The truly remarkable aspect of L'Arche is how they have been able to draw people from all walks of life, many of whom come simply as volunteers who are willing to spend time being present to the least of these. "In these communities," Vanier writes, "men and women with disabilities can develop in a spirit of freedom. We live together—those with disabilities and those who wish to have a deep and sometimes lasting relationship with them. We laugh and cry and sometimes fight with one another; we work, we celebrate life, and we pray together."[2]

Vanier has spent countless hours reflecting on the power of broken people. His thoughts and writings provide a map of his own journey and provide direction for us as well. The weak—in this case, those with mental disabilities—have a hidden power that we often fail to recognize or acknowledge. They are able to expose the common brokenness we all share. Those who live and work at a L'Arche community have found that they do not need to mask or cover over their brokenness, their weakness, and their frailty. Instead, they share it. They talk about it. They embrace it. And when they do, a great power is unleashed in their midst. Vanier is convinced that this is the supernatural power of the God who inhabits our weakness.

---

2 Ibid., 2.

Many who come to L'Arche are forever changed as they discover the simplicity of being with other people who live and serve out of their brokenness.[3]

When I listen to Jean Vanier speak, when I read his books and consider his way of life, I am struck by his absolute insistence on the power of weakness for the Christian. When I compare my leadership training and preparation for ministry with Vanier's experience, the contrast is stunning. "We are afraid of showing weakness," Vanier says. "We are afraid of not succeeding. Deep inside we are afraid of not being recognized. So we pretend we are the best. We hide behind power. We hide behind all sorts of things. However, when we meet people with disabilities and reveal to them through our eyes and ears and words that they are precious, they are changed. But we too are changed. We are led to God."[4]

Vanier has found an ardent friend, admirer, and theological ally in Stanley Hauerwas. Hauerwas has long considered Vanier's life at L'Arche to be a particularly revealing example of God's heart for all Christian communities. He notes the way L'Arche demonstrates that those who are willing to live together in profound brokenness learn that they can only do so by embracing *gentleness*. This, Hauerwas believes, must become normative in order for all church communities to begin to image Jesus.

Gentleness is not a quality I hear talked about in many leadership circles. You won't find a chapter on being a gentle leader in the latest church leadership books. I haven't heard anyone speak on it at any of the conferences I've attended. But Hauerwas sees gentleness as a key defining quality of Christian leadership. In fact, several years ago Hauerwas and Vanier collaborated on a short collection of essays

---

3 One of the men who followed Jean Vanier's lead was Henri Nouwen. Nouwen left a successful career in academia (Notre Dame, Yale, and Harvard), to live the last twelve years of his life as a part of the community Vanier established in Canada (L'Arche Daybreak in Richmond Hill, Ontario). You can read Nouwen's testimony of the power of brokenness in his book *Adam: God's Beloved* (New York, NY: Maryknoll, 1997).

4 Stanley Hauerwas and Jean Vanier, *Living Gently in a Violent World* (Downers Grove, IL: IVP, 2008), 64.

called *Living Gently in a Violent World*. In his chapter entitled "The Politics of Gentleness," Hauerwas tells the story of Daniel, whose disabilities were so severe that his parents no longer wanted him. After moving from one institution to another, Daniel came to live at L'Arche. Daniel was in such intense pain from being rejected that he had constructed impenetrable walls around his heart.

Hauerwas writes that extreme cases like this have much to teach us about the human condition. All of us have been deeply wounded in one way or another over the course of our lives. To get by in a rough-and-tumble world, we learn how to build walls of protection around our wounds. These walls allow us to navigate our world without feeling the constant pain involved when someone puts their finger on our wound. When others brush up against our lives, they do not touch our wounds; they merely touch the walls we have constructed to hide our wounds. But there is a problem with these walls. The same walls we construct to protect ourselves also keep out the presence of God and the presence of a healing community. Hauerwas insists that the walls we have built around our hearts can only be breached through gentleness.

As a pastor and a Christian leader I find that I regularly encounter points of decision, forks in the road, and I find that I must choose a path forward. Through the influence of Vanier and Hauerwas, I've come to realize that my job as a leader is to choose the way that will most honestly expose my own brokenness. I often ask myself: Which of the choices before me will best allow me to be present to the brokenness of others? This might sound like an odd leadership principle, but when deciding on a course of action, I pursue those steps that will most effectively allow me to speak or live out of my own brokenness and allow those around me to do the same. Which choice will best reveal my weakness and my dependence on God? Which option requires me to rely on God's power, not my own? It is all I can do to resist the impulse to hide

> I will often ask myself which step I can take that will most effectively allow me to speak or live out of my own brokenness and allow those around me to do the same.

my own brokenness. I don't naturally want other people to know my struggles. I want to pretend as if I have my act together. But that is not where the power of God resides. The power of God resides in weakness.

This is not always palatable for some Christian communities. After all, the prodigal son and the loving father are not the only characters in Jesus' parable. There is also an older brother, and his presence will be felt in every church community. Some of our friends will not like to worship with deeply broken people. They will find their presence uncomfortable and unpredictable. It will create too much tension for them.

Each week on a Sunday morning in our little church, there are typically about twenty to thirty men and women who are living off the grid. Most of them are actively living in the throes of addictions so terrible that they have completely disrupted their lives. It's not easy to worship with people like this, people who have not learned or are unable to hide their brokenness from the rest of the community. The hardcore homeless bring with them mental illness, addictions, criminal records, patterns of deceit and violence, sometimes weapons, drugs, and negative attitudes. They bring everything we have been trained to hide from others. And when they don't hide these things, their presence sometimes feels like a jarring slap in the face.

In Jesus' parable, the older brother is repulsed by the presence of his younger brother. There will always be some who feel the same way when broken people are present. That's one of the reasons this book is called *Shrink*. If you choose to care for the "least of these," you have to give up the aspiration to draw a crowd. American Christianity is comfortable with older brothers, and while they will embrace the occasional prodigal, the church is not naturally comfortable with people who haven't gotten their act together. In Jesus' parable, the older brother resented the prodigal son for squandering the father's wealth. Like many contemporary older brothers, he may have also secretly believed that the wayward child was having the good life, enjoying himself at his and his father's expense.

Older brothers have a cancerous problem. The same struggles and brokenness the prodigals struggle with are present in older brothers' lives as well, but they are hidden so that others cannot see them. The older brother looks on the brokenness of his struggling sibling with contempt and self-righteous pride. And this pride is toxic to his soul.

When Jesus told the story of the prodigal son, he ended by leaving a clear choice for the Pharisees in his audience. There are two paths—two options remaining open to them. Either join the father and become like him—more loving, accepting, generous, and forgiving—or remain proud and resentful, outside the party. Sadly, many of our churches today are filled with older brothers, and so these churches are not places where prodigals feel welcome.

Consider the contrast between the two brothers in Jesus' parable. When the younger son insults his father by asking for his inheritance, he does so in private. But the older brother publicly embarrasses his father. There is a party going on at the house. Their neighbors have come. Everyone is celebrating. The older brother would have important duties to the family in that social setting, but he refuses to identify with his father and younger brother. He sits outside the party and pouts. So the father comes out, away from the gathering, to meet the older brother. He leaves the party and goes outside to his sulking heir, saying, "You know everything I have is already yours. Come in to the party, son! Your little brother is back. Let's celebrate as a family again."

The older brother refuses. Swimming in his own resentment, he makes his accusation: "This son of yours . . ." With those four words, he effectively places himself outside the family. He continues, ". . . who has squandered your wealth with prostitutes." Jesus never mentioned prostitutes when he described the far-off country, so this comment actually reveals the heart of the older brother accurately. How many nights did the older brother lie awake imagining the debauchery of his younger brother, secretly wishing he could enjoy it? His resentment fueled his judgmental anger. "I bet he's off gambling, drinking, whoring around the country," he accused, and his hatred only grew.

Because the older brother is unable to see his own brokenness, his own offense, he places himself outside the family and cuts himself off from the love of the father. In the end, the older brother is the one who is miserable. Because he could not see or admit his own brokenness, he effectively cut himself off from grace.

Friendship with the broken will always be offensive to the self-righteous. Many people will simply choose to leave your church. Some of the most painful moments of my ministry life have been when people left our community, choosing to place themselves outside our church family, usually citing our church's inability to meet their needs. I watch them go with a heavy heart every single time, wishing they could somehow connect with the idea that everything they need in order to be healed is already in this place. All they have to do is stick around long enough for their hearts to wake up to what is right in front of them. But if you choose to embrace broken people, some people will opt out, and your church or ministry is likely going to shrink.

> Because he could not see or admit his own brokenness, he effectively cut himself off from grace.

BROKENNESS AS A LEADERSHIP VIRTUE

So what does brokenness look like as a leadership virtue? It has everything to do with growing in friendship with the people around us. Engaging with broken people, especially those like my friend Bob who are unable to hide their own limitations, leads to deep and profound friendship—the type of friendship we seldom see in our society today.

Hauerwas tells us that Aristotle distinguished between three types of friendships: friendships of *use*, friendships of *pleasure*, and friendships of *virtue*. In a friendship of *use*, it is often hard to know whether we are just hanging out with a friend or if we are really networking to get ahead. These relationships are valued because they help us get to where we want to go. Friendships of *pleasure* are built on mutual enjoyment and interest. We engage in these friendships only as long as they are fun, and we quickly abandon them when our enjoyment runs dry. Friendships of *virtue*, Aristotle believed, are the highest form of friendship because they are based on equals recognizing virtue in one another and building the kind of friendship that can be sustained over time.

"Aristotle would not have thought it possible," Hauerwas says, "for a friendship to exist between people who are mentally disabled and those who are not,"[5] whether they were friendships of use, pleasure, or virtue. Yet Vanier's life and the existence of the L'Arche communities all around the world speak to a different reality. Friendships with damaged, wounded, broken, and impaired people are possible, Vanier says, because, "when the poor and weak are present, they prevent us from falling into the trap of power — even the power to do good — of thinking that it is we who are the good ones, who must save the Savior and his church."[6]

Brokenness is the only ground available to us on which all human beings stand as equals. We are all broken, and it is by relating to one another in humble acknowledgment of our brokenness that the power of God is unleashed in our midst. Brokenness, as it turns out, is an essential leadership virtue.

> Brokenness, as it turns out, is an essential leadership virtue.

To embrace the virtue of brokenness within Christian community, one must embrace a new mode of being a leader, and this will not be easy. Early on when I had just begun to write my blog *Paperback Theology*, I confessed some of the struggles I was having with the concept of limited atonement and double imputation — two theological issues connected to Calvinism. I had previously accepted them but was now beginning to question them.

Immediately I was attacked on my blog by several people within our church body. I'll never forget one parishioner telling me that I owed it to the church to leave ministry for a while, go figure out what I really believed, and then come back to ministry (or not). There was clearly no room for conversation about these issues. When I didn't comply, his family left the church. Another was openly critical,

---

5 Ibid., 91.

6 Jean Vanier, *Drawn into the Mystery of Jesus through the Gospel of John* (New York: Paulist, 2004), 238.

attempting to get others to leave with him. He went so far as sending a snarky email to a large number of our church members as he left, telling them they were wasting their time following a leader who didn't know exactly what he believed.

I believe this is one of the reasons why so many pastors are profoundly lonely. From that moment on in my ministry, I promised myself that I would never pretend to be something I am not, or to allow people to think more highly of me than they should. I committed myself to being vulnerable and sharing my questions, my brokenness, my weaknesses as often as I can, even when I teach on Sunday mornings.

Undoubtedly, this has hindered growth in our church, but I will say that I have seldom felt lonely. In that sense, my life and ministry are quite different from the average senior pastor's. I am not held on a pedestal at my church. My congregation is now used to me confessing my own limitations, speaking openly about my uncertainties, and hearing me acknowledge that I don't know what the next steps are for us as a church. Some people prefer certainty, promises, and confident guarantees that I know what I'm doing and I have the answers. Those folks never seem to stick around for long. But I can't bring myself to fake it. That kind of ministry isn't honest, nor is it real. Sharing my brokenness has kept me and our leaders in a much healthier place. Instead of feeling isolated and lonely in our carefully constructed persona, we talk and share our struggles. We have grown in intimacy through our shared brokenness.

When leaders act like we have it all together, when we hide our own brokenness, we become lonely. This loneliness, Vanier believes, is like a disease from which we must allow ourselves to heal. "Loneliness," he writes, "is something essential to the human heart."[7] It is an inescapable part of what plagues every person. And this movement—from loneliness to community with others—is fundamental to the gospel. We experience the power of the gospel as we find new brothers and sisters and grow as a family among the people of God.

Vanier notes that when you work with those who are mentally

---

7 Vanier, *Becoming Human*, 7.

disabled, most people believe that the true "success story" is for a mentally disabled person to learn to live on their own — self-sufficiently. The end goal is often greater autonomy, less dependence on others. But Vanier believes that the opposite is the goal of the church as a community. Independence does not lead to healthy relationships; instead, it leads to loneliness and, in the case of many of those he works with, alcoholism. "The problem" he writes, referring to the L'Arche community, "was not that they lived alone but that they lacked a network of friends. It always comes back to belonging."[8]

> Independence does not lead to healthy relationships; instead, it leads to loneliness.

This is axiomatic for the church today as well. Vanier again: "We have to discover more fully that the church is a place of compassion and fecundity, a place of welcome and friendship."[9]

We are wired by God for this type of familial connection. What endangers our health is not a lack of autonomy or independence; what endangers our health is loneliness, being cut off from others and only depending on ourselves. The abundant life is not a life of radical individualism; the abundant life is a life of mutuality and relationship characterized by participation in the new community of God. The leader's first job is to cultivate this kind of connection. And the only way we can do this is by being vulnerable ourselves — relating to others in and through our own brokenness and weakness and failure and loss.

At one point in my own relationship with Bob, I finally realized that there was nothing I could ever do to fix Bob's problems. Sure, I could help him from time to time. But my goal, my responsibility, was not to fix him. Only as I released this did I begin to see the amazing power that Bob had as a broken vessel, ready to be filled and used. Instead of seeing Bob as a project to be finished or a problem to fix, I began to see Bob as a friend to love and to be loved by.

Bob would not be able to perform for me or produce any tangible

---

8 Hauerwas and Vanier, *Living Gently*, 37.
9 Ibid.

results for me. When I accepted this, I found I was able simply to live in relationship with Bob, to be his friend. I stopped trying to figure out how he could help my ministry; I stopped worrying about whether I was having "fun" being with Bob. Only then was I able to truly listen to Bob. I began to really see him, maybe for the first time. I came to rely on him as a friend.

I also began to listen to the voice of God as it was mediated to me through Bob's presence. "Learning to listen," Hauerwas writes, "is basic to the gentle character of life in L'Arche."[10] On many of those short rides from Bob's house to the church, I would talk with him about what I was preaching that day. Bob would share words and thoughts with me, words I would scribble on the margins of my sermon notes, and I would share them with the congregation. Often, they were deeply impactful.

In case I haven't been clear—all of this was deeply disturbing to my leadership life, my self-identity as a leader, and my ideas about what I was supposed to be doing. I began to realize that many of my ministry friendships and relationships with people in my congregation were nothing more than friendships of use. I found that I was unskilled at relating to other people in their brokenness, and I was not nearly comfortable enough allowing them to see my own brokenness. I saw that I had constructed walls around my heart that only the gentleness of a hopelessly addicted, injured, and vulnerable former homeless man could break through.

What can leaders learn by engaging in friendship with those who cannot help us to achieve anything? They bring the power of brokenness to our churches. We learn to be gentle, to be patient, to love others not for what they do for us or even for the enjoyment of being with them, but simply as a friend in Christ. Most of the prevailing wisdom among church leaders today is nothing but an attempt to cover over, reduce, mitigate the impact of, or erase our own brokenness. But it's impossible. We learn to mask our fears, our inadequacies, our uncertainties, and our weaknesses. We gravitate toward the *strong*, *powerful*, and *robust* and downplay the way of the *broken*, *gentle*, and

---

10 Ibid., 79.

weak. We may talk about weakness or extol the example of Jesus, but in our own lives—it just doesn't make sense.

Instead, we are driven to succeed because *our identity is all wrapped up in what we can achieve.* Our identity as leaders is wrapped up in our accomplishments, and any acknowledgment of brokenness or weakness feels and smells like failure. And it is true—much of this does look like failure. Shrinking your church will feel like failing. Shrinking your ministry will feel like you aren't accomplishing anything of worth or value. The church that follows the way of Jesus, the downward path, the road to the cross, is made beautiful not through triumphalist growth strategies but in discovering the power of God present in weakness.

I am convinced that learning to expose our own brokenness is one of the basic qualifications for leadership among the people of God. God doesn't need experts in the latest models, strategies, and techniques. He needs broken people who can sit with other broken people and appreciate them as precious children of the Father, prodigals returning home. When we sit with someone who is so broken that they have nothing to offer us that will help us get ahead, nothing that is of use to us, nothing that will enhance our reputation, and little that is of pleasure, then we are forced either to walk away or to stay long enough to begin to recognize the spark of the divine living within them—even in their humble state. Only then can we begin to see our own power, wholeness, usefulness, and competency as a roadblock instead of an advantage. We learn to recognize that the power of God is not perfected in our strength, but in our weakness.

Chapter 10

THE NECESSITY OF PATIENCE

*The movement that Jesus begins is constituted by
people who believe that they have all the time in the
world, made possible by God's patience, to challenge the
world's impatient violence by cross and resurrection.*
—Stanley Hauerwas

*Have courage for the great sorrows of life and patience
for the small ones; and when you have laboriously
accomplished your daily task, go to sleep in peace.
God is awake.*
—Victor Hugo

TERRA INCOGNITA

I have always been a fan of old maps—maps of any kind, really, but especially old maps because they give us this great snapshot of what people knew about the world at a particular time. Sometimes they were way off. Sometimes they were surprisingly accurate. Often when it came time to draw a part of the land mass that was yet to be explored, cartographers would label those regions *terra incognita*— "the unknown land." There was more out there, they just didn't know how much, nor could they give any detail. So cartographers would make an educated guess and label it *terra incognita*.

There was a sense of danger associated with the phrase. Uncharted territory was assumed to be a dangerous place. On some old maps on the territories labeled *terra incognita*, they would write HIC SVNT DRACONES ("here be dragons"—which sounds much scarier if said in a pirate voice), or HIC *SVNT LEONES* ("here be lions"). It was all meant to warn people that this place is dangerous. The moment you cross over into *terra incognita*, you are functionally lost. Nobody knows what's out there, and nobody's coming to get you. If you get in trouble, you'll have to find your own way out.

In her book *A Field Guide to Getting Lost*, Rebecca Solnit plays with this idea of *terra incognita*, relating it to human spirituality and the soul.[1] Solnit says that in the same way an explorer agrees to get lost in order to press into new territory, so anyone who wants to experience growth and wholeness as a person must be willing to get a little bit lost now and then in order to venture beyond the limits we now know.

One of Solnit's close friends is part of a search-and-rescue team in the Rockies. She told a story of a lost eleven-year-old boy who was deaf and losing his eyesight. The boy was became lost during a late afternoon game of hide and seek. Because he was deaf, he was particularly hard to find. He had been blowing a whistle given him for just such an occasion, but could not hear how close he was to a nearby stream. The roar of the water made his signal impossible for those searching for him to hear. After a harrowing night on his own, the sun came up, and he started blowing his whistle again. The search-and-rescue team finally found him, very cold but okay.

The experts say that the key to survival is knowing you are lost. That's why kids are found more often than adults. Kids don't stray as far. They usually curl up in a sheltered place and wait for help.

Navigating the forest involves paying attention to weather, landmarks, trails, the route you are taking, the movements of the sun, and if need be, the moon and the stars. You need to recognize the way the land slopes, the direction of running water, and a thousand other things that are immediately understood by those who are literate in

---

1 Rebecca Solnit, *A Field Guide to Getting Lost*, (New York, NY: Penguin, 2006).

the language of the forest. Most people who get lost don't speak this language. So they immediately panic.

Solnit says that to be lost means that the world has suddenly "become larger than your knowledge of it."[2] That's *terra incognita*. Your surroundings have pushed beyond the limits of your wisdom.

Hunters are among the best at getting lost. They run off in hot pursuit of some wild beast. In the excitement their *hippocampus* shuts down, and they stop making mental maps. By the time they realize they don't know where they are, their bodies are so full of adrenaline that even though they know they should stay put, they usually try to walk out of trouble, making things worse.

I've never been lost. This is nothing special, since we now live in a world in which we can always know where we are. Most of our world is paved and marked well enough that few of us have ever been truly lost. We might have been turned around or headed the wrong way. But we don't have much experience with being truly lost. This is probably a good thing because we are so dependent upon our GPS systems in our cars and cell phones, we hardly even know how to read a map, much less navigate by the night sky—or our wits. If we ever really do get lost—spiritually, existentially, or God forbid, physically—we become subservient slaves to our limbic system—fight, flight, or freeze. We lack the basic tools needed to survive in *terra incognita* when we can't push the locate button.

It hasn't always been this way. Solnit poked around in the historiography of the nineteenth century and learned that people back then were rarely lost. A century ago, being off course by a day or two or spending a few extra nights in the wild was not uncommon. Daniel Boone once said, "I was never lost in the woods my whole life, though once I was confused for three days."[3] For him it was a legitimate distinction. He knew he would stumble onto something he recognized sooner or later, and in the meantime he knew what to do.

Solnit says that says that Sacagawea's main role in the famous Lewis and Clarke campaign was not really to navigate. Her main role

---

2 Ibid., 22.
3 Ibid., 13.

was that she made everyone comfortable, because *she* was so comfortable. These guys were experienced scouts, trappers, and explorers, but it was different for Sacagawea—the forest was her home. She knew what plants they could eat and understood many native languages, and her infant child signaled to every tribe they encountered that this was not a war party. She was completely at home in the wilderness. And it made everyone around her calm.

Calm was extremely valuable, because all explorers are *functionally lost*. Although Lewis and Clarke had never seen these places before, they did have a rich body of experience on which to draw. This gave them the one thing most lost people never have: *patience*. Even though the world had suddenly gotten larger than their knowledge of it, they did not panic or become anxious. They had Sacagawea, plus a whole set of competencies formed through years in the wilderness.

Being lost, as Solnit says, is mostly a state of mind.[4] This, I believe, is true not only in the backwoods of Colorado, but also in regard to the soul and the human experience. Two people can undergo the same exact life experience, one feeling completely anxious, and the other bearing it with calm patience. The difference is usually a rich body of experience with *terra incognita*. If being lost is what happens when we realize that the world is suddenly larger than our knowledge of it, then maybe that experience is a spiritual necessity. We'll never reach anything like spiritual maturity without it. Most of all we will never learn the virtue of *patience*.

The Bible has a term of its own for *terra incognita*. It's called the wilderness. The story of Israel is one trip after another into the *terra incognita*. Over and over we see that God performed some pretty good work with people who are good and seriously lost.

FORTY YEARS

"The Lord said to Moses, 'Send men to spy out the land of Canaan, which I am giving to the Israelites'" (Num 13:1–2). It was smart. The Israelites were fresh out of a four-hundred-year stint in Egyptian

---

4 Ibid., 14.

slavery. They were not heavily armed. They needed to figure out just what they were getting themselves into in this campaign to inhabit the land promised to their ancestors. So Moses took a representative from every tribe and sent them through the Negev into the hill country to see what they could see.

In a scene that reminds me of Han Solo and Luke Skywalker being carried after being captured by the small Ewoks, the spies came back from the Promised Land carrying a cluster of grapes so phenomenally large that it had to be suspended on a pole between two men. "The place is everything we could ever dream of. Flowing with milk and honey is an understatement. But [hemming and hawing] there's a little problem."

To be honest, the problem wasn't little at all. In fact, there were colossal beasts in the land, huge bloodthirsty warriors, the sons of the Anak, who were descended from honest-to-goodness giants. The response of the spies was nearly unanimous: there was no way they could win if they went in and tried to take the land.

But two of the spies disagreed. Caleb silenced the people. "You guys are crazy. I think we should do it," he said. Joshua stood beside him and agreed, declaring, "They are no stronger than we are." But the other spies started a whisper campaign. They said that compared to these supermen, they felt like mere grasshoppers. The ancient Nephilim lived in the Promised Land. Sons of the gods, half-bloods who had one mortal and one immortal parent, were waiting to destroy Israel. There was no way. The grumbling continued until everyone was flat on their backs with fear.

Joshua and Caleb were livid. They ripped their clothes. They screamed and hollered. They told the entire assembly they wore ladies underwear, called them so-and-sos, and questioned their family heritage, but to no avail. The people had lost heart.

When Yahweh delivered his people from slavery in Egypt, he wanted to take them straight into the Promised Land, but they could not muster the courage. Centuries of Egyptian slave drivers had robbed them of the imagination they needed in order to be free.

If you break down the structure of the book of Numbers in the Old Testament, the first two chapters give instructions on how they are to arrange the camp. The third and fourth chapters talk about the role of the priests. Chapters 5 and 6 talk about how to keep the camp holy. Chapters 7 through 10 refer to the dedication of the tabernacle and the way that God will lead them.

Then in chapter 11 there is a shift. The people start to grumble. They don't like the manna God is giving them. Never mind the fact that ten minutes ago God was leading them out of Egypt and parting the Red Sea. They have moved on from all that and now they want some better food.

By the time we reach chapter 13 nobody is surprised when the spies come back quaking in fear. Everyone except Joshua and Caleb is terror struck, which is exactly what the reader expects. These people, whose imaginations were so thoroughly shaped by slavery, simply did not have the capacity to see a different way of life.

When the allies began liberating concentration camps in the last days of World War II, they encountered a strange phenomenon. Sometimes, after liberating the camp, the prisoners would refuse to leave. The barbaric combination of forced labor and savage violence had conditioned the prisoners and stunted their imaginations. Sometimes, it would take days to help them find a way to leave their prison behind. That's the power slavery holds over the human imagination.

Joshua and Caleb told everyone who would listen that they were sure the Lord would go before them and that they could accomplish anything with God's help, but the people refused to listen. They even began a small rebellion, saying, "Let's choose a new leader and go back to Egypt" (Num 14:4).

Then in Numbers 14 there is a pivotal passage (14:26–35) in which God says that he has counted their numbers—hence the title. God knows who they are. He has inspected every one of them—young and old, great and small. Yahweh has peered into the hearts of his people, knows what they are thinking about doing, and is displeased with their disobedience. This entire generation cannot find the courage or obedience necessary *because they simply can't imagine it.* So Yahweh decides to lead them into *terra incognita.*

Forty years it took for God to give them a new *orientation* in which they could stop thinking like slaves and start thinking like children of God. The wilderness is all about a change in orientation. The Israelites began with an *old orientation*: slavery. God wanted to give them a *new orientation*: freedom. The only way to get them from their old orientation to a new orientation was to lead them into a time of profound *disorientation*. The Israelites thought they knew what kind of world they were living in — a world where only Pharaoh could provide. God would move them to a place of disorientation in which the world was suddenly much larger than their knowledge of it. When they emerged on the other side, they would know a little more about their world.

Often it seems as though the only way God can do what God is trying to do with his people is to get them good and lost. Stanley Hauerwas says that the wilderness is the place reserved for learning how to go on when you don't know where you are.[5] It's as though, if we're going to be ready for the times when life circumstances leave us nowhere, we will need to have practiced being lost.

In his book *Walden*, Henry David Thoreau says that never to be lost is to never really live. Thoreau writes, "It is a surprising and memorable, as well as valuable, experience to be lost in the woods any time ... not till we are completely lost, or turned round ... do we appreciate the vastness and strangeness of nature. Not till we are lost, in other words, not till we have lost the world, do we begin to find ourselves, and realize where we are and the infinite extent of our relations."[6] The wilderness is about learning who we are, where we are, who God is, and how it all relates together. There is a sense in which the wilderness is a kind of a grace.

When Jesus ventured into *terra incognita* to be tempted by the devil, it says that he was led into the wilderness by the Spirit of God (Matt 4:1). He wasn't being punished. He wasn't off course. He was there because he was being led. He was being led because there was something God wanted Jesus to experience, something essential to his mission that could only be learned in the wilderness.

---

5   This is the title of chapter 1 in Stanley Hauerwas, *Wilderness Wanderings* (Boulder, CO: Westview, 1997).

6   Henry David Thoreau, *Walden*, (New York: Crowell, 1910), 226–27.

Many of the saints were lost at some point. Abraham and Sarah, for example: God didn't even say where they were going, but along the way Abraham learned to hear the voice of God when nobody else on the planet could. When Elijah was lost in the wilderness, running from Queen Jezebel, it took forty days for him to learn that God's voice is often so soft it's like a whisper—a lesson he learned only when he became patient and still (2 Kings 19). Moses and the children of Israel spent forty years lost in the wilderness, and by the time they got to the Promised Land, they were ready to fight wars armed with trumpets.

Only the patient will survive the wilderness. If we get panicky and try to run, we'll never make it. We must learn to see the wilderness as a means of grace—the place where God takes us from time to time, to give us a new orientation and to break us out of the patterns that will end in failure.

In the wilderness Israel and her leaders were forced to rely on God for even the most basic necessities of life. If they needed food, they had to trust in God to provide manna for the next day. If they needed water, Moses would strike a rock with his staff, and God would bring it forth. They had no maps of the wilderness; all they had to go on was a cloud by day and a pillar of fire by night.

What the wilderness taught the children of Israel, maybe more than anything else, was the *patience* required to wait on God to move. When they felt restless, they had to learn how to still their own hearts and quiet their own fears. They learned the patience necessary to resist becoming constantly stirred up by the pressing concerns of the moment. God soon formed a new imagination among his people. By the end of their time in the wilderness, their reaction to struggle was no longer to freak out or wail, for they had become the patient people of God.

Forty years they wandered, learning to trust God—failing sometimes and succeeding others—until every single person from that sad, wounded, and faithless generation had died except for Joshua and Caleb, two brave soldiers and Israel's next appointed leaders.

THE TASK OF RE-SCRIPTING

I sometimes think about the patience of Joshua and Caleb during that journey. I picture them running up to the tent where Moses stayed asking, "Are we there yet? Are we there yet?" I wonder if they walked around the camp, occasionally poking their head through a doorway to see if one of the holdouts from the older generation had died yet. I know I would have. What extraordinary patience it must have taken to wait on God, especially given the fact that they were ready to go from the beginning.

Rebellions, plagues, poisonous snakes, the orgy at Shittim, grumblings, and skirmishes, and finally all-out war—it must have been a strange life for Joshua and Caleb. In the end, all of their friends were dead. One by one, the spies who had gone with them into the land of milk and honey and had lost heart were buried in the wilderness. And the wandering continued.

When I was in college, the *Grumpy Old Men* movies came out. The stories were fun enough, but the real magic was the chemistry between the old, has-been actors who still knew how to make us feel something deeply. One of my favorite lines comes from the second movie and the ninety-five-year-old character played by Burgess Meredith. "According to all of them flat-belly experts," he says, "I should've took a dirt nap like thirty years ago. But each year comes and goes, and I'm still here. Ha! And they keep dyin'. You know? Sometimes I wonder if God forgot about me." I wonder if that's how Joshua and Caleb must have felt—forgotten by God.

The patience of Caleb and Joshua in the wilderness is the kind of patience required of you and me if we wish to learn how to live through times of disorientation. The contemporary church in the West has been taken captive by our culture. Like the children of Israel in Egypt, our imagination has been shaped, not by the story of God, but a slavery to individualism, consumerism, and nationalism. While most Christians in the West point to secularism, failing morality, and rising decadence as the reason the church is losing ground, the truth is that we have lost our ability to worship only one God. We are held captive by a story that is not rooted in Scripture;

we have lost our grasp on the story of God and our confidence in God's ability to breathe life into the church. Somehow we are going to have to learn to let that modern story go.

In September 2005, the Old Testament scholar Walter Brueggemann sat with a group of church leaders for a theological conversation. He brought along a working document that he called his "Nineteen Theses," a series of convictions he had developed over the years that he hoped would seed their discussion time. Brueggemann's theses have much to teach us about the virtue of patience in leadership.[7]

- Thesis 1: Everybody lives by a script. The script may be implicit or explicit. It may be recognized or unrecognized, but everybody has a script.
- Thesis 2: We get scripted. All of us get scripted through the process of nurture and formation and socialization, and it happens to us without our knowing it.
- Thesis 3: The dominant scripting in our society is a script of technological therapeutic military consumerism that socializes us all, liberal and conservative.[8]
- Thesis 4: That script, enacted through advertising and propaganda and ideology, especially on the liturgies of television, promises to make us safe and to make us happy.
- Thesis 5: That script has failed ... the script of military consumerism cannot make us safe and it cannot make us happy. We may be the unhappiest society in the world.

---

7 A recording of these Nineteen Theses is available at: http://soupiset.type-pad.com/soupablog/Brueggemann_19_Theses.html. A written record of these Nineteen Theses is located here: http://119.161.74.13/articles/20798.htm.

8 In Brueggemann's first reading of Thesis 3 he calls the script "technological therapeutic consumer militarism." In the rest of his discussion of the nineteen theses, including an immediate comment on Thesis 3, Brueggeman uses "military consumerism" instead of "consumer militarism." This is why my version of Thesis 3 varies from other versions I have seen. I think Brueggemann misspoke in his first reading of Thesis 3 and corrected this throughout the rest of his presentation.

- Thesis 6: Health for our society depends on disengagement from and relinquishment of that script of military consumerism. This is a disengagement and relinquishment that we mostly resist and about which we are profoundly ambiguous.

Brueggemann's first six theses offer a stunning description of our society. We are constantly scripted by the liturgies of our culture. We are given a story that is meant to shape our lives and our imaginations, and for the most part we are completely unaware that this is happening. Brueggemann calls the script our culture hands us technological therapeutic military consumerism. I usually shorten this to: *individualism, consumerism, and nationalism.* This script promises to make us safe and happy, but it has utterly failed.

The health of our society depends on our ability to disengage from that failed script. The problem, as Brueggemann sees it, is that we do not have the energy to disengage. Most Christians feel profoundly ambivalent about disengaging from the dominant script of our society. We like the script. Even if we know this script is an illusion, we resist any attempts to move away from it. We are like the Hebrew people fresh out of Egypt and completely ambivalent about changing stories.

While these first six theses describe the problem, as well as the task, that is facing the contemporary Western church, what I find most inspiring about Brueggemann's "Nineteen Theses" is what he says next. In the theses that follow, he describes the task of ministry for those who serve the church:

- Thesis 7: It is the task of ministry to de-script that script among us. That is, to enable persons to relinquish a world that no longer exists and indeed never did exist.
- Thesis 8: The task of de-scripting, relinquishment, and disengagement is accomplished by a steady, patient, intentional articulation of an alternative script that we say can make us happy and make us safe.
- Thesis 9: The alternative script is rooted in the Bible and is enacted through the tradition of the church. It is an offer of a

counter-metanarrative, counter to the script of technological therapeutic military consumerism.

The task of ministry involves de-scripting ourselves and others from a story we are told by our society—a story that cannot make us safe or happy—and re-scripting ourselves in the story we call the gospel. The task of ministry involves the prophetic recognition that the story our society tells is a story about a world that no longer exists, and indeed it has never really existed outside of our own warped imaginations. The only way to de-script and re-script, Brueggemann says, is to tell a better story, and to tell it with relentless *patience*.

When I'm describing my job as a pastor, the job to which I'm calling everyone I work with in my congregation, this is what I say: *We are trying to switch stories.* We are working to change our stories from the old, tired script of individualism, consumerism, and nationalism, a failed script and a lie. And the health of our world depends on our ability to leave that old story and join God's new story. The only way to do this is through a *steady, patient, intentional articulation of a better story*, the story we call the gospel. Changing stories is not simple or easy. It's like editing a book, revising chapters, changing the plotline: it requires patience. Ministry is *patient* work.

The day Jesus emerged from the tomb a new world broke into our old world—a world of resurrection. In this new resurrection world, life springs forth from death. But only for those who are willing to see the world in a completely new way. In this new way—the Jesus way—your life is found when you lay it down for the sake of others. Most of the time this will not make the least bit of sense. Most of the time dying to yourself and dying to others will feel like a complete waste of time, and nobody in our society will cheer you on or encourage you—yet another reason the Jesus way of life will require a great deal of patience.

Entering into this new resurrection reality means nothing less than the wholesale relinquishment of the narrative of our culture. The only way this will happen is if we immerse ourselves in the Story of God—the script of the gospel. This story, Brueggemann says, is far from monolithic. It is full of tension. It is disjunctive and sometimes borders on incoherent. It has been raggedly glued together over centuries by scores of different authors and communities, and it cannot be wrapped up into a neat package with a bow on top.

The process of re-scripting will involve the kind of deep disorientation we experience in the wilderness. Changing stories will create tensions and arguments and divisions that we cannot anticipate ahead of time. All along the way we will need to resist the temptation to leave *terra incognita* too quickly, for we will need all the tension we can stomach if we are to really change.

The process of switching stories will be different for each of us, so we must learn to wrestle with the tensions — and with each other — and especially with the God who stands behind the story speaking the words by which we live. "The nurture, formation, and socialization into the counter-script with this illusive, irascible character [God], is the work of ministry. We do that work ... by the practices of preaching, liturgy, education, social action, spirituality, and neighboring of all kinds."[9]

Brueggemann's final thesis asserts that the work of ministry is indispensable because there is no other place in Western society where we can actually engage in the work of exchanging scripts. Those who are called to serve the church must never stop chasing, never stop striving after the task of re-scripting. The work of ministry is truly a work of love for the world — even as the world is trying to script us into its false story. Ministry is about loving a world that is actively trying to deceive us and persecute us. This is why we need passionate patience — the kind of patience that can endure injustice.

Those who begin to live the story of the gospel will find themselves taking on the vulnerability of those on the margins, speaking up for those who cannot speak for themselves. Christians serve those who live on the margins of the culture, often precisely because they don't fit the story line of the world. When the story of Western society has completely used you up and left you wasted, you may become more open to a different story, more ready to explore. The marginalized have fewer allegiances to the status quo, because the status quo

---

9 Walter Brueggemann's 19 Theses: Number 11.

has beaten the life out of them for too long. More than anything else, it will take great patience to love, and in loving to be peaceful, and in being peaceful to be nonviolent in our approach to our task of re-scripting ourselves and those we mean to serve. Changing stories cannot be done by force or through coercion. It requires patience and grace, a gentleness that willingly engages broken people.

THE CHURCH AND POWER

Palestine was once the beating heart of the Christian faith. Early Christians were an often-persecuted and powerless minority. Under Emperor Constantine, Christianity came into favor, and soon into great power. Yet today there are hardly any Christians to be found in Palestine, and those who remain are largely persecuted and culturally irrelevant. The heart of the Christian faith migrated to Western Europe, as Christianity came into greater power and dominance than ever before. But today the great cathedrals of Europe serve more as museums than centers of community life. For a short time, it seemed that the center of gravity for the church might shift to North America, but the American church seems to be following the same pattern of power followed by decline as Western Europe.

Church leaders in North America are scrambling for new models, strategies, and techniques that will arrest this downward momentum. As demographics and culture shift in North America, church leaders discover that old ways of being the church no longer work. Innovation and radical changes are all the rage, and everyone is longing for a silver bullet. As all of this is happening in the United States, the heartbeat of global Christianity has quietly migrated to the Southern Hemisphere and the rapidly expanding church of the global South. While the American church struggles to reinvent itself, God's global work has shifted. How did this happen?

There are many factors at work, but at least some of the causes have been a constant emphasis on church growth methods and a reductionist version of the gospel. The gospel of American Christianity has largely been focused on teaching people how to get into heaven when they die instead of on teaching them everything Jesus commanded—how to live in the way of the cross. The powerful pull of individualism, consumerism, and nationalism has left the North American church somewhat impotent. Yet many church leaders steadfastly refuse to accept that the American church is in decline.

All of this leads me to ask some questions.

What if expansion and growth are *not* God's plan for North America right now?

What if God *wants* the American church to shrink?

What if God is *pruning* a Christianity that has become bloated with affluence and power?

What if God's work in North America means that our churches will decline in numbers, a decline that prepares us for something new?

What if the church in North America has entered a season of disorientation in the wilderness?

In his book *The Prophetic Imagination*, Walter Brueggemann argues that God always resists any attempt to co-opt his mission, whether by a church, a religion, or a government. God is free, and the moment we try to co-opt God to support our projects—social, political, or otherwise—we begin to distort God's nature into whatever story we believe will allow us to gain and hold power. Those who attempt to co-opt God to consolidate their power and control will soon find God has organized against them.[10]

This may explain what happened centuries ago in Palestine and more recently in Europe. Could this be what is happening now in North America? Honestly, I'm not all that convinced by arguments that suggest we are losing numbers because we have become too secularized, because we have become lax on social issues such as abortion or gay marriage. The reason for our decline has less to do with the culture around us and more to do with the fact that we (the church) have co-opted God and used him as the rationale for power.

Christianity is, at its core, a minority religion. Those who fol-

---

10 Walter Brueggemann, *The Prophetic Imagination* (Minneapolis: Fortress, 2001), 21–25.

low Jesus must follow him in vulnerability. Christians don't have any formal power or influence in the world. Those who try to accomplish God's mission through power cannot follow Jesus in his work, because the way to follow Jesus is the way of powerlessness. The way of Jesus leads us to the cross.

The church has never done well when it has had power. That the American church has not done well with power is at least partly to blame for the declining role of Christianity in our culture. Much of what passes for Christianity in North America is not all that concerned with the mission of God or living in the way of the cross. Rather, much of what passes for Christianity is little more than a religious rationale for the exercise of state power. Christianity, in this sense, has morphed into the civil religion of the Western world.

In order to adapt Christianity to this new role of being the American civil religion, the gospel had to be sterilized and rendered impotent and harmless. The Jesus of the gospel is replaced with Santa Claus: sentimental, commercialized, powerless, and fake — nothing more than a means of getting into heaven when you die. Anytime this happens in the church, God takes a step back. God will not be co-opted to serve the goals of the powerful.

The story of the church is not meant to be a narrative of rising to power, nor is it supposed to be a story of progress and expansion. The story of the church is meant to be a story of patience — a story of the vulnerability of people called to pursue a whole new way of relating to God and each other. The story of the church is meant to be the patient rearticulation of this alternative story in the midst of a culture that refuses to listen. But this is not who we are right now. Rather, we are wandering around in *terra incognita*. But it won't always be this way.

So patience will be needed to lead our churches through the wilderness. Patience to refuse church marketing, hype, and sensationalism to grow our congregations. Patience to bypass the quick fixes and the easy, packaged solution. Patience to endure ridicule from an

> The story of the church is meant to be the patient rearticulation of this alternative story in the midst of a culture that refuses to listen.

increasingly secular culture that considers our faith to be primitive and unsophisticated.

TRUSTING IN THE FUTURE

Here is what Caleb told the people as he was receiving his inheritance:

> I was forty years old when Moses the servant of the LORD sent me from Kadesh Barnea to explore the land. And I brought him back a report according to my convictions, but my fellow Israelites who went up with me made the hearts of the people melt in fear. I, however, followed the LORD my God wholeheartedly. So on that day Moses swore to me, "The land on which your feet have walked will be your inheritance and that of your children forever, because you have followed the Lord my God wholeheartedly." (Josh 14:7–9)

This is a stunning scene. The forty years was over, and God's people had arrived, once again, on the doorstep of the Promised Land. But this time it was different. Caleb and Joshua were there, ready to follow God with wholehearted devotion. But now they were not alone. The entire nation of Israel now shared their vision, their passion to follow God in obedience and take the land that had been promised.

The forty years had been good to the former spies. Caleb boldly declared to the people:

> Now then, just as the LORD promised, he has kept me alive for forty-five years since the time he said this to Moses, while Israel moved about in the wilderness. So here I am today, eighty-five years old! I am still as strong today as the day Moses sent me out; I'm just as vigorous to go out to battle now as I was then. Now give me this hill country that the LORD promised me that day. (Josh 14:10–12)

After the long wilderness wanderings, the people were not wilting from God's judgment. On the contrary, they had confidence. They had learned to depend on God's provision for so long that they had begun to really trust God again for their lives. They were now a people with imagination, with ability to trust in the future God had promised them.

When my younger son, Lewis, was only four, we took him and his brother to a water park. There were several slides and water rides for the kids. My older son, Nick, is a bit of a daredevil, and he'll ride just about anything, but Lewis is a little more tentative. We tried to coax Lewis onto one of the slides, but he was pretty sure he didn't want a piece of that. So he stuck to the pools and the fountains.

After an hour or so sitting on a little plastic raft circling the lazy river, Lewis kept bringing up the waterslide, talking about it apprehensively, but with curiosity.

"I don't want to do that waterslide. It looks scary."

"That's okay, buddy," I'd say. "You don't have to if you don't want to."

"If I did go on that slide, I'd be safe though, right?"

"Yeah, I think you would be fine," I answered.

"Does anybody ever get hurt up there?"

"I don't think so, son."

This went on for about fifteen minutes. Subtle questions. Moments of silence. More questions. Then I started to mess with him a little bit.

"They had to make sure it was safe when they built it, right, Dad?" Lewis said.

"Yeah, but when are any of us *really* safe?" Lewis elbows me in the ribs.

"But you could never die on that thing, right, Dad?"

"Well, you know, Lewis, there's a chance in everything." He smacks me and laughs.

Finally, my four-year-old gets up the nerve to say, "I think I'd like to try going down that waterslide."

My wife went to the bottom of the slide to catch him, and I walked with Lewis up several stories of stairs to the top, where he waited nervously in line. His big brother went first to show him how easy it was, and then it was my little guy's turn.

For as long as I live, I'll never forget that moment. Lewis sat down on the mat at the top of the slide, put each hand on a side of the slide to push off, and then he twisted his body completely around and looked back at me. He didn't say a word; he just looked at me with this stark, serious look. He stared right into my eyes. I smiled and said, "If you don't drown, I'll see you at the bottom." He smiled real big, spun around, pushed off, and took off down the slide.

It took a lot of patience not to rush Lewis while he tried to imagine himself riding on the waterslide that scared him so much. If I would have pushed, prodded, or hurried him at any point, that would have been the end of it. It would have never happened. In fact, at a couple of points I actually tried to stoke his disorientation and keep him thinking about it. It takes patience in order to midwife a new beginning.

My son, whom I love so much, was poised on the edge of something really cool. But it was also a bit scary and unknown. Instinctively, he did two things right. First, he spent a significant amount of time patiently waiting, talking to his father, investigating his doubts, being honest about his fears, and asking all of his questions. He didn't make a move until he was ready, until he had built up enough courage that he could actually imagine doing something that scared him to death. Second, poised at the moment of truth, he took a good long look back at his father, gathered his strength, and then pushed off in faith.

Lewis experience the movement from old orientation, through disorientation, to new orientation. The imagination we must access in order to switch stories from the dominant narrative of our culture to the narrative of the gospel only comes through *terra incognita*. Learning to switch stories takes time and a ton of patience. Disorientation, with all of the requisite doubts and questions and fears and tensions, has to happen. It's the liminal space in which we wrestle with the Father, allowing him to help us imagine the world the way God sees it.

Caleb and Joshua had been there all along. They were daredevils ready to try anything. But the children of Israel weren't ready for the Promised Land. They couldn't imagine doing something that risky. So they had to sit in the Father's lap for a while and learn how to have confidence in his power and provision. They had to ask all of their questions and get all of the grumbling out of their system. They had to entertain all of their darkest fears. I cannot imagine how much patience it took for them to wait. They must have had so much faith — so much trust that God actually knew what God was doing.

I dream of those moments when, like Caleb and Joshua and the children of Israel kissing the wilderness good-bye and crossing the Jordan, we step out and storm the castles. Moments where decades of patience pay off and we see God move in amazing ways. I hope for those days, and I often think about them. Yet I also know that most of life isn't spent in those moments. Most of life is lived in the ordinary, not the spectacular. Most of my days will be spent learning to be patient while God moves in me and around me, on my behalf.

I wonder about the church these days. I wonder if we have the kind of patience we will need in order to be faithful in obscurity, without a lot of positive results to which we can point. I wonder if we have the capability to produce truly patient leaders—leaders who are confident not so much in their own theologies and doctrines, but who are confident in God, trusting in God no matter what. Or we keep on chasing the spectacular and sending out press releases. One thing is for sure: we will never have the patience for this if we remain completely immersed in our culture's story of world domination and success. This is, after all, what it means to be born again. We have to leave behind the old world that is dying and passing away, and be reborn—re-scripted—into a new story of hope and resurrection.

If we are to switch scripts from the story of success, power, and expansion without limits to the story of patient reliance on God, it's going to take a lot of courage. This move will require leaders who have enough patience to sit with their people for decades and allow them to ask all of their questions. It will require leaders with the patience to allow a whole generation to pass, missing the point all the while, until a new generation can hear the story of God with fresh ears.

Max Weber famously said that politics was like the slow boring of hard boards. I think ministry is like that. Ministry is the slow boring of hard boards, which requires exceptional patience. Anyone who engages in the task of ministry will certainly risk their own sanity. Church growth is meant to be measured not in weekly attendance numbers, but in decades and half-centuries. If that is true, then patience is a leadership virtue none of us can afford to go without.

Chapter 11
THE STRUGGLE FOR FIDELITY

FIDELITY, n. A virtue peculiar
to those who are about to be betrayed.
—Ambrose Bierce

Most of the lasting lessons I've learned in ministry have come through failure. I've blown important relationships and ignored essential responsibilities. I've made strategic blunders and factual errors that have cost our church dearly. I've misjudged people's character and have placed my trust in wrong things. Yet I remain convinced that these failures have been beneficial. Failure has been one of my best teachers.

We all fail. Failure is an inevitable part of being human. Even much of what we call success has its root in failure. Michael Jordan was cut from his high school basketball team. Albert Einstein didn't speak until he was four years old and was considered not very bright. Oprah Winfrey was demoted from a news anchor job because she was thought to be unfit for television. Walt Disney was fired from a newspaper for lacking imagination. Thomas Edison was called stupid by his teachers. The Beatles were told they didn't have a great sound and rejected by Decca Recording Studios. Dr. Suess was rejected by twenty-seven publishers. Abraham Lincoln had a long list of failures, including eight election losses and a nervous breakdown.

> Much of what we call success has its root in failure.

From Michael Jordan to Abraham Lincoln, the difference

between failure and success is not a spark of genius—it is fidelity. It's what Eugene Peterson calls *a long obedience in the same direction.* These were people who never quit.

My favorite 1980s film is Cameron Crowe's *Say Anything.* It's a film about the soft-spoken, neurotically sweet Lloyd Dobbler. Growing up in the 80s, most of my friends wanted to be like Ferris Buehler; I wanted to be Lloyd Dobbler. I once tried to get my wife to name our first son "Lloyd Dobbler Suttle." She refused. She's wise. I digress ... In the last scene of the movie, Lloyd and his girlfriend are on a plane headed for the United Kingdom to chase a dream of love and adventure when his girlfriend has a moment of pause. "Nobody thought we would do this," she says. "Nobody really thinks it can work, do they?"

"No," Lloyd responds. Then, after a long pause, he says, "You just described every great success story."

How true that is. In fact, if you poke around and study the great success stories, you'll usually find a truckload of failure somewhere. One of my favorites is the story behind the success of Harry Potter. J. K. Rowling, the famed author of the series—now the bestselling book series of all time—was a total failure for a long time. After finishing the Harry Potter series, Rowling was asked to speak at a Harvard commencement ceremony. She chose to speak, not about her successes, but about her failures. "I think it fair to say that by any conventional measure, a mere seven years after my graduation day, I had failed on an epic scale," Rowling said. "An exceptionally short-lived marriage had imploded, and I was jobless, a lone parent, and as poor as it is possible to be in modern Britain without being homeless. The fears that my parents had had for me, and that I had had for myself, had both come to pass, and by every usual standard, I was the biggest failure I knew."[1]

Yet, in the words of Lloyd Dobbler, Rowling had just described

---

1 J. K. Rowling, Commencement Address at Harvard University, "The Fringe Benefits of Failure, and the Importance of Imagination," June 5, 2008. Quoted from the transcribed remarks as posted on the site of the *Harvard Gazette.* Accessed 12/13/2013, http://news.harvard.edu/gazette/story/2008/06/text-of-j-k-rowling-speech/.

every great success story. Rowling went on to share how her failures had stripped away what was nonessential to her life, her personality, and her work. Her failures helped her to face hard realities and focus her energy on what she felt called to do — the only thing that really, truly mattered to her. As it turns out, that one thing was writing a book about a little boy who lived in a cupboard under the stairs and had no idea he was a wizard.

Some of the most important moments of our lives will come through our failures. But the difference between a failure that becomes our undoing and a failure that becomes a redemptive part of our story is nearly always *fidelity*.

I have this theory. I think God uses our lives *against* us. God takes the events of our lives that are painful — things we do and things that have been done to us — and uses them against us. He takes hold of the jagged edges of our lives and our stories and uses them to scrape away everything that is killing us. God takes our failures in hand and makes them the instrument by which he can grind down our rough edges, peel away the death that traps us there, and free us to become fully human. This will only happen to the person who sticks around long enough to make it through the extended period of pain. The problem is that most of us don't have the stomach to press on, even when it looks like we are completely failing. We have lost any concept of fidelity.

LOVE IS FIDELITY OVER TIME

On the night that Jesus was betrayed by Judas, all of the rest of his disciples scattered and fled. Jewish leaders took Jesus and put him on trial: a farce, a kangaroo court. They trumped up charges, hired false witnesses to testify against him, and sentenced him to die. We don't know exactly where the disciples spent that evening, except for Peter and presumably John. John was allowed to witness the proceedings; Peter was stuck outside standing by a fire.

Because it was a cold night, Peter was warming himself by a charcoal fire in the courtyard when a woman recognized him and accused him of being a friend of Jesus. Peter tried to laugh it off, but she persisted. Still Peter continued to deny any association with Jesus. I find it odd that Peter chose to stay out there by the fire. After all, John was just as close to Jesus, and he was inside the proceedings, apparently not fearing for his life. So what was Peter afraid of? The Scripture tells us that one of the people warming himself around the fire had been at Gethsemane and was a relative of the man whose ear Peter had cut off. Perhaps Peter was afraid that he would be arrested as well. Or maybe he was just embarrassed. It's possible he was just proud and didn't want to be associated with Jesus in a crowd of hostile people.

We really don't know why Peter denied Jesus. But we do know that he did it three times. I can picture Peter weeping bitter tears as the sun rose the next morning and he realized what he had done. Soon his friend and teacher would be crucified, and it would be too late to seek forgiveness.

Several weeks later, after the resurrection, the disciples were confused about what to do, so Peter and several others went back to what they knew best: fishing. They went out at night on the Sea of Tiberias, but caught nothing. Early in the morning, a bystander called out to them with a strange request: try the other side of the boat. Peter obeyed, and when the nets became strained with fish, Peter felt that old familiar feeling he'd often had when he was around Jesus. He didn't even wait for the boat to land; he just dove into the water and swam for shore.

This is the third time Jesus appeared to his disciples (including Peter) after his resurrection, but to this point Jesus and Peter had not yet talked about that night in the courtyard. The tension had to be thick there. Sitting in front of another charcoal fire, Peter was once again questioned about his loyalty to Jesus. It's not hard to imagine Peter believing his failure disqualified him for ministry. He was no longer fishing for men, he was just fishing—and not even doing that very well. Peter was no longer the rock; he was just plain old Simon.

That's how Jesus addressed him (see John 21:15–17). Jesus said, "Simon, do you love me?" The word for love here is *agapaō*, unfailing love.

Peter answered, "You know I love you." The word for love here is *phileō*, friendship.

Jesus tried again, "Simon, do you *agapaō* me?" Again Simon said, "I *phileō* you."

Jesus asked again, only this time he switched words to *phileō*. "Simon, son of John, do you *phileō* me?" Are you really my friend?

Peter was hurt. Jesus' question was a dagger to his heart. "Lord," he said, "you know all things. You know that I *phileō* you."

It's almost as if Peter couldn't even bring himself to say the word *love*. The best he could do was friendship.

When Jesus had asked these Jewish men to follow him three years earlier, he called into question everything they thought they knew about their lives. Jesus confronted Roman and Jewish power, and he said and did things that only Yahweh was allowed to say and do. He healed people and cast out demons. He accepted the outcasts and confronted the powers.

Then Jesus went and got himself killed. Peter simply didn't get what was happening.

What Peter did know was that he had failed at fidelity. He had turned his back on his friend in the hour of his greatest need. Denying Jesus was a failure of fidelity. And standing here on the beach in front of his risen Lord, Peter is trying to avoid making a promise that he knows he cannot keep. For the first time, Peter began to comprehend what was required of him to honestly say "I love you" (*agapaō*) to this man. And he couldn't bring himself to do it.

My wife and I started dating in 1989 and continued to date all through college. We had our ups and downs, but we really knew each other and loved each other. After graduation she got a job and I went to grad school in a different town. We tried to keep dating, but it wasn't going well. We had five years and a lot of our hearts invested in this relationship, but we both knew something was not right. Once while we were on the telephone, we found ourselves at a watershed moment. I told her that I thought we either needed to get on with it and get married or we needed to just let it go. I said, "I know what I want. I want to marry you. What do you want?"

I'll never forget what she said: "I know that I love you, Tim. I'm just not sure it's the marrying kind of love."

Her answer was brilliant, but at the time I thought it was just a tactful way to say, "It's not me, it's you." More than that, however, her words showed a deep understanding of what love would require. We had been through a lot together. Kristin knew exactly what was required in order to say "I love you" to me, and she wasn't sure she could do it. Her reply was mature and wise.

When Jesus said, "Simon, do you love me?" Peter knew exactly what he was getting himself into—what loving Jesus would require. He also knew that he had failed to live in fidelity to those requirements once before.

Loving Jesus would make hefty demands on Peter's life. Loving our enemies sounds so great in theory, but when they are arresting your leader and nailing him to a cross, it can get pretty real. Peter had failed once already, so when Jesus put the question to him on the beach, Peter's eyes were wide open. He was no longer brash and bold. He was humble, unsure of himself, aware of his failures, aware of how much fidelity to Jesus would require.

I have great respect for Peter's answer. It's truthful. Peter knew that his actions in the past did not justify empty promises. Peter had begun to understand that the deep kind of *agapaō* love that Jesus requires cannot be expressed in words. The kind of love Jesus was calling forth from Peter is expressed in a life of faithfulness and fidelity to Jesus over time. Loving Jesus isn't just something you say with your lips; it is lived with your life. And Peter now understood this. The author of John's gospel then writes of this beautiful ceremony on the beach, where Jesus reinstates Peter and tells Peter that he will, indeed, live this life of love for Jesus.

When I think of this moment, I'm reminded of that day on the phone with my future wife, when she told me she couldn't commit herself until she knew she could live up to it. We were in love, but was it the marrying kind of love? That was twenty-five years ago now, and I can tell you it was indeed the marrying kind of love. We have lived in fidelity to one another and our children for all those years. My wife works hard for our family, keeps faith, forgives, hopes, and loves us. I have no doubt that she loves me, because she has lived in fidelity to that promise for twenty-five years.

Jesus tells Peter, "I need you to get back in the game, man. Feed my sheep. Yes, you failed. You blew it. Still, I believe in you. You will follow me again. My enemies will become your enemies. And they are going to stretch out your hands just like they stretched out mine [a reference to Peter's future death]. You are right Peter. I know you love me. And you are going to go where I've gone because you are willing to live in fidelity to me" (see John 21:18–19).

Love is more than just something we say, even if we mean it. Love is a way of life.

Love requires *fidelity over time.*

Kristin and I broke up that day and didn't speak again for almost a year. During that time we were each on journeys of growth and redirection. I changed my career path and headed back toward ministry. I imagined a whole new vocation for my life. Kristin did intense soul work, making her faith her own, not just something that was connected to me, but something that was welded to the foundation of her life whether or not I was going to be in it. I shudder to think how our marriage would have struggled without that year apart.

Yes, our relationship "failed" that day on the phone. We separated and went our own way. But that failure was the seedbed of a happy and fruitful marriage. It laid the foundation for years of fidelity.

> Some theologians tell us that *agapē* is a kind of love that only God can achieve — that humans can't ever achieve *unconditional love*. But I disagree. I believe *agapē* is within our reach; *we just aren't allowed to say it.*

Some theologians tell us that *agapē* is a kind of love that only God can achieve — that humans can't ever achieve *unconditional love*. But I disagree. I believe *agapē* is within our reach; *we just aren't allowed to say it.* Like Peter on the shore of the Sea of Tiberius, we shouldn't be too eager to make claims about how much we love Jesus. All we can do is get on with the business of living in fidelity to Jesus all the days of our lives. Our lives become our declaration of love and worship. And when we wash up on the other shore and Jesus picks up our lifeless bodies and breathes new air back into our lungs and we see him face-to-face—then we get to say it: "Yes, Lord, I love you."

Until then, we don't get to claim to love as God loves. The only way we can speak is by living in fidelity—both to God and to each other.

WE'VE DECIDED

Throughout this book, I've wanted to hold up different ways in which faithfulness to God defines the goal of life and ministry. At the heart of faithfulness is the word *faith*. *Faith* is a significant word for Christians. We walk by faith, not by sight. We have one Lord, one faith, one baptism. We are saved by grace through faith. In all of these statements from Scripture, the word used is the Greek word *pistis*, which we translate as "faith."

In our culture, the word *faith* has come to mean something like trust or belief. Having faith in Jesus is typically taken to mean that we believe certain things about him and that we trust him for certain benefits. While this is true, it doesn't come close to describing the fullness of what is involved in *pistis*. Trust and belief are part of *pistis*, but the semantic field is wider, including ideas akin to what we mean when we talk about love, loyalty, devotion, confidence, allegiance, and faithfulness. Perhaps the best translation of *pistis* is the word "fidelity." We cannot have faith without fidelity.

This is true not only in the way that we relate to Jesus, but also the way we relate to one another. We see in his letters, for example, that Paul is concerned about unity among Jesus' followers. Over and over he refers to the church as the body of Christ. Paul understood that the church was more than just individuals who had a common association; it was one body with many parts. Who we are as people is constituted by the church. To be a "person" names not a thing, but a relationship. In other words, what it means to be a human being, as human was intended by God, will

> We cannot have faith without fidelity.

only become clear as we find our lives and our identities in this new community.

If you cut off a toe or gouge out an eyeball, the whole body will feel it. Paul made it clear that the way we relate to one another matters. Leaving the body is no small affair. This is why I constantly preach fidelity to the people in our church. In a consumerist, church growth culture, fidelity is a pretty tough sell. We are raised to assert our individuality, our freedom, our right to choose. It's tough to embrace the idea that we are supposed to lay those things down in order to live in fidelity to our church community.

I often say that the two most dangerous words I ever hear as a pastor are, "We've decided." Those two words are the prefix to all kinds of pain. We've decided ... to leave the church. We've decided ... to get a divorce. We've decided ... we are not sure we buy any of this Jesus stuff anymore. The ubiquitous "we've decided" shows us the extent to which radical individualism has taken root in our churches. The word "we" in this sense is used to exclude oneself from relationship. It shows that a person has formed their identity and is making choices apart from any sense of union with the rest of the body.

Decisions like these violate the unity of the body. Worship of God should involve the whole of our lives, so a decision made privately to leave a church means that we are severing deep bonds of friendship and community. Our relationship with the church community is meant to be reciprocal. The words "We've decided" or "I've decided" are a sign that individualism has so pervaded our lives and our Christian faith that we believe we are authorized to make decisions on behalf of everyone else in our community without consulting them. If it is so easy for us to leave one another, what does that say about the depth and quality of our relationship to one another in Christ? Do we truly belong to one another at all?

Breaking fidelity is tragic, especially when I know that if a family or person were to bring their decision to the rest of the body, there would usually be an opportunity for their hurts and wounds to be healed. And even when the hurt cannot be healed or if something else is at work—moving to a different town for work or finding a church with a different focus—bringing the decision to the body can affirm that this calling is from God. When the body is given a chance to affirm these decisions, there are no scars, no resentment, no bitter feelings. The community can affirm that God has called them to a different place, lay hands on them, and send them out— even if they are sending them to a church right across the street.

In his book *The Church*, Wolfhart Pannenberg writes about the unity of the body of Christ: "The unity of all Christians is not some optional feature of the nature of the church, which is desirable, but can, if necessary, be dispensed with." Without unity the church cannot be the church. Pannenberg goes so far as to say that "the being of the church itself is in question if its unity is not realized."[2] A visibly disunited church fails to image God.

I sometimes wonder what would happen if we could institute some sort of church-swapping freeze. Think about it. What would it be like if we could just freeze the church "marketplace" and require that everyone simply stays right where they are? What would change? Would it affect the way we see one another? Would it change our level of commitment to one another and to our church community? Would it cause us to speak up about unhealthy situations? If we couldn't just leave when things get tough, would we begin to roll up our sleeves and get to work tending to the health of the body? Would we finally engage in the mission of God?

I realize we can't force people to live in fidelity, but we can choose fidelity ourselves. Don't leave when things get tough. Stay and help figure things out. Yes, your church is going to fail you in many ways. But the only way that our failure becomes fatal is when we divide over our failures. Fidelity—long-term faithfulness to one another and to God—means that we stick around long enough to see those failures become the seedbed of something beautiful.

After several years of welcoming homeless people to our congregation, we finally raised some money and bought a building. We had been meeting in a local high school, and the janitor had allowed us to use some of the locker rooms to help the homeless people get

---

2 Wolfhart Pannenberg, *The Church* (Louisville: Westminster John Knox, 1983), 27.

a shower each week. Many of them came to count on that weekly shower. We also liked the idea that people were coming to church to get clean.

When we bought a building, we spent an extra fifteen or twenty thousand dollars to make sure we had new bathrooms that included showers. The problem was that they were located next to our children's ministry. Often our kids got an eyeful on their way to class.

At the same time, our atrium space was not as big as the rented high school. All of a sudden we felt crowded—right on top of each other. As more and more of our friends living on the street began coming each week, we went from a dozen or so homeless to as many as thirty on a given Sunday morning. This led to a significant change in the culture of our church. Some of our members grew uncomfortable and were frustrated by these newcomers who came to church drunk, belligerent, or so hung over they would fall asleep in the service and snore loudly. We were routinely enduring disruptions of the worship service and other inappropriate behavior. Our children stay in with us during the first half of the service, so they were getting quite an education on why we just say no to drugs. All of this caused a fair amount of friction, and it led us to take a hard look at the ministry and to be honest about our own limitations. So we called a congregational meeting to discuss what this ministry was doing to the culture of our church.

And we had an amazing time together.

We reminded each other that our faithfulness doesn't depend on our ability to solve every problem perfectly. When we have an issue brewing in our church, we're not going to ignore it; we're going to face it head on. We laughed when I said the phrase "I told you so" gets a bad rap. It's actually a good sign when someone says, "I told you so," because it means they've stayed around, even when things got tough. It means they were willing to speak up for what they believed in at the time. They told the truth, and nobody had to leave to keep the peace. I shared my hope that *everyone* in our church would be willing to stick around long enough to say one of two things: either "I told you so," or "You were right and I was wrong."

After this meeting, we built some new teams, recruited new leaders, started some new procedures, and fought to regain some intentionality over the developing culture in our church. I wish I could say that it's all gone perfectly, but we have made some mistakes along the way. We will always have to work to create a worship experience that will honor God and shape our lives in ways that bear fruit. Yet we have stayed together. I think that's the ballgame.

Sometimes people in our congregation still leave feeling frustrated after a rowdy Sunday morning filled with disturbances. We've had to confront some of our members when they are disrespectful in our worship time or to some of our other members. Yet people keep coming back, again and again. It's as though we've come to accept the fact that we are all a bunch of ragamuffins, so the most beautiful thing we can do with our lives is to live in fidelity to one another.

LEARNING TO STAND

Fidelity is *faithfulness over time*. If we want to live in fidelity—sticking together for the long haul—we will have to fight and struggle for it. As with all of the virtues, fidelity cannot be fully achieved or realized in this life, but it can be practiced. On the path to fidelity, much of what we need to learn will come to us through our struggles and failures.

When Brené Brown talks about parenting, she says that the virtues you want your child to develop will be born out of their struggles. Her research tells us that struggle is the seedbed of health for your child. Failures, disappointments, and difficulties are what they need (as we do, for that matter) in order to become healthy, mature adults. One of the problems, Brown says, is that our society conditions us to believe that everything should be "fun, fast, and easy."[3] In the midst of difficult situations that might tax our resolve to live in fidelity, we are quick to think, "This is supposed to be easy; it's not worth the effort, or this should be easier: it's only hard and slow because I'm not good at it."[4]

---

3 Brown, *Gifts of Imperfection*, 66.
4 Ibid.

You've probably heard about the "helicopter" parent who keeps careful watch over their child's affairs, their schedule, and their grades—all to make sure they are safe and successful. While we all love our kids and hate to see them struggle, if we helicopter in and solve every problem for our children, they will never learn what it means to strive and push through failure in a healthy way. They will never learn how to live in fidelity, how to be faithful over time. Fun, fast, and easy are significant roadblocks to fidelity. We are wired for struggle, so it isn't something to be feared or resisted. Struggle is where the good stuff comes from.

Often the impulse to win and resist struggle and failure is fueled by misreadings of Scripture. Ephesians 6 contains one of the more well-known passages from the Bible. In this chapter we read instructions about the armor of God and how to engage the principalities and powers against which we struggle. The entire chapter is filled with military themes and the imagery of the battlefield. We often read this with a competitive lens, and we plug in our cultural values of winning at all costs.

But Paul here seems intent on clarifying our goal, adding some realistic nuance. He tells us that the end toward which we are striving is to *stand*: "Put on the full armor of God, so that you can take your *stand* ... so that ... you maybe be able to *stand* your ground ... and after you have done everything, to *stand*. *Stand* firm then ..." (Eph 6:11–14). Paul's vision is that the church would know how to stand, how to be faithful, how to live in fidelity and commitment to Jesus and one another.

In the waning days of World War I, the famous Second Battle of Marne was fought. The Germans had won several victories and had almost made it to Paris. In fact, their artillery was actively shelling the outskirts of the city. The Germans had the Allied forces on the ropes and were hoping to finish them off. They sent fifty-two divisions against the Allies' thirty-four, hoping this would decisively turn the battle and help Germany win the war.

The Second Battle of Marne was a decisive battle, but not in the way the Germans intended. Over three days, from July 15 to July 18, 1918, the tide of the war turned. Ludendorff, the German high commander, remarked before the battle: "I was convinced ... that before the first of September our adversaries would send us peace proposals.... That was on the 15th. On the 18th even the most optimistic among us knew all was lost. The history of the world was played out in three days."[5]

Shortly after the Second Battle of Marne, the majority of the American fighting force arrived on the field. The decisive battle had been fought, and most of the U.S. soldiers were just getting to Europe. But once they arrived in full force, over four million strong, everyone knew the war was truly over. No matter what the Axis powers could throw at them, the Allied forces would stand. The United States gets credit for helping to win the war, but in truth, our main contribution was providing our allies with the ability to stand after absorbing so much loss. The tide of the war had already turned; now it was a matter of faithfully holding out until the fighting was over.

This is a picture of the kind of work Christ has given to us, his church. The decisive battle has already been won for us through Christ's cross and resurrection. Now our job is simply to stand firm. We must resist the corrupting influences, powers, and principalities of our day and age that keep us from living as God's new creations, living out our resurrection lives.

Living in fidelity to Jesus means following in the way of the cross, learning how to stand when those around us fall. The battle in which we are engaged is not a battle that we need to win — it has already been won for us. Our job is to stand — to live in *fidelity* to Jesus no matter what the cost and no matter how hard we have to struggle to do so.

> Living in fidelity to Jesus means following in the way of the cross, learning how to stand when those around us fall.

Have you ever noticed that nearly all of the armor recommended by Paul in Ephesians 6 consists of defensive equipment? The belt of truth, the breastplate of righteousness, the shoes made ready to proclaim the gospel of peace, the shield of faith, the helmet of salvation — all of those are defensive weapons. The only offensive

---

5 David McCullough, *Truman* (New York: Touchstone, 1992), 119.

weapon we are given is the sword of the Spirit—a weapon that is ultimately beyond our control, whose offensive power is dependent on God's power and grace.

God is not asking us to win a great battle. He's done that already. He wants us to learn how to stand, and he has equipped us precisely for this task. Our calling is not to wage an all-out assault on the kingdom of darkness. Our job is to organize our common life together in such a way that we image God to all creation—to live in such a way that our existence stands in stark contrast to the rest of the culture. Our lives are meant to be lives of fidelity as we withstand the onslaught of a culture hell-bent on making us into just another community.

But we are *not* just another community. The church is not the Rotary Club, or the Boy Scouts, or a glorified book club. We are the body of Christ, and we are in a real battle. But we are not an assault team; *we are an army of resistance, and our job is to stand.*

Spiritual warfare isn't primarily about slaying people in the Spirit or casting out demons. It's not like the work of exorcism we see in the movies, rebuking the devil and waiting for a girl's head to spin around. Spiritual warfare is what you and I do when nobody else is looking. Will I be honest or will I lie? Will I be faithful or will I compromise? We stand or fall on these decisions—fidelity hangs in the balance every moment of every day.

We need the armor of God because we are going to wake up tomorrow and must decide whether we will live in fidelity to our marriage. We have to decide if we are going to be patient with our children; whether we will work hard for our employers even when it's a drag; and whether we can worship with people who are messed up, disruptive, and addicted without judging them and casting them away. *Spiritual warfare doesn't happen in the spectacular; it happens in the mundane.* It's about how we live our lives moment to moment—in fidelity to Jesus. If we dig deep and practice integrity, peacemaking, mercy, justice, faith, hope, love, gentleness, and everything else, our churches will stand strong in the midst of a flailing culture.

Chapter 12

A PRACTICAL BUT NOT PRAGMATIC CONCLUSION

*My father was a better bricklayer than I am
a theologian. I am still in too much of a hurry.
But if the work I have done in theology is of any use,
it is because of what I learned on the job, that is,
you can lay only one brick at a time.*
—Stanley Hauerwas, *Hannah's Child*

Remember the movie *Armageddon*, the blockbuster film starring Bruce Willis? An asteroid was heading for the earth, a global killer, and the plan was to fly a team of oil drillers out to the asteroid on the space shuttle, land on it, dig a deep well to the center, and blow it up with a nuclear warhead ... Plausible, right?

As it turns out, this is a real thing. NASA has a program called the NEO, or Near Earth Object program. They track all of these huge asteroids that are orbiting our solar system and think about how to deal with them if one ever posed a threat. The current thinking on how to avert an impact, however, has nothing to do with the Bruce Willis scenario.

What scientists would do is launch a satellite to intercept the asteroid while it's still far away from the earth. The satellite would get as close to the asteroid as it possibly could without actually touching it. At that close proximity, the satellite would exert a tiny gravitational force on the asteroid ... just a tiny little bit. By getting really close to the asteroid, and exerting a small amount of gravitational force on it, the relatively small satellite could actually change the trajectory of a giant, global killing asteroid.

It's a real thing; it's called "gravitational coupling."

This whole scenario depends on the ability to intercept the asteroid while it's still a long way off. A tiny change in its trajectory while it is still thousands of miles away would be enough to steer it far clear of the earth.

As pastors and church leaders we have many influences, and it is important for us to think carefully about who we are allowing into close proximity to our lives and ministries. We have to be careful with our relationships and choose leadership archetypes and mentors carefully, because those choices are critical. Those whom we allow to draw close today will act like gravitational coupling for us and for our churches. They will have a significant impact on the trajectory of our life and our work, especially miles and miles down the road.

Instead of looking to the cabal of bigger, better, higher, faster, stronger leaders who are selling successful models, strategies, and techniques, church leaders must be finding something small to imitate. We need healthy influences. We need archetypes and mentors who share our vision of the church and the kingdom, because over time the tiny force and almost imperceptible influence they bring to bear on our lives and our ministries can have a big impact. Healthy influences will change the quality and direction of everything to which we are committed. The decision we make to allow someone to come close to our hearts and to shape us is a precious decision, and we have to make it carefully.

The church leadership conversation in North America is clearly focused on success. So once a leader has decided to opt out of the mainstream, where do we go for ideas and influence? Especially since even the more cutting-edge ministry stuff—nearly everything with the word *missional* in the title—still suffers from the same fatal dose of pragmatism ... what *works*, more than what is *faithful*.

Finding influences can be extremely difficult, but it is an important part of our task as leaders. We need influences not so we can copy what they are doing, but so we can have hope that it's actually possible to lead a church in a different direction. All of us need trust-worthy guides along the way so that we can be encouraged, ener-gized, and passionate about serving the church.

PRACTICAL STEPS

I do not want to end on a pragmatic note after I've tried so hard to steer clear of pragmatics throughout this book. However, I do want to offer a little bit of my perspective on how anyone can make some of the moves I've been making. I want to give just a few steps that you can take if you are inclined to investigate more about pursuing faithfulness over success.

In this final section I'm aiming for something practical, but not pragmatic. What follows is just a page or two out of my own play-book, a few influences and sources that have served to shape my life and ministry.

From Models to an Ecclesiology

There are no shortcuts when it comes to theology. Building a robust ecclesiology involves a slow gradual change of your paradigm. Much of the process of building an ecclesiology involves *unlearning* things that are already settled in your mind. A significant part of the task of re-scripting involves subverting the old script. It's a long process, but it's worth it.

I have in mind some wise guides that have served me well over the years as I attempt to construct a coherent, adaptive, and captivat-ing ecclesiological vision. If you are looking for some practical steps, these are some wise guides to follow.

First, sit down and read *Resident Aliens* by Stanley Hauerwas and William Willimon as fast as you possibly can. Don't mark it or take notes, just fly through it. Then read it through again, slowly this time, taking notes as you go. While you are reading the second time, start listening to Hauerwas lectures online (there are dozens of them free online). Drink in his vision of the church. It will serve you well.

Next read *The Prophetic Imagination* by Walter Brueggemann, *For the Life of the World* by Alexander Schmemann, and *The Divine*

Conspiracy by Dallas Willard. These will frame the task of ministry and help to clarify not only where we often go wrong, but how we might approach our ecclesiology with practical ministry in mind.

A few ecclesiology texts that I found important are *The Church in the Power of the Spirit* by Jürgen Moltmann and *The Church* by Wolfhart Pannenberg. *Missional Church* by Darrell Guder and others should be required reading, although it can get a little pragmatic at times. After that I would start in on anything written by Eugene Peterson and Leslie Newbigin.

Finally, you have to read *Jayber Crow* by Wendell Berry. When he says *land*, think *parish*. When he says *farm*, think *church*. Reading Wendell Berry's fiction can quite probably give you the best ecclesiological vision possible.

From Strategies to Stories

Pastors and church leaders have to learn how to become professional story catchers. I am constantly taking down stories in my journal and filing them away for future use. I have in my mind a constant refrain: *The kingdom of God is like* ... When I run into people, places, things, and events that shed light on that refrain, I write them down. I share them liberally. Stories are the currency of ministry.

We can learn a lot about the dynamics of narrative by reading those who are thinking about story. Donald Miller's book *A Million Miles in a Thousand Years* is a great starting point. You can also read books on writing and the creative process to learn more about story. I suggest taking creative writing classes or even courses on literature.

One of the most fruitful things I've done is to read memoirs of great writers and pastors. Frederick Buechner has written extensively about his own life. *The Sacred Journey, Now and Then,* and *Telling Secrets* are three short memoirs that I think of often as I go about my daily tasks of ministry. Eugene Peterson's memoir *The Pastor* is required reading for leaders. Read books on the task of writing. There are good ones by Annie Dillard and Anne Lamott. Reading Rebecca Solnit and John Jeremiah Sullivan can teach you about how to tell and write a story.

If memoir or nonfiction isn't really your thing, reading fiction is possibly the best training. Finding redemptive stories, especially as they pertain to the journey of faith, is essential to the ministry life. One of the most fruitful sources in my life has been the novels of Chaim Potok: *My Name Is Asher Lev* and *The Gift of Asher Lev*, along with *The Chosen* and *The Promise*, are all stories on which I draw deeply when I'm attempting to understand what it means to be a part of the people of God and of what God is doing in the world.

Once a year we do a Sunday morning series called *Storyaoke*. For several weeks, we spend our sermon time listening to the story of one person from our congregation. They share their lives and tell stories of struggle and healing. We've had folks share stories of intense loss, trials, eating disorders, addictions, hitting rock bottom, getting lost, and being found. These are potent moments. We have come to learn the power involved when we have the courage to be vulnerable and to let other people into our lives as we tell our own stories.

Another new tradition for our church is that we spend the four weeks between All Saints Day and Advent telling the stories of great saints of the church. This past year we spent one week each on people like Corrie ten Boom, Dorothy Day, St. Francis, and William Wilberforce. The stories of the saints who have gone before us give us archetypes we can follow and seed our imagination for what it means to live a faithful life.

Another practice I'm committed to as a pastor is to use the Old Testament regularly in preaching. I try to spend at least a third of the year working with stories from the Old Testament. These texts contain such a rich narrative history of the church. When I'm working in the New Testament, I tend to traffic much more consistently in the gospel texts and the history—anything that is saturated with stories.

From Techniques to Virtues

Virtues are the basic building blocks of Christian leadership. The pursuit of virtue in my life is where I spend most of my leadership energy. The central leadership virtue is *vulnerability*, which has to live at the heart of any ministry committed to living in the way of Jesus. All of the other virtues stem from that central embrace of vulnerability.

The Enneagram personality type has been one of the most

important elements of my leadership journey. I have asked our entire staff to become students of the Enneagram and to learn how to use this language in our everyday lives, especially in our relationships with each other. The Enneagram is a tool that allows us to take a step back from our lives and observe our own behavior. As we begin to see the little games we play, little dramas we inhabit, little tricks we use to protect our fragile egos, we begin to grow tired of them. They lose power over us. And we begin to grow in virtue instead. The Enneagram isn't about discovering our strengths and taking them out for a drive to see what we can accomplish with them. Instead, the Enneagram is about learning the way of descent, the way of Jesus. Leaders must deal with our own egos if the virtues are to be free to flourish and grow in our lives.

Here are a few of the go-to books I recommend in this section. *The Gifts of Imperfection* by Brené Brown is a good place to start. Pete Scazzerro's book *The Emotionally Healthy Church* can teach some practical habits with an eye toward emotional and relational wholeness. I return constantly to Eugene Peterson's *The Contemplative Pastor* as I go about the daily tasks of ministry.

Richard Rohr has been helpful in terms of creating a vocabulary of descent that I can share with the leaders in my church. His work on subverting dualistic thinking and the power of the contemplative life have left an indelible impact on our church staff.

If you feel the need to read books reflecting directly on the task of leadership, I recommend *In the Name of Jesus* by Henri Nouwen, *Cross-Shaped Leadership* by John A. Berntsen, and *Intuitive Leadership* by Tim Keel.

CONCLUSION

Falling back into the bigger, better, higher, faster, stronger narrative will be a constant temptation for any church leader. When our congregation is struggling, I'm tempted to try and force God's hand with a new strategy or model. One of the litmus tests I have found helpful is to run my decisions through a kind of gauntlet set forth by Henri Nouwen in his great leadership book, *In the Name of Jesus*.

Nouwen says that the three temptations Jesus faced in Matthew 4:1–11 are the same temptations we all face as we attempt to shepherd the people of God.

The first temptation—to turn the stone to bread—Nouwen calls the temptation to be *relevant*. This is the temptation to deal with the pressing issues of the day. After forty days of fasting, the only thing that could matter would be food, right? Yet Jesus refused to deal with the relevant issue of hunger. Nouwen says, "I am deeply convinced that the Christian leader of the future is called to be completely irrelevant and to stand in this world with nothing to offer but his or her own vulnerable self."[1] I think he's right.

Another temptation is to be *powerful*. "I will give you the kingdoms of this world."[2] The question here is simple: Will Jesus power up in order to achieve his goals? Will he raise an army, kill the Romans, and become the new ruler of the day? This is the gut check we all struggle with from time to time: the temptation to gain power without suffering.

"Let me save you a little time," the tempter said. "I think I see where you are going. Let me just give it to you. You won't have to even raise a finger. Quick caveat, though, you just have to bow down to me one time. Just a little bow … no big deal."[3]

Jesus refused. In so doing he demonstrates that playing the power games of the world, even for legitimate purposes, will involve bowing down to illegitimate lords and rival gods. Nouwen says, "What makes the temptation of power so seemingly irresistible … is that power offers an easy substitute for the hard task of love. It seems easier to be God than to love God, easier to control people than to love people, easier to own life than to love life."[4] Power is a shortcut that avoids the necessity of relationship and sacrifice. We need to find ways to lay down power and embrace vulnerability and weakness.

---

1   Henri Nouwen, *In the Name of Jesus: Reflections on Christian Leadership* (New York: Crossroads, 1989), 17.
2   Matthew 4:9, paraphrase.
3   Matthew 4:9, paraphrase.
4   Ibid., 77.

The final test Jesus faces is the temptation to be *spectacular*—to throw himself off the temple so that God will send angels to his rescue. Jesus could have created a splash that day, but he didn't do it. He refused to entertain the crowds with the spectacular and the impressive.

This is a huge question for ministry in our time because the spectacular is so big in our culture. In a world where the spectacular is king, God is looking for leaders who will dare to do a small thing faithfully.

Anybody who has been married has run into this, as has anyone who has worked at the same job for years. The challenge is never the crisis or the spectacular feat. The challenge is the day to day, the moment to moment. To live in fidelity to a spouse who is far from perfect, to work hard when the boss is out of town, to get up and give your day to a job when it is not immediately clear why it makes any difference to the world ... these are the ordinary decisions we all have to face in secret. Our culture loves the spectacular and disdains the ordinary. Jesus seemed to know that the ordinary is where all the good stuff happens.

Nouwen notes that nearly everything the tempter tempted Jesus with on that day, Jesus would do eventually. The *what* turned out to be exactly the same stuff; it was always the *how* that was in question. Although he did not turn stones to bread that day, later on he did feed the hungry, sometimes by miraculously producing bread. Although he refused to grasp power that day, he did become the world's true Lord. But Jesus' kingdom would come not through politics as usual. It would come through weakness, vulnerability, and peace. Although he didn't take the leap off the temple that day, he did jump eventually. Jesus went to his death the way all of us must go: trusting in God to raise him from the dead—not as a means of testing God, but in complete obedience to God's calling for his life.

And it's the *how* that matters most for us as well. The *what* will almost never kill us. It will always be the *how*, because you cannot pursue the kingdom in illegitimate ways and still expect to find it.

If we choose to engage in ministry—whether we do so as pastors or lay leaders—we can be sure that we will face the same three temptations Jesus faced: the temptation to be *relevant, powerful,* and *spectacular.* There are churches all over the country knocking themselves out week after week trying to chase relevance, power, and all things spectacular. If we want to become involved with Jesus, we cannot continue to chase those things. The kingdom comes only through the wise and judicious practice of vulnerability and weakness. When we embrace those things, we place ourselves exactly where we need to be in order for God's power to break through, heal our broken hearts, and restore our broken world.

My prayer for the church is that leaders will crop up all over the place, ready and willing to embrace the way of Jesus. My hope is that a new generation of leaders is being raised up right now who are unwilling to allow the culture to set the agenda for the church. Instead of chasing after pragmatic success, I pray for those who have the courage to pursue faithfulness no matter what the perceived results may be. I pray that we'll have the humility to see that we have no right to quibble with the results of our ministry life. We only have the duty to be faithful in all the small things and leave the results in the hands of the loving God who holds our future.